The North American Beef Industry in Transition: New Consumer Demands and Supply Chain Responses

HD9433.N72 B76 2008
0134111 537715
Brocklebank, Andrea M.

The North American beef
 industry in transition :
   c2008.

THE NORTH AMERICAN BEEF INDUSTRY IN TRANSITION: NEW CONSUMER DEMANDS AND SUPPLY CHAIN RESPONSES

ANDREA M. BROCKLEBANK, JILL E. HOBBS
AND WILLIAM A. KERR

Nova Science Publishers, Inc.
New York

Copyright © 2008 by Nova Science Publishers, Inc.

All rights reserved. No part of this book may be reproduced, stored in a retrieval system or transmitted in any form or by any means: electronic, electrostatic, magnetic, tape, mechanical photocopying, recording or otherwise without the written permission of the Publisher.

For permission to use material from this book please contact us:
Telephone 631-231-7269; Fax 631-231-8175
Web Site: http://www.novapublishers.com

NOTICE TO THE READER

The Publisher has taken reasonable care in the preparation of this book, but makes no expressed or implied warranty of any kind and assumes no responsibility for any errors or omissions. No liability is assumed for incidental or consequential damages in connection with or arising out of information contained in this book. The Publisher shall not be liable for any special, consequential, or exemplary damages resulting, in whole or in part, from the readers' use of, or reliance upon, this material.

Independent verification should be sought for any data, advice or recommendations contained in this book. In addition, no responsibility is assumed by the publisher for any injury and/or damage to persons or property arising from any methods, products, instructions, ideas or otherwise contained in this publication.

This publication is designed to provide accurate and authoritative information with regard to the subject matter covered herein. It is sold with the clear understanding that the Publisher is not engaged in rendering legal or any other professional services. If legal or any other expert assistance is required, the services of a competent person should be sought. FROM A DECLARATION OF PARTICIPANTS JOINTLY ADOPTED BY A COMMITTEE OF THE AMERICAN BAR ASSOCIATION AND A COMMITTEE OF PUBLISHERS.

LIBRARY OF CONGRESS CATALOGING-IN-PUBLICATION DATA

Brocklebank, Andrea M.
  The North American beef industry in transition : new consumer demands and supply chain responses / Andrea M. Brocklebank, Jill E. Hobbs, William A. Kerr.
      p. cm.
  Includes bibliographical references and index.
  ISBN 978-1-60456-121-0 (hbk. : alk. paper)
 1. Beef industry--North America. I. Hobbs, Jill E. II. Kerr, William A. (William Alexander) III. Title.
HD9433.N72.B76 2007
338.1'762130973--dc22
                                  2007044359

Published by Nova Science Publishers, Inc. ≃ New York

CONTENTS

Preface		vii
Chapter 1	New Consumer Food Requirements and the Challenge for the Agri-food Industry	1
Chapter 2	The Beef Industry In The North American Marketplace	7
Chapter 3	The Economics of Supply Chains	27
Chapter 4	A Framework for Assessing Supply Chain Relationships	45
Chapter 5	Cow-Calf Operators and Changing Supply Chains	71
Chapter 6	Supply Chain Alliances	109
Chapter 7	Insights for the Agri-food Sector	141
References		149
Appendix A:	Cow-Calf Operator Survey	157
Appendix B:	Beef Alliance Survey	167
Index		175

PREFACE

Since the signing of the Canada US Trade Agreement between the United States and Canada in the late 1980s the continental beef industry has gone through a process of deep integration. Further, there has been a major shift in consumers' approach to food consumption centered on more healthy lifestyles, product safety, convenience and variety. Consumers have become more discerning with respect to where their food comes from and how it was produced. Increased scrutiny is given to production practices – organics, drug residues, broken needles in injection sites, environmentally friendly methods – as well as intrinsic factors such as fat content, nutrition, 'ready to eat', and a host of other food product attributes that had barely entered the lexicon of most food consumers twenty years ago. Supplying foods that provide the new attributes desired by consumers has become a central part of the competitive strategies of agri-food firms. The beef industry is one of the largest sectors in the agri-food industry yet it initially struggled to respond to changing consumer tastes and the strategies of its competitors. In recent years, however, the beef industry has responded strongly to these challenges. However, this is requiring major changes in the organization and coordination of business transactions and relationships within the beef sector – from suppliers of genetics through to supermarkets. This book provides an in depth analysis of the factors providing the impetus for change in the North American beef industry and how the industry responded to the challenges. The beef industry story provides lessons for other agri-food industries attempting to respond to rapidly evolving food markets.

Our purpose in writing this book is to provide insights into the process whereby industries respond to a rapidly changing marketplace and, in particular, industries with complex supply chains consisting of many actors. The agri-food industry provides an excellent example of a market that is evolving rapidly in ways few would have contemplated even a few years ago. The beef industry has exceedingly complex supply chains that must coordinate complex resources such as genetics, extensive grazing, precision feeding strategies, high tech processing, cold chain logistics and food safety protocols. The interaction between changing demands and the beef industry's responses to an evolving marketplace provide the focus of the book. The book examines the process whereby the beef industry is making the transition from a supplier of commodities to a provider of differentiated products with attributes tailored to individual consumers. The book then provides a theoretical basis for the examination of evolving supply chains and a means by which the industry's response can be assessed using modern quantitative methods. Case studies are developed to dig deeper into the transition the beef industry is experiencing. Insights are drawn for other agri-food sectors facing similar challenges.

Ranchers have always had a special place in the cultural heritage that defines North Americans, and beef has been the premium product in the dietary hierarchy in traditional North American cuisine. As urban dwellers who are generations removed from agricultural production now overwhelmingly make up the consumer base, the image of cattle producers is buffeted by new customer priorities such as animal welfare, environmental sustainability and the ability to determine the place of origin of their food. As the proportion of food consumed at home declines and consumers seek to expand their range of culinary experiences, food from cultures where beef is not a mainstay of the diet have gained more prominence. These restaurant experiences are increasingly being reflected in the near table ready products on offer in supermarkets. While consumers are still likely to enjoy a good steak, other traditional beef products now struggle for consumers' attention against a host of new competitors. Some of these new competitors are beef based, but even with these products the consumer's experience is formed by spicing and complementary ingredients as much as the beef. Thus, the implications of the response of the beef industry to the changes buffeting the sector goes beyond strictly commercial concerns and will determine the place of beef and the industry's participants in the evolving North American culture. We think it is a topic worthy of investigation.

Andrea Brocklebank
Calgary, Canada
Jill Hobbs
Saskatoon, Canada
William Kerr
Saskatoon, Canada

Chapter 1

NEW CONSUMER FOOD REQUIREMENTS AND THE CHALLENGE FOR THE AGRI-FOOD INDUSTRY

INTRODUCTION

From the perspective of the majority of consumers in North America the industry vying for their food budget is extremely competitive. The choices they are presented with anytime they wish to eat are extensive and varied – a sushi restaurant two blocks away, a pizza that can be delivered in twenty minutes, a steak in the fridge that can be thrown on the barbeque, frozen burritos that can be popped in the microwave, noodles in a pot that can be ready as fast as a kettle can be boiled, a fast food burger joint with a drive through window that can be reached in ten minutes – and the list goes on. The choices in a modern supermarket are difficult to comprehend – thousands of products from hundreds of countries – fresh, frozen, freeze dried, smoked, canned, organic, low fat, low cholesterol, sugar coated, baked fresh, made without wheat flour, fair trade, kosher, choice grade, etc. If the particular supermarket doesn't measure up there is likely one close by that is "greener" or cheaper or that has better quality produce. It is a buyers' market. While the competition for the consumer's food budget is fierce, that does not mean that all the players in the market are competitive firms, clearly there are large corporate entities in any facet of the industry from McDonalds to Walmart to Costco to Whole Foods to Nabisco to Nestle that find the food industry an attractive place to do business. Even for these giants the competition for the consumers' patronage is intense.

The heart of this competition is providing the consumer with a greater range of choices largely through increasing the attributes of products. Instead of there just being lettuce to buy, now there is non-organic and organic lettuce to choose from. In addition to head lettuce there is also pre-washed lettuce leaves and pre-washed, chopped lettuce ready for salad to choose from. Sometimes new attributes are added without changing the product – corn flakes are now endowed with the attribute of being a "traditional" breakfast cereal that you have "trusted" since you were a child. While most new attributes start out as being unique as a way to attract additional customers, some gain widespread acceptance by consumers and are added by competitors to their products so that a new standard is created.

Underlying the changing choices provided for consumers are complex supply chains that move food products through many hands from farms to being purchased by the final consumer. Given the dynamics of competition for the consumers' food budget, these supply chains must be able to adapt and change to be successful. This adaptability must be present as food products move down the supply chain from farms to the consumer but it also must be present as information flows back up the supply chain from the consumer to farms. Complex supply chains require that many actors must be co-ordinated, they must be provided with incentives to be consistent when needed and to change when necessary and they must receive technical information on how to improve both their products and the efficiency with which they are produced. Success over the long run also means that all members of the supply chain that are willing to adapt to change must prosper.

Competitiveness based on product diversity is a relatively new phenomenon in the agri-food industry. For much of the 20th century competitiveness in the agri-food industry followed the industrial sector and was linked to exploiting available economies of scale to lower costs. This was achieved through standardization. At the farm level standardization was manifest in both larger and more specialized farms. Standardization at the farm level was often assisted through the establishment of grades by governments. In food processing, over time small local dairies, abattoirs, flour mills, bakeries, fruit packers, etc. were replaced by large scale operations that utilized production methods similar to those pioneered in industries such as automobiles and consumer appliances. These changes were assisted by significant technological improvements in transportation and the ability to preserve products through packaging, canning, freezing and vacuum packing, etc. that allowed both inputs and final products to be moved great distances. In retail, local butchers, green grocers, general stores and fishmongers were largely replaced by first supermarkets and latterly by supermarket chains. Restaurant chains moved eating out from an "event" experience to a "mass market" phenomenon and garnered an ever increasing share of the consumer's food budget. Both supermarket chains and restaurant chains were able to capitalize on economies of scale in centralized supplies and distribution. Consumers benefited from ever lower food prices and the proportion of their income spent on food consistently declined.

While competitiveness defined by product diversity has clearly been on the rise since the 1990s, economies of scale have not yet been fully exploited as the size of farms continues to increase and meat packing plants as well as other food processing facilities continue to expand in size, Walmart and Costco become food retailers and globalization means that market size is no longer constrained by national borders. Hence, at the moment competitiveness in the agri-food industry is defined by two forces – standardization and diversity – that appear diametrically opposed (Isaac et al., 2004). Entrepreneurs and corporate executives in the agri-food industry will continue to identify and act on opportunities to lower costs by scaling up their operations but increasingly opportunities are being found in providing variety for consumers through adding attributes to food products. Many of those attributes are less tangible that those that came from standardization such as freshness and consistent portions. Organic, animal welfare friendly, transfat free, certified Angus, free range and a host of other attributes cannot be readily identified by consumers when products are purchased and, hence, require that consumers both be informed of the existence of the attributes and assured that the information is true. This requires a different type of business relationship all along the supply chain from the farmer that produces a free range chicken to the retailer that markets some chickens as having been raised in a manner considered as being "free range". Responding to the challenges of re-orienting supply chains to be able to respond to competitive pressures relating to the provision of new product attributes for consumers has proved far more challenging for entrepreneurs, farmers and managers in the agri-food industry than exploiting economies of scale. The ability to rise to this challenge will determine success in the agri-food industry. Most important, competitive success will increasingly be determined less by the innovative activities of individual firms and more by the performance of all of the actors along the entire supply chain acting in concert. Supply chains that fail to adapt and actively coordinate their activities will see their market shares decline. This can be true for competing supply chains within the same industry and supply chains in different industries. For example, if the poultry supply chain is better able to respond to the challenge than those providing lamb, pork or beef then the market share of poultry will expand relative to competing meats.

Understanding and assessing the ability of supply chains to respond to the competitive challenges facing the agri-food industry in the 21st century requires a different set of tools than those required to understand supply chains governed largely by the incentives provided by prices determined by broad-based (often commodity) markets. The neoclassical paradigm which underpins the training of most economists is not particularly helpful in assessing supply chains organized through exclusive and non-transparent contracts and proprietary flows of information along segmented supply chains. More insights can be gained using modern theories of industrial organization and particularly the transaction cost approach found in new institutional economics paradigm (Hobbs, 1996a). This is the approach used in this book. The book focuses on the competitive challenges faced by the North American beef industry and how the industry is responding to those challenges while keeping in mind the broader forces operating in the agri-food industry outlined above.

THE NORTH AMERICAN BEEF INDUSTRY

While there was a degree of integration between the US and Canadian cattle and beef industries prior to the signing of the Canada-US Trade Agreement (CUSTA) in 1988, it can be agued that this agreement spurred considerable changes to the flow of cattle and beef in North America. The North American Free Trade Agreement (NAFTA) which added Mexico as a regional trading partner in 1995 little changed the forces for change brought by the CUSTA and, while Mexico's beef cattle industry has seen increased flows of animals into the US, Mexico's beef industry is much less integrated with the dominant US industry than Canada's. Hence, we will not treat the Mexican industry as an integral part of the North American industry in this book.

Prior to the CUSTA, the orientation of the flows of cattle and beef in the US and Canada were primarily east-west in nature. This was particularly true in Canada where large numbers of live animals were shipped from Western Canada to Central Canada by rail each year. In addition, policy distortions in the transport of grain, which is primarily produced in the Canadian prairies, discouraged cattle production in Western Canada – the "Crow Rate" pricing of grain movements – and actively encouraged livestock feeding in Central and Eastern Canada – the Feed Freight Assistance transport subsidy. In the US cattle feeding was concentrated in the Midwest and to a lesser extent in states further west such as Colorado with calves flowing into the feeding areas from the west and south and beef moving to the large urban centres on the east coast and to the rapidly expanding market in California.

By 1988, however, the primarily east-west orientation of the beef industry was feeling the stress of strong economic forces that pulled more in a north-south direction despite the distortions caused by Canadian transportation policy and border effects. Midwestern beef packers were confident they could competitively access consumer markets in heavily populated Southern Ontario and Quebec (Hobbs and Kerr, 1998) Beef processors in Western Canada, and particularly those located in Alberta, perceived opportunities in the California market (Gillis et al., 1985) while cattle producers could identify a range of lucrative markets for live animals in the US (Kerr and Ulmer, 1984, Kerr, 1985).

While formal trade barriers such as tariffs in the cattle and beef sectors prior to the CUSTA were relatively low and benign (Kerr and Cullen, 1985) there were a considerable number of non-tariff barriers that increased the risk of engaging in cross-border transactions in cattle and beef (Bruce and Kerr, 1986; Kerr, et al., 1986). The CUSTA attempted to deal with a number these trade irritants and removed the remaining small tariffs. The NAFTA's, unique at the time, investment provisions – Chapter 11 – improved the security of foreign investment and encouraged "greenfield" investments in, and acquisitions of, facilities targeting cross-border movements beef products. While the CUSTA's mechanisms for removing non-tariff barriers were only partially successful (Kerr, 1988), the positive attitude surrounding the agreement quickly led to a considerable north-south re-orientation of cattle and beef movements in North America. Cattle and beef began to flow south out of Western Canada while considerably increased quantities of beef began to flow from the Midwestern US into Central Canada. West to East movements of live animals in Canada virtually ceased. There was a considerable expansion in the beef industry in Western Canada. There was also some evidence of deeper market integration with counterflow movements of products to take advantage of niche market opportunities (Kerr and Hobbs, 1992).

While the effect of these changes was not as dramatic in the US given that the industry there is approximately ten times the size of the Canadian industry, the general result was the creation of a North American market where prices move together closely and arbitrage is observed throughout. This integration mirrors much of the broader NAFTA experience whereby once separate markets have become indistinguishable (Moodley, et al., 2000). The interdependence of the US-Canada market has remained dominant in the beef trade of both countries despite offshore opportunities for diversification of markets in Asia, and in particular in Japan (Kerr, et al., 1994; Hobbs and Kerr, 1994)) and Korea (Kerr and Correll, 1993). The continuing strong interdependence was most strongly illustrated in the market disruption caused by the discovery of bovine spongiform encephalopathy (BSE) – sometimes called "mad cow disease" in North America in 2003 and the subsequent closure of the US-Canada border to beef and live cattle movements(Loppacher and Kerr, 2005). The disruption was felt strongly on both sides of the border with the economic cost being particularly heavy in Canada. Even stronger proof of the power of the forces fostering market integration was the extremely rapid return to normal North American cattle and beef flows when the border eventually re-opened. This was in spite of clear evidence of the risks associated with transborder transactions.

North American market integration is not complete, however, as a number of non-tariff barriers to trade still exist – the US-Canada border still matters in trade flows. Some trade irritants remain despite the obvious benefits available from harmonization – differing grading standards for beef being one of the most obvious examples (Hayes and Kerr, 1997). Anti-dumping and countervail are still available for protectionist purposes (Kerr, 2006a) and harassment of foreign firms (Barichello, 2007). The NAFTA mechanisms that were expected to promote the harmonization of sanitary and phytosanitary standards (SPS) and other technical barriers to trade have not worked as intended (Kerr, 2006b) and multilateral efforts have, as yet, not been able to harmonize SPS regimes – as illustrated by the handling of BSE in North America (Kerr et al., 2007). While many in the beef industry see the benefits of market integration others still seek protection – one example is US legislation to mandate "country of origin" labelling for beef (and a number of other food products) (Kerr and Hall, 2003).

Despite the sometimes significant disruptions to cross-border cattle and beef movements that have arisen since the signing of the CUSTA due to the failure to totally remove non-tariff barriers to trade, the forces of market integration have clearly dominated in the two decades of the CUSTA/NAFTA trade regime. The integration of the North American beef market, however, only provided a canvass upon which the larger changes affecting the beef industry over the same period could be painted.

THE BEEF INDUSTRY'S COMPETITIVE CHALLENGE

Surveys of North American consumers consistently show a strong relative preference for beef compared to its major competitors, pork and chicken. Despite having a preferred product the second half of the 20th century was a difficult one for the beef industries in both the US and Canada – and latterly the integrated North American marketplace. Pork and particularly poultry increased their market share at the expense of beef. The main reason was the declining relative price of chicken and pork. Part of this story is biological. Much of the productivity gains – which lead to declining costs – over the last sixty years has come from improved genetics. The poultry industry is blessed with both multiple offspring and a short generation interval – an ideal situation for rapid genetic improvement. The hog industry also has large litters and a shorter generation interval than beef. While artificial insemination in beef helped to speed genetic progress in beef and particularly dairy cattle, a beef cow only typically produces one offspring and there is a long lag between when a heifer is born and when it can be bred. While there is evidence that beef producers have done well given the hand they have been dealt on the genetic front (Kerr, 1984; Kerr, 1982), the rates of genetic improvement are inevitably less rapid that for beef's major competitors. In addition to providing cost saving technical improvements, genetics assisted the poultry and pork industries ability to standardise – through reduced genetic variation. As suggested above, standardisation was a major mechanism for achieving economies of scale.

The poultry and pork industries have been able move to large scale production in the live animal segments of their supply chains. Economies of scale in poultry and hog barns are augmented by the ability to reduce the vicissitudes of weather that comes from interior housing – leading to greater standardization. In the beef industry, while feedlots have grown considerably in size garnering considerable economies of scale, the cow-calf segment of the industry is primarily based on grazing resources whose geography inhibits large scale operations in most cases – although very large ranches certainly exist. Further, grazing resources tend to be geographically diverse, meaning that there are considerable transportation costs associated with assembling sufficient animals to fill a feedlot that can reap the advantages of economies of scale. As poultry and hog operations do not rely on grazing resources, assembly costs can be considerably reduced or eliminated entirely. The net result is that the beef industry has not benefited from economies of scale to the same degree as its competitors.

Leaving aside the constraints imposed due to the slower rates of genetic improvement that can be achieved and geographically dispersed grazing resources, beef industry participants have long been in the forefront of technological improvement (Kerr, 1991) and have been willing to rapidly adapt to changes in economic incentives (Considine et al., 1986). As a result, the beef industry has made considerable gains in animal feeding efficiency, animal health management, financial management and in the benefits brought to managerial efficiency due to the computer revolution. Individual firms all along the beef supply chain – cow calf operations, feedlots, slaughter facilities, further processors, transport companies, and retailers – as well as their various support industries from nutrient suppliers, to packaging firms to rendering firms have all taken on board, and sometimes created, new technologies.

While individual firms in the beef industry have been instrumental in improving efficiency, it is difficult to make the same case for beef supply chains taken together. The relationships between firms along the supply chain is competitive (and often acrimonious) instead of cooperative – or more correctly firms spend too much effort on attempting to increase their portion of the benefits arising from a transaction relative to the efforts they put into increasing the benefits arising from cooperating to better coordinate the supply chain. There is very little trust among those who engage in transactions up and down beef supply chains. In contrast, the poultry and pork supply chains are much more closely coordinated through the use of complex contract and sometimes vertical integration along segments of the supply chain. Initially this closer coordination was an important innovation to improve standardization and, hence, economies of scale. Having learned to cooperate or integrate to achieve standardization, beef's major competitors were better placed and more experienced in cooperative approaches to supply chains to respond to consumers' desires for diversity in product offerings. Cooperation to provide standardization can be adapted to provide new attributes such as "drug free" or "environmentally friendly" than when there is little trust among supply chain participants and information flows among members is inhibited due to information being viewed as a strategic weapon in attaining a larger share of the benefits arising from a transaction. How beef supply chains (and their constituent firms) adapt to the demand for diversity among consumers will determine the future prosperity of the beef industry and its share of consumers' expenditures on food. While this book cannot provide definite answers as to how the beef supply chains will perform relative to their close competitors, it does provide some insights into the process thus far. The reader can draw their own conclusions.

Chapter 2

THE BEEF INDUSTRY IN THE NORTH AMERICAN MARKETPLACE

AN OVERVIEW OF THE NORTH AMERICAN BEEF INDUSTRY

Each year approximately 200 million metric tons of meat is produced worldwide. Of the total meat produced, 42 percent is pork, 25 percent is beef, 25 percent is chicken, 5 percent is lamb and goat meat, and 3 percent is turkey meat (International Beef Industry Congress, 2003). Currently, the largest beef producer in the world is the United States, which produces 24 percent of the world's total production (Agri-Food Trade Service Fact Sheets, 2003). Canada is the tenth largest world producer and produces approximately 1.2 million tons of beef or 2.5 percent of the world's total production (Agri-Food Trade Service Fact Sheets, 2003).

Prior to the emergence of Bovine Spongiform Encephalopathy (BSE) in Canada and the U.S. in 2003, Australia and the United States were the dominant participants in world beef export markets, having a 23 percent and 16 percent share of total world beef export volumes respectively. Canada followed closely with a 15 percent share of total world beef export volumes in 2001 (International Beef Industry Congress, 2003). Canada exported the majority of its beef into the United States and Mexico. In 2003, 78 percent of Canada's exports moved into the US and 10 percent was exported into Mexico (Agri-Food Trade Service Fact Sheets, 2003). Other major export markets for Canadian beef included Japan and South Korea. Cattle and beef exports are important to Canada, as they are its largest agri-food export. By 2002 these exports were valued at four billion dollars (Canfax Research Services, 2002). The discovery of BSE led to worldwide market closures to exports of beef from North America. Over time, those restrictions have been gradually eased and export patterns are returning to normal but some former markets were still restricted in 2007.

In both the US and Canada the beef industry is also the single largest component of domestic agricultural markets (Agri-Food Trade Service Fact Sheets, 2003). Approximately 0.7 percent of Canada's gross domestic product and slightly less than 1 percent of the US gross domestic product is derived from sales of beef (Agri-Food Trade Service Fact Sheets, 2003). From a different perspective, Canadian farm cash receipts from the sale of cattle and calves totaled $7.8 billion in 2001, 22 percent of total farm receipts (Canfax Research Services, 2001).

With a current cattle inventory of around 13.8 million animals, Canada's cattle herd is about one-fifteenth the size of the US herd (Agri-Food Trade Service Fact Sheets, 2003). Canada's beef feeding industry is regionally concentrated, with approximately 71 percent of all fed cattle production occurring in the western province of Alberta. Ontario is the second largest beef producing province in Canada and produces 18 percent of all fed cattle (Canfax Research Services, 2002). The underlying reason that Alberta has become an epicenter for beef production and processing in Canada is the significant production cost advantages which exist. Economies of scale in both production and processing have also emerged as a result of the industry's regional concentration. In North America, Alberta consistently ranks among the six largest breeding herds and feeding areas along with Texas, Kansas, Nebraska, Colorado, and Iowa. (Unterschultz, 2000).

The North American beef industry can be broken down into four main sectors. The first stage can be divided into two further segments that include seedstock producers and commercial cow/calf operations. Seedstock producers focus on the production of high quality purebred cattle that are sold to commercial operations to assist them in establishing a desired genetic production base. Commercial cow-calf producers raise calves from birth to 400-600 pounds when they are then weaned. In the second stage, cattle feeders background or feed these weaned calves out to heavier weights so that they can be finished on high-energy diets in feedlots. Feedlots represent the final stage in the feeding process. Calves are typically fed to weights in the 1,000 to 1,300 pound range at which time they are ready for slaughter. The entire feeding cycle from the birth of calves on commercial operations to slaughter can range anywhere from twelve to eighteen months (Unterschultz, 2000). After cattle reach slaughter weight they are sent to the packer to be killed and processed. The degree of processing can vary significantly with some beef being processed into ready-to-eat products; some being packaged for placement in retail meat counters, some being tailored to the requirements of the restaurant and food service sectors, while the largest portion of beef production is boxed and sent to retailers for further processing into packages suitable for home consumption.

Each of the sectors varies considerably in their market structure and degree of concentration. Seedstock producers and commercial cow-calf producers vary widely in size, ranging from many small "lifestyle" farms to large commercial operations. The average herd size in Canada in 2001 was 53 head (Statistics Canada Website, n.d.). These segments of the industry have remained relatively unchanged throughout the 1980s and 1990s and have been characterized as being perfectly competitive with many individual sellers that have small herds of cows used to produce offspring that funnel into the rest of the beef supply chain (Alberta Agriculture Food and Rural Development, 2001). It has been argued that the cow/calf sector has always been less concentrated than other sectors of the beef industry because calf production requires more land, labor, and management per unit of output. In particular, many ranches in this sector rely on natural, site specific grazing resources that are geographically dispersed. Further, costs associated with monitoring production on a large cow-calf operation may be extremely high due to the necessary dispersion of animals over a large geographic area. This has resulted in this segment of the beef industry being less conducive to the economies of size that have increased the concentration in other sectors of the beef industry (Barkema and Drabenstott, 1990). Typically, average production costs remain relatively constant as the number of calves produced on an operation increases until very large sizes are reached and consequently very little consolidation has occurred in the cow-calf sector (Barkema et al., 2001).

While relatively constant average production costs and high monitoring costs have not encouraged widespread consolidation in the cow-calf sector, some consolidation has become evident in recent years, as fewer farms became larger in size across North America. This consolidation has been in response to reduced access to markets and price differentials, which have arisen because large feedlots and processors prefer to deal with fewer and larger suppliers. In Canada, 40 percent of the herd is located on farms with over 123 head of cattle. In the US, the largest 3.5 percent of cow-calf operators are producing about a third of the calves and the largest 9 percent of cow-calf operators account for approximately half of the cattle in the US (International Beef Industry Congress, 2003). The remainder of the US cow-calf sector is in herds of less than a hundred head. Thus, while some consolidation is apparent, the majority of commercial cow-calf animals continue to be located in smaller herds (International Livestock Congress, 2002). On the whole, a high level of concentration is not expected due to the geographic, capital and management constraints faced by cow-calf operations.

In the feedlot sector, concentration and consolidation is much more evident. Over the past twenty years the average size of individual feedlots has increased, while the number of feedlots has fallen. This trend has occurred because feedlots have been able to exploit economies of size in cattle feeding. Savings were gained by spreading the costs of fixed investments across a large number of animals (Barkema et al., 2001). Feedlots have also been able to take advantage of economies of scale generated by a constant flow of emerging technologies that reduce their variable costs (Brester, 2002). These include improved feed programs that increase feed efficiency, new health management protocols and medical treatments, and continually evolving identification systems, which in some cases use electronic scanners and databases to improve current tracking and record keeping systems. The latter may contribute to considerable gains in managerial efficiency.

For example, the number of large-scale feedlots (+10,000 head) in Alberta increased from 12 to 33 between 1991 and 2002 and the percentage of total beef production derived from these operations has increased from 31 percent to 58 percent in the same time period (Canfax Research Services, 2002). A similar trend exists in the US, with the largest 2 percent of feedlots now producing approximately 85 percent of all finished cattle and the top three feedlot companies producing about 10 percent of all finished cattle (International Livestock Congress, 2002).

Concentration and consolidation becomes even more evident when examining the packing and processing sector. Since the early 1980s, the number of beef packing plants in the US has declined from more than 600 to 170 (Barkema et al., 2001). Beef processing in the U.S. has moved into the control of fewer and larger companies. The market share of the largest four firms increased from thirty-three percent in the early 1980s to more than 80 percent by 1998 (Pearcy, 2000). The four largest packers are comprised of two publicly traded companies, Tyson Foods/IBP and ConAgra, one private company, Excel/Cargill Foods, and one farmer-owned cooperative, Farmland National Beef. In Canada, the concentration ratio is also increasing, with over 70 percent of all beef currently being processed by three major packers, as compared to the situation in 1991 when only 43 percent of beef was processed by the same firms (International Beef Industry Congress, 2003, 1). The major packers operating in the Canadian beef processing industry are Excel/Cargill, Tyson Foods/IBP and XL Foods Ltd.

The concentration in the packing and processing sector in both the United States and Canada has been a result of shifts in consumer demand and subsequent efforts to trim costs. Economies of size played a key role in generating cost savings. In the last decade new technological developments have expanded the mechanization of plants, improved processing capabilities, increased product innovation, and positively impacted the overall efficiency of plants. Putting in place this technology requires high levels of capital investment. This has limited the ability of smaller high-cost plants to compete with larger plants that can distribute the sunk costs over a larger production base and, consequently, enjoy a lower per-unit cost. Smaller high-cost plants have exited from the industry. The amount of new entry into the industry is limited due to the significant capital investment that is now required.

In addition to the four main sectors in the beef industry, the other crucial link in the beef supply chain is with retailers and food service, which sell the final product to consumers. In terms of the retail sector, supermarkets across North America have consolidated to reduce costs, capture market share, and to benefit from more effective and efficient coordination in all operating areas. For many food retailers, especially in the US, much of the consolidation is being driven by the competitive threat of Wal-Mart and other large discount retailers that have latterly added retail food sales to their stores (Allan, 2002). Traditional grocery stores have relatively low gross margins and low per unit profits, while discounters like Wal-Mart often have half their gross margin and double the profit margin due to their high volumes, lower labor costs, and high turnover (Meeting the Market: Growth through Strategic Alliances, 2002).

The ten largest supermarket chains in the US control 62 percent of food grocery sales. The largest of those is Wal-Mart, second largest is Kroger, and the third largest is Albertsons (International Beef Industry Congress, 2003). In Canada, there is even more concentration in the food retailing sector with the six largest supermarket companies representing 86 percent of all food grocery sales. The top six supermarket companies in the US only represent 37 percent of all food grocery sales although they tend to be regionally concentrated (Kubas and Simmons, 2000). The largest four firms in Canada are Loblaws, Sobeys, Canada Safeway, and Metro.

TRENDS IN BEEF CONSUMPTION

Until a recent turn around, the beef industry had experienced twenty years of declining consumption. The market share for beef remained relatively stable from the mid-1950s to the early 1970s and peaked in 1976 at 52.4 percent of meat consumption (Purcell, 2002). Since then, the market share for beef has declined, while pork and chicken have grown in popularity among consumers. In Measures of Changes in Demand for Beef, Pork, and Chicken, 1975-2000, Purcell (2000) estimates that beef consumption in the US declined by 42 percent during the last two decades of the 20th century.

Declining consumption for beef is also apparent in Canada. From a peak annual consumption of approximately fifty kilograms per person in 1975, Canadian consumers now purchase only slightly more than twenty kilograms per capita. Even more significant is the widening gap between Canadian and US beef consumption patterns, with Canadians now consuming 15 percent less beef than their American counterparts (Unterschultz, 2000).

While the market share and consumption of beef has declined, inflation adjusted retail prices for beef have fallen. Figure 2.1 plots yearly beef consumption from 1980 to 2002 using a deflated beef price index. From the scatter plot it is easy to see that along with consumption, inflation adjusted beef prices dropped significantly over the 1980s and 1990s. Hence, despite a decrease in real prices a decline in the demand for beef has occurred. An important trend to note is that while the demand for beef has declined, poultry demand has increased. Per capita consumption of poultry has risen from 18 kg in the early 1970s to just over 35 kg in 1999 and poultry consumption is projected to continue to increase in the future (Purcell, 2000).

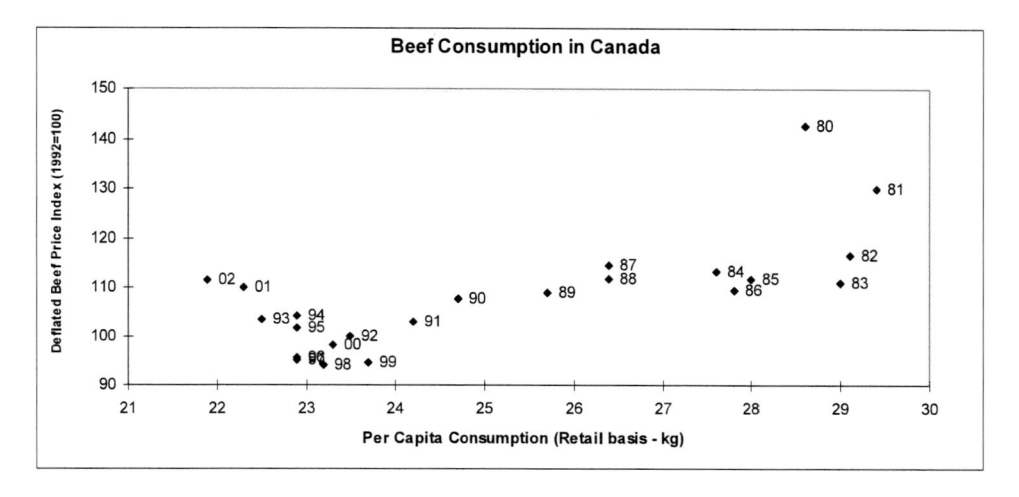

Figure 2.1 - Beef Consumption in Canada between 1980 and 2002
(Deflated price index 1992=100) Source: AAFC Red Meat Information
Source: http://www.agri.gc.ca/redmeat

In examining declining beef consumption and rising poultry consumption, the question arises as to what has caused these changes in consumption patterns. Changes in the relative prices of beef and chicken can explain a portion of the change (Atkins, et al., 1989). Beef prices have typically always been higher than chicken prices on a per unit basis, but the ratio of these prices has increased during the last two decades, from 2.5 in 1976 to 2.9 in 1989, making beef more expensive relative to chicken (Brester et al., 1995; Barkema and Drabenstott., 1990). Investment in poultry research and product innovation increased substantially during this same period. This assisted in reducing production and processing costs, which subsequently lowered retail chicken prices. Lower relative poultry prices have led consumers to substitute away from more expensive beef and to purchase more chicken (Brester et al., 1995).

Changes in the relative prices of beef and chicken can only explain a portion of the total change in consumption, with the substitution away from beef towards poultry being largely attributed to the increased production of consumer oriented products by the poultry industry. Besides lowering production costs, substantial investments in the poultry industry have led to the production of consumer oriented products. By offering a wide array of convenient, high quality, nutritious, and value-added products, the poultry industry has recognized and benefited from a changing consumer (Marsh et al., 2000).

Consumers are caught up in an on-the-go lifestyle and increasingly demand consistent, high-quality, convenient food products. This is in large part due to the increasing participation of women in the work force. In the US, the percentage of females in the labor force rose from 43 percent in 1970 to 60 percent in 1998 and for women ages 35 to 44, the participation rate is as high as 77 percent (Kinsey and Senauer, 1996). As a greater proportion of females enter the labor force, less time is available for meal preparation. The poultry industry was better able to recognize this trend due to its inherent ability to take a more consumer oriented approach as a result of the vertically coordinated nature of industry, which will be discussed in the next chapter. Poultry is also more amenable to product differentiation, as it has a neutral taste that makes it more versatile and amenable to flavoring, coating, and spicing.

Other demographic factors have also negatively impacted the demand for beef including slower population growth, greater ethnic diversity, smaller households, an aging more health conscious population, and rising disposable incomes (Kinsey and Senauer, 1996). Slower growth in the Canadian population implies that total food sales are not likely to grow very much, if at all. Greater ethnic diversity means that consumers are demanding a wider variety of products than have typically been provided by the beef industry.

Disposable incomes have been rising in North America because of an increased number of dual income households, smaller family sizes, and a general rise in the earnings of higher income North Americans. As a result of this increase in income, there has been a growth in the demand for an even wider range of convenience oriented, value-added, nutritious products. Consumers have become increasingly discriminating and less price conscious with food becoming more than just fuel; instead it is becoming a pleasure and wellbeing indicator (Meeting the Market: Growth through Strategic Alliances, 2002). This change implies that other attributes besides price have become important, with the five major attributes being nutrition and health, food safety, food quality, environmental and animal welfare, and convenience (International Livestock Congress, 2000)

Even though consumers are spending less time preparing meals, they are paying more attention to cholesterol levels, fat, food safety, and other health concerns that are perceived to be related to the use of genetically-modified feeds, hormones, antibiotics, and non-organic inputs in meat production. The beef industry, as it is currently structured, has been poorly placed to respond to consumer demands for these attributes. One example of this is the continued production of marbled beef that was popular with consumers in the 1970s. While consumers are increasingly concerned about purchasing low-fat and low-cholesterol meat products, the beef industry, unlike the poultry industry, failed to adjust their product offerings to meet consumers' demands for differentiated products that provide new attributes (Purcell, 1993).

Consumers have also become more demanding when it comes to the quality, consistency, and palatability of the foods that they consume. In the 1990 US National Beef Quality Audit, meat tenderness was ranked the second most important quality characteristic for beef consumers, while overall uniformity and consistency was the most important (Hudson and Purcell, 2003). Several studies show that the beef industry has failed to provide consistently tender products to consumers. In a survey conducted in Alberta, over 30 percent of steaks and 35 percent of roasts purchased in a six month period in six supermarket chains were ranked as unacceptable for tenderness by a trained panel in a laboratory setting (Brewin and Ulrich, 1999). In a survey done in Canada, 44 percent of the consumers surveyed felt that buying beef was a game of chance with respect to whether the quality they received met their expectations (International Livestock Congress, 2002).

Although the beef consumption has declined it continues to be a significant source of protein in the average diet, accounting for 6.7 percent of total retail counter sales and 35.1 percent of every retail meat dollar in Canada (Unterschultz, 2000). In order to regain and maintain market share from other proteins, the beef industry needs to develop products that meet the changing demands of consumers. Successfully increasing demand means that the five principal demand drivers, as identified by consumers, must become the industry's focus: (1) consistency, quality, and palatability, (2) health and nutrition, (3) food safety, (4) environmental sustainability and animal welfare, and (5) convenience products (International Livestock Congress, 2000,). At the 2003 International Beef Industry Congress, Randy Blach, an analyst with US-based Cattlefax, summarized this idea by explaining that, "the consumer is the boss and as a result to expand demand, increase market-share, and improve profitability the beef industry must deliver a more consistent, convenient, consumer-oriented product" (International Beef Industry Congress, 2003).

CONSUMERS AND BRANDED BEEF PROGRAMS

Beef has traditionally been marketed as a generic product, with consumers purchasing beef products with broad quality characteristics and then transforming them into meals in their kitchens (Barkema, 1994). Consumers have typically not chosen beef based on differentiated quality characteristics, but this is slowly changing as the industry begins to focus on increased product differentiation and "branded beef" in an effort to better satisfy consumer demand. Branded beef is seen as a move in the right direction as a brand provides a promise to consumers that the product will deliver consistently the qualities consumers demand (Smith, 2000).

Ideally, existing grading systems should enable consumers to identify and choose products that will satisfy their demands for different attributes. The problem with existing grading systems is that the number of attributes being demanded has increased so that grades no longer provide sufficient information signals to consumers. Further, the attributes demanded vary significantly from consumer to consumer, outstripping the ability of the traditional marketing system to classify and identify all of the important attributes (Barkema, 1994).

Both Canada and the US have existing grading systems that are designed to grade beef based on different characteristics. Canada's top grades are Canada Prime, Canada AAA, Canada AA and Canada A, which differ mainly by the amount of marbling in the meat. Other characteristics that are taken into account during the grading process are colour, age, and the yield of the carcass. The US system for grading beef is very similar to the Canadian system, with USDA Prime, USDA Choice, USDA Select and USDA Standard close to being equivalent to Canada Prime, Canada AAA, Canada AA, and Canada A respectively (Beef Trade Website, 2003).

Even within the existing Canadian and US grading systems there is a failure to identify adequate proxy variables for different measurements of quality such as tenderness. Current standards grade on marbling, which does not provide an accurate or consistent measurement of tenderness. This means that even within the same quality grade, tenderness can vary considerably and may result in a negative eating experience that could reduce consumer confidence and consequently the demand for beef (Lusk et al., 1999).

Branded differentiated products are an alternative to reliance on grades to signal attributes of a product, creating a system whereby consumers recognize the meat and its associated characteristics through a particular brand (Lusk, 2001). Brands also provide consumers with a guarantee by the brander that they will receive the same quality every time they consume a product. In this sense brand "quality" is defined as consistency, tenderness, flavour, source verification, process verification, food safety, or any other specific characteristic that is demanded by consumers and provided under a particular brand (International Livestock Congress, 2002).

With the creation of branded beef products, the potential for niche markets to emerge is increasing. Product differentiation can be used to appeal to smaller groups of consumers that are willing to pay a premium for beef that includes the characteristics that they demand (Peterson and Phillips, 2001). Consumers may be willing to pay a premium if branded products lower their transaction costs. With branded products, consumers face less uncertainty with regards to the quality of the product. Lower information costs are incurred, as less time is spent searching among products and monitoring products to determine which one will provide a given level of quality. This results from the guarantees of consistency and uniformity provided under a brand name. Given the savings in transaction costs derived from consuming branded products, consumers are often willing to pay more for them.

The willingness of consumers to pay a premium for branded beef is critical to the ability of branded beef products to improve profitability in the beef industry. While branding a retail product can be advantageous there are also added costs to consider (Lusk, 2001). These costs are typically associated with the additional production and segregation costs incurred to meet the identity preservation requirements of branded beef programs, as well as costs of safeguarding any asset specific investments that have been made.

If a firm differentiates its product on the basis of a specific quality or attribute, then an animal produced with that particular attribute must be separated from other animals throughout the supply chain (Lusk, 2001). Segregation and identity preservation costs will vary significantly and depend on the type of attribute being guaranteed and how easy, or difficult, it is to produce and detect this attribute along the supply chain. The production of a particular attribute may also require specific physical or human capital investments that will result in additional costs, which will be discussed in the next chapter. Total costs will also depend on how many firms along the supply chain are involved in the production of a particular attribute. The costs associated with monitoring and preserving a particular characteristic will increase as the number of supply chain participants required to produce the attribute increases.

Very little research is available that focuses on consumers' willingness to pay for branded beef programs that guarantee specific attributes. Instead, most of the literature focuses more generally on the increased demand for different attributes. A small number of studies have focused on consumers' willingness to pay for tender, more consistent beef products including Lusk et al. (1999) in 1999 and Fuez and Umberger (2001). This type of research is important given that lack of tenderness and low overall uniformity and consistency have been identified as the most important quality concerns for beef consumers.

Lusk et al. (1999) found that consumers exhibited a preference for tender steak. Blind taste tests revealed that 72 percent of consumers preferred tender steak relative to tough steaks and

36 percent of consumers were willing to pay an average premium of US$1.23/lb for a steak that was guaranteed to be tender (Lusk et al., 1999). In the same study, when information was revealed to consumers regarding the tenderness of the steak together with a taste test, 90 percent preferred tender steak and 51 percent were willing to pay an average premium of US$1.84/lb for a guaranteed tender steak (Lusk et al., 1999). The significance of both of these tests is that consumers are able to distinguish between varying levels of tenderness and are willing to pay a premium for a guaranteed level of tenderness.

A large proportion of the participants in this study failed to recognize government grades as an indicator for quality even though these grades are intended to inform consumers of beef quality (Lusk et al., 1999). Current Canadian and US grading systems do not sufficiently segregate carcasses for tenderness. Consequently, there is a potential for industry participants to develop different branded beef programs that promote increased coordination along the supply chain to provide a guarantee of quality to consumers. In return, they should obtain a premium price for their product and have fewer unsatisfied consumers.

BRANDED BEEF PROGRAMS

In the past few years beef demand in the US has begun to turn around. Since 1998, after nearly 20 years of continuous decline, demand in the US has increased each year (Purcell, 2002). These increases in demand have been attributed, in part, to the increasing efforts of the beef industry to produce differentiated value-added branded products that better meet consumer demands (Kovanda and Schroeder, 2003). In 1998, producer and processor brands accounted for between 10 and 12 percent of the total market share of US beef (Allan, 2002). It has been suggested that this could rise to 50 percent before 2010 (Lamp, 1998). Similar information is not available for Canada, but the percentage of the total market share of beef marketed through branded beef programs in Canada is probably lower than in the US given that the emergence of these programs has been slower in Canada. The slower emergence of these programs may help to explain part of the 15 percent difference between the Canadian and US quantity demanded per capita – consumers in Canada have less access to branded beef, and hence the attribute signals it provides. Consequently, Canadians have continued to consume alternative meat products.

A number of marketing arrangements are being used in the effort to provide branded products, and they vary based on their program specifications, management structures, and coordination mechanisms. Beef is differentiated in a variety of ways, with the likelihood of success of a particular brand depending on the costs versus consumers' willingness to pay (Lusk, 2001). Tenderness is one of the most frequently branded attributes. Other programs are differentiated as "natural" products that are hormone and/or antibiotic free and in some cases even free of any genetically-modified feeds. A further extension of this market is the production of organic beef products and "safe" beef products, which are promoted as being free of E-coli and other bacteria. The latter is typically accomplished by implementing a Hazard Analysis – Critical Control Point (HACCP)-based management and monitoring program that identifies risk areas and implements protocols throughout the production and processing stages to reduce these risks.

Markets have also arisen for leaner beef with a low level of marbling, targeting consumers who are concerned with lowering their cholesterol and fat intake. Other branding initiatives include beef that has been produced in a particular region, is grass-fed, is environmentally friendly, animal-welfare friendly, of a particular breed, or is presented in a convenient value-added product format. Attributes that are often included in branded beef programs, in combination with those mentioned above include source-verification, process-verification, product freshness, appearance, and a particular USDA or Canadian grade.

In terms of the mechanisms used to improve vertical coordination, there is no single format for developing a particular branded beef program. Vertical coordination varies significantly and often depends on which supply chain member initiates the program and what attributes are being guaranteed, as this will determine the involvement of different supply chain members in a particular program. Currently, four dominant supply chain structures can be identified and include brand licensing programs, marketing alliances, new-generation cooperatives, and externally coordinated programs.

Brand licensing programs have most commonly emerged under the auspices of existing purebred breeding organizations. These programs typically require that cattle meet a certain genetic template, specific to a particular breed. They create value by centering the program on a branded product that uses breed as a proxy to convey a certain standard of quality to the consumer (Anton, 2002). Licensing programs tend to be very loosely coordinated with the only requirements being that participants are certified to sell beef under the program name and that the breed of cattle entering the program are verified through visual inspection and/or genetic records (Anton, 2002). The largest existing licensing program is the Certified Angus Beef (CAB) program run by the American Angus Association. Similar programs to the CAB program are emerging, including the Certified Hereford Beef program run by the American Hereford Association.

Branded programs have also been initiated by packers, processors, and retailers under a marketing alliance. These programs differ from brand licensing programs in that they are owned by operations that purchase finished cattle from cow-calf operators and/or feedlots via a marketing alliance that uses a grid pricing system with more detailed program specifications[1]. Marketing alliances, and their associated grid pricing systems, typically have particular quality, yield, and process requirements, creating incentives for cow-calf operators and feedlots to produce animals that yield the desired quality traits (Anton, 2002). The production of high quality animals that meet all program requirements is rewarded with premium prices above a set base price. The production of low quality animals results in discounts and even direct exclusion from the program.

Prior to the emergence of grid-based pricing systems, cattle have traditionally been sold on a live animal basis, with pricing based on the average traits of an entire pen of cattle. This type of pricing has occurred despite well-documented sizeable differences in value among animals. Basing price on average quality results in the market failing to send the appropriate price signals to producers regarding the quality attributes demanded by buyers (Kovanda and Schroeder, 2003, 4). Marketing alliances that use grid-based pricing systems have been

---

[1] Grid pricing systems price cattle based on carcass quality, which is determined by the measurement of several different elements that often include carcass grade, carcass weight, yield grade, and rib-eye size. This differs from a live-weight pricing system where cattle are priced based on a visual inspection of the live animal and animal weight.

suggested as one method of improving information flow and reducing quality variation. With grid pricing cattle are priced on carcass quality and producers are provided with incentives to produce cattle with specific quality traits and to improve the overall quality of their cattle (Unterschultz, 2000). Cattle are typically graded on two dimensions in a grid-based system. Firstly, a quality grade is used to measure the taste and palatability of the meat. The maturity of an animal is also taken into account, as older animals are generally thought to be tougher and have a less desirable taste. Secondly, the amount of edible meat or yield of the carcass is considered (Beshear and Lamb, 1998).

New generation cooperatives are also emerging as a means of producing branded beef products. Cooperatives are typically producer-owned entities that take a systems approach to branded beef production. The primary goal of cooperatives is to enhance the flow of information to members, to reduce production costs, and to increase profitability (Beshear and Lamb, 1998). Their focus is to create new efficiencies by implementing uniform practices within each segment of the supply chain and by coordinating production, processing, and marketing through alliances with other sectors of the industry (Kovanda and Schroeder, 2003). This type of system may facilitate the creation of stronger incentives for cow-calf operators to focus on improving quality.

The management structure of new generation cooperatives is much more formal than the previous types of branding arrangements discussed above. To ensure the stability and longevity of the program, membership of new generation cooperatives is often fixed and members are usually required to invest equity into the venture through the purchase of shares that come with certain rights and obligations (Anton, 2002). Shares establish a two-way contract between members and the cooperative, which requires members to sell a certain number of cattle through the cooperative and requires that the cooperative take delivery of these cattle (Boland and Katz, 2000). Investment in a cooperative also establishes that the beef will be produced, marketed, and processed in a specific manner. Often a grid-pricing system is used, which provides incentives for members to comply with the program requirements. Further, in addition to the premiums and discounts provided on the grid, closed cooperatives may pay dividends or bonuses to members that market cattle through their program (Anton, 2002).

New generation cooperative is a term that has been applied to fifty or so beef industry cooperatives in the US thus far (Boland and Katz, 2000). Ranchers Renaissance, US Premium Beef, and Rancher's Choice are all good examples of cooperatives that are driven by cow-calf operators and that are aligned with other supply chain members such as feedlots, packers and retailers to produce branded beef products.

Externally coordinated branded beef programs are less common than any of the other formats discussed. The underlying approach of this branding strategy is to create a fully vertically coordinated supply chain with the initiative being driven by a newly formed corporation instead of an existing supply chain participant. The majority of these operations have only existed conceptually, with limited success when programs are actually put into operation. This type of program has not been neglected completely, however, as the underlying structure of these programs is seen to be a possible method of producing beef for large-scale branded beef programs in the future. Future Beef Operations was the first such initiative in the US. It attempted to coordinate cow-calf producers, feedlots, packing/processing, and retailers through the formation of a new entity (Roybal, 2001).

Although this initiative failed, it provides some insights into how future branded beef programs might be coordinated.

The types of supply chain coordination outlined above constitute a broad framework. Within this framework, significant variations can occur in terms of organizational and management structure. Many different value chain alliance structures have emerged within the industry and each is unique in certain aspects. However, identifying common features in a broad framework is useful in an analysis of the reasons behind different methods of vertical coordination.

Regardless of the type of coordination mechanism chosen, the success of a branded beef program depends on identifying a niche market and building brand loyalty (Hayes et al., 2003). Operations must be able to achieve a scale of production large enough to justify the costs of creating and maintaining the differentiated brand among consumers (Hayes et al., 2003). They must also be able to ensure a consistent and year-round supply of product to retailers and other end-users. Lastly, management must be able to assert control over supply. Without supply control entry will occur and production will expand to capture premiums until no premiums exist in the market. In order to limit this self-defeating increase in supply, brands must be based on some fixed attribute or membership must be limited through the use of membership fees, property rights, licensing requirements, or strict production standards that limit eligibility (Hayes et al., 2003).

Existing programs have been examined with respect to their objectives and program requirements. Although program structures can vary significantly, several commonalities exist. Ward (2001), surveyed different alliances in the US beef industry and found that the stated objectives in over half of the alliances mentioned a customer focus, beef industry improvements, improved communication between stages, and product enhancement. Over three-quarters of the alliances spanned more than three stages of the production and marketing process in an effort to improve information flow through the supply chain (Ward, 2001). About one-third of the alliances had various forms of licensing agreements, non-participation penalties, certification requirements, and/or required investment/fees to provide a level of commitment (Ward, 2001). Over half of the alliances required the use of a specific breed and had some requirements for source verification (Ward, 2001).

BRANDED BEEF CASE STUDIES

To illustrate how branded beef programs have developed, it is useful to examine a number of case studies. Several programs are examined in order to provide examples of the different management structures outlined in the previous section. Case studies of Certified Angus Beef, Decatur Beef Alliance, Ranchers Renaissance, and Future Beef Operations are discussed. These programs were selected as they all had a similar objective of providing an overall high quality, consistent, tender beef product. It is important to note that while these case studies provide an insight into the different methods of supply chain coordination that are emerging in the beef industry, many programs exist that vary from the case studies presented. The purpose of these case studies is to provide a snapshot illustration of what is occurring in the industry, while recognizing that these four structures are not the only ones that have emerged.

Certified Angus Beef

The Certified Angus Beef (CAB) brand was started in 1978 and is the industry's oldest, largest, and most successful brand. CAB operates as a non-profit division of the American Angus Association, which is comprised of more than 28,000 Angus breeders. The goal of the program is to produce high quality, tender, flavourful beef. The CAB functions independently with the guidance of a nine-member board of directors with a mission to increase demand for Angus cattle through its branded beef program (Certified Angus Beef Website, n.d.). Approximately 500 million pounds of beef are marketed through the CAB program annually (Kovanda and Schroeder, 2003). The program has grown by about 30 percent each year and sells products in the US and fifty other countries in more than 8,000 restaurants and retail locations. Nonetheless, the CAB program has less than a one percent share in the US market (Brester, 2002).

The focus of the Certified Angus Beef program is to produce consistent quality products with an emphasis on brand integrity. The grading of CAB is done by the United States Department of Agriculture and the Canadian Beef Grading Agency rather than using in-house grades by processors. No herds are "certified" and no living Angus cattle are actually "Certified Angus Beef". Rather, after meeting the live specification of being at least 51 percent black-hided, the program has eight further carcass specifications. On average, only 17.3 percent of evaluated Angus cattle qualify to be sold under the Certified Angus Beef brand (Certified Angus Beef Website, n.d.). The focus of the program is to provide price incentives to improve cattle quality and increase the percentage of cattle accepted in the program. Since inception, some cow-calf operators that specialize in Angus cattle have focused on producing animals that are suitable for the CAB. Some of these producers have achieved an acceptance rate of more than 50 percent (Certified Angus Beef Website).

The Certified Angus Beef program differs from other programs in that it does not own cattle or beef products during any part of production or processing. Instead, the CAB program licenses packers, processors, distributors, retailers, and restaurants to harvest, fabricate, and merchandise Certified Angus Beef product. Financial rewards are derived along the supply chain through the preserved integrity of the brand by tracking product from the cow-calf operation to the processor level with a tagging system that is exclusive to the program. To be eligible for the tagging program, the Angus Association must certify cow-calf operators as producing animals that are Angus or Angus-cross. Although the existing tagging system is not a complete farm to plate traceability system, it allows for supply chain participants to achieve premiums through the identification of acceptable animals and a value based marketing system (Certified Angus Beef Website, n.d.).

An experimental auction combined with a consumer survey in 2002, which valued steaks with different attributes, suggested that consumers were willing to pay an average premium of US$2.33/lb for CAB products compared to generic products (Kovanda and Schroeder, 2003). The higher consumer demand and willingness to pay for CAB products has translated into fed cattle premiums of US$2.00 to $5.00 per-hundred weight. A portion of this premium is typically passed back to the Angus cow-calf operators when calves are purchased by feedlots (Certified Angus Beef Website, n.d.). Given the program's focus on breed, relatively little supply chain coordination is required to preserve product identity and to pay participants for the desired attribute. This is because the characteristic is visible during the entire production process as well as the initial stages of processing.

While packers, retailers, and other merchandisers do market Certified Angus Beef and must purchase licenses, there are no long-term commitments required by cow-calf operators and feedlots (Certified Angus Beef Website). Typically, formal agreements between packers, feedlots, and cow-calf operators are not necessary to ensure a constant supply of beef cattle into the CAB program. This is because the program requirements are broad enough that a large supply of cattle is available to fill them through more informal arrangements. Indirectly, a certain degree of commitment does arise, as in deciding to target the Certified Angus Beef market, cow-calf operators make a voluntary decision to align production with CAB breed and quality requirements. Hence, they have an incentive to attempt to achieve the premiums associated with the program. Quality requirements in this case are fairly minimal; once beef has been identified as being from an Angus animal it must grade as either USDA Prime or Canada Prime to fulfill the program's requirements (Certified Angus Beef Website).

The Certified Angus Beef brand is an interesting system in that it uses fairly narrow grading requirements to fulfill its guarantee of tenderness. Aside from cattle having to be Angus, they have to grade as either the top 35 percent of USDA Choice or USDA/Canada Prime. There is little formal research on the relationship between breed and meat quality. Hammack (1998) suggests that the Angus breed has a higher level of marbling than other breeds, and marbling is related to tenderness and flavour.

Decatur Beef Alliance

Decatur Beef Alliance is a marketing alliance that began in 1994 and is managed by Decatur County Feedyard in Kansas. Decatur County Feedyard is a privately owned feedlot that has been in operation since 1977 and has a one-time capacity to feed 35,000 head of cattle. Approximately 90 percent of the cattle fed in the lot each year are run through the alliance. More than 130 cow-calf operators throughout the United States currently participate in the program and approximately 50,000 head are being processed each year through the alliance (Weibert, 2004). The mission of the alliance is to produce consistent, quality beef at the lowest possible cost and provide the highest quality service to both feeders and packers through the use of all available technology and proven techniques. The goal of the program is to avoid "average management", as there is tremendous range in animal growth patterns and carcass value. By penning cattle together from start to finish in the typical feedlot and, hence, ignoring these differences, creates carcass discounts and inefficiencies in the production process that increase costs. Thus, traditional management practices often result in a final product with considerable inconsistency in quality. Instead of managing pens of cattle "on average", the Decatur Beef Alliance manages each individual animal to its optimum genetic endpoint (Weibert, 2004).

The alliance is partnered with Excel's processing plant in Dodge City, Kansas. A quality-based grid pricing system is used, where cow-calf operators are paid for high quality, high yielding cattle. The grid has high premiums and large discounts in order to provide incentives to focus on the production of top quality cattle. The alliance does not own a particular brand, but instead directs its production towards existing brand programs run by Excel, which include Certified Angus Beef, Sterling Silver, and Ranchers Registry. All of these brands focus on providing customers with consistent, tender, and flavourful beef.

The alliance chose not to develop and own its own brand for several reasons. The owner of Decatur County Feedyard, Warren Weibert stated, "Developing a brand through an alliance is tremendous in terms of the large volumes typically required and the amount of organization required to ensure ongoing supplies are available. Large amounts of capital must also be available to develop, market, and sell a brand." (Weibert, 2004) Aligning with Excel also has an advantage in that Excel has a large processing capacity and the production can be easily absorbed into the plant's processing activities. Consequently, the alliance is not limited in what it supplies to Excel on an ongoing basis and future growth is also not limited. This reduces the degree of coordination required to ensure adequate supplies, which is often significant for alliances that are the sole supplier to one particular brand, as they have to ensure an ongoing and constant supply of product. At the same time, Excel also benefits from the partnership with Decatur, as the alliance creates a constant, predictable, flow of cattle into the plant and into its high end programs, reducing the time spent searching for and procuring cattle.

Program requirements for cow-calf operators entering into the program are minimal. Specific production protocols are not required, but instead recommended production guidelines are provided in an effort to enhance cow-calf operators' returns. They must commit a minimum of sixty head of cattle of the same sex into the alliance and are charged an alliance fee of US$5/head and an additional US$0.02/head/day on feed. The feedlot is flexible in terms of the ownership of cattle and will purchase up to a one-half interest in cattle entering into the alliance in order to reduce the capital commitment required by cow-calf operators. Currently about forty percent of cow-calf operators retain ownership and the feedlot partners with the remaining sixty percent of suppliers (Weibert, 2004).

In terms of commitment, cow-calf operators can enter into the program at anytime. Once they enter their cattle into the program they have to sign a feeding agreement that stipulates those cattle are part of the alliance and that the feedlot is responsible for marketing their cattle. The latter is done on the basis of individual animal performance. Cattle are tagged with an electronic ID tag upon entering the feedlot. Once cattle have been in the lot for 70 days they are sorted twice based on different quality indicators and co-mingled in mixed ownership lots in order to optimize cattle performance on the grid. Therefore, an individual cow-calf operator's cattle may be in several different lots and will be sold at different times (Weibert, 2004). The electronic ID tags manage information on an individual animal basis.

The idea behind Decatur's system is that electronic ID tags and co-mingling avoid the problems associated with one cow-calf operator's cattle being separated into one lot throughout the production process, which often results in inefficient lot sizes and groups of cattle that vary in terms of weight and finishing times. The sorting process centers on the use of the Micro Beef Technology ACCU-TRACTM Electronic Cattle Management System, which allows the feedlot to measure and sort individual cattle based on different quality and economic indicators. To implement the ultrasound technology and sorting system the feedlot spent approximately US$650,000. It also pays a yearly license and data management fee to Micro Beef (Weibert, 2004).

The feedlot alliance has incurred costs to implement the system and also has higher ongoing costs as a result of the increased management and sorting that occurs in the program. The alliance fees cover the increased management and marketing costs and the cost of the electronic identification tag. While the feedlot receives some payback directly, the system it has implemented also enhances the paybacks received by cow-calf operators and the quality of information that they have access to. Cow-calf operators that perform well within the alliance usually increase the number of head they enter into the program, and they also typically progess to retaining ownership. For the feedlot, less time is spent procuring cattle; they have a more constant income stream as a result of custom feeding fees, and are able to operate at an optimum capacity.

Cow-calf operators in the program are located throughout the United States, with the majority being from Kansas, Nebraska, Wyoming, and Montana. Feeder calves are assembled and fed at Decatur and then sent to the Excel processing plant in Dodge City. A key element in the success of the alliance is that it markets all of its cattle into one Excel plant. Besides premiums, the alliance is providing cow-calf operators with data on carcass performance. For this data to be reliable the alliance must focus on selling to one plant in one location, as opposed too moving around and reducing the traceability of animals and the flow of information. Excel provides the alliance with weekly market access and manages the data through an in-house electronic tracking system. There is no written contract or commitment between the alliance and Excel in terms of the number of cattle to be supplied. Consequently, the alliance can focus on selling cattle based on their optimal finishing times. Furthermore, it does not have to spend a great deal of time gathering and managing data from several different processors (Weibert, 2004).

The cattle from one individual cow-calf operator may be sold through several different lots at different times. After the last animal is sold, suppliers receive information on individual animals – close outs – that include their feedlot performance, measured carcass data and the programs that individual animals were allocated to, a net return statement based on premiums received and costs incurred, and a comparative report that compares the cow-calf operator's cattle to others in the alliance. Particularly important is the focus on the overall net return instead of simply the premiums received, as this balances premiums against the increased costs incurred to obtain those premiums.

The Decatur Beef Alliance is a fairly flexible marketing alliance. Cow-calf operator requirements are low and commitment to the program is limited to one production cycle. Alignment with one Excel processing plant and its branded beef programs reduces the marketing effort required by the alliance and allows for the formation of an ongoing partnership that benefits both the alliance and the packer. The alliance has grown at a rate of 10-15 percent each year and has been quite successful in achieving its goal of producing high quality cattle that return premiums to the cow-calf operator in addition to the provision of quality information (Weibert, 2004).

In 1999, 99.74 percent of the cattle marketed in the alliance had a yield grade of 3 or better, 57 percent made Choice grade or better, and 97 percent made Select grade or better. Outliers in the program totaled 3.37 percent compared to an industry average of 9.71 percent (Decatur Beef Alliance Fact Sheet, 2003). Hitting such a high quality target through the focus on individual animal management rather than average lot management resulted in participants receiving average premiums of US$15/head. Timely marketing on the grid resulted in additional producer premiums of US$5-10/head (Decatur Beef Alliance Fact Sheet, 2003). Decatur has focused on continuously looking at different opportunities to provide differentiated beef products and to add value at the cow-calf, feedlot, and packer level. Marketing alliances, such as the Decatur Beef Alliance, are structured in a way that allows for different segments to maintain their independence and a large amount of flexibility, while still being able to increase transparency of information and add value along the system.

Ranchers Renaissance

Ranchers Renaissance is a new generation closed cooperative that commenced operation in 1997. Ranchers concentrated in Texas and Colorado own it, but others are located as far away as Alberta. Ranchers Renaissance is a vertically aligned beef production system based on the creation of partnerships between ranchers, feeders, a processor (Excel), and retail end users (Ranchers Renaissance Website, n.d.). The stated goal of the cooperative is to bring together all industry players to build trust, better understand the consumer, lower costs, share information, improve the quality of beef being produced, and ultimately share in the additional value created by a branded beef program (Pearcy, 2000).

Using a value-based marketing system where producers and others in the supply chain are paid for a high quality product, the cooperative's mission is to create "a customer-focused, vertically coordinated beef production system, with profits derived from increased efficiency and consistent, high-quality finished products" (Ranchers Renaissance Website, n.d.). The finished products derived from the Ranchers Renaissance cooperative are sold under several retail product labels including King Soopers' Cattleman's Collection, Harris Teeter Rancher, Sobey's Select, and Safeway's Angus Ranchers Reserve. All of these brands guarantee their beef products to be consistent, tender, and flavourful (International Beef Industry Congress, 2003). The labels that Ranchers Renaissance products are marketed under are owned by the respective retailers. The cooperative itself does not own a brand name label, as in the retail environment a rental fee must be paid to gain shelf space for a product. This space is quite expensive to rent and cooperatives often cannot afford to pay the fees. Participants (cow-calf operators) are limited in the amount of investment they are willing to make in order to participate in a cooperative and if the capital requirements are substantial it is unlikely the cooperative will be able to recruit participants. Instead, cooperatives often prefer to produce for brands that are store owned (Butler, 2003).

Unlike marketing alliances that often focus on guaranteeing attributes that are measured under existing government grading programs, producer-driven cooperatives, such as Ranchers Renaissance, tend to rely less on current grading standards as a measurement of quality and have more detailed program specifications. The programs discussed previously typically do not require members to comply with detailed specifications, as the increased identity preservation and monitoring requirements would require a considerable amount of resources. In a new generation cooperative, members are driving the program and can more readily observe whether program specifications are met. They are likely to also be more motivated to follow program requirements given that they own the program and will profit directly from its success.

Under the Ranchers Renaissance system, twenty-three quality control points verifying genetics, source, production and processing procedures, animal health and welfare, and feed programs have been implemented in order to provide consumers with quality assurance and a consistently tender product. Third party verification ensures that all members comply with specifications and electronic ear tags are used to collect data on each animal, which is then shared among all segments of the supply chains (Ranchers Renaissance Website, n.d.).

As a closed cooperative, membership is required in order to produce beef under the Ranchers Renaissance program. Membership is broken into two classes, A and B, which are based on the number of cattle supplied to the program. In order to be in Class A, members must provide a high volume of animals, whereas Class B members are required to provide a lower volume of animals. Fees vary based on membership class, with class A members, paying a one time entry fee of US$25,000 and from there the fee moves to as low as US$2,500, with the fee being determined based on the number of head an individual is committing to market through the cooperative. Currently there are 21 Class A members. Several of the Class A members individually own and process around 30,000 head of cattle through the program each year. Higher initial investments are required for larger suppliers given that they are providing a large percentage of the animals that flow through the program. Their long-term commitment is necessary to reduce variability in quality and to ensure the long-term stability of the program.

New members are interviewed in order to ensure their operations will fit within the requirements and that they are willing to provide a long-term commitment to the program. Their operations are also audited to ensure that they comply with all production standards and program regulations. Audits to ensure compliance are conducted by a third party. In addition to initial inspections, evaluations of all ranchers, feedlots, and the packer are performed each year (Butler, 2003). A yearly fee of US$3.00 per head is also assessed in order to cover promotion and administration costs. The cooperative is a non-profit organization and any remaining funds at the end of the year are dispersed for research or redistributed to members (Ranchers Renaissance Website, n.d.).

Ranchers are required to commit a minimum number of cattle each year based on a three year rolling average of their prior commitments. Each feedlot has to guarantee feeding space to a certain number of Ranchers Renaissance cattle each year in addition to paying an initial membership fee similar to that paid by cow-calf operators. Every lot of cattle is contracted with Excel in order to coordinate production and ensure a constant flow into packing plants. Four key retailers, which include Kroger, Harris Teeter, Sobeys, and Safeway are also contracted to purchase a given quantity of beef each year under their various brand names (Butler, 2003). Commitment between cow-calf operators and feedlots is achieved through required initial investments and incentives provided by premiums based on quality performance. Contracts are used to ensure the commitment between Ranchers Renaissance and the packer and retailer. A mutual relationship exists with these partners, as they both have an incentive to maintain their association with the program. Packers gain from the premiums received and retailers gain from the ability to sell a differentiated beef product that increases their sales of meat.

John Butler, the President of Ranchers Renaissance, stated that the most important element for success of the program has been the long-term commitment of all participating members (Butler, 2003). As ranchers retain ownership of the product until it is sold to the retailer, alignment of the entire supply chain is necessary in order to ensure that each segment of production and processing adheres to the quality and process control standards of the cooperative. An incentive-based grid pricing system is used to reward all supply chain members, with payments based on the end performance of cattle. In addition to compliance with program specifications, which will improve the conformity of the cattle produced, the grid measures the performance of cattle based on specific yield, marbling, texture, and colour criteria (Butler, 2003). Since inception, the Ranchers Renaissance approach to producing branded beef products appears to have been very successful, with the cooperative processing over 200,000 head of cattle in 2003 and achieving over 30 percent growth since production began in 2001 (Butler, 2003).

New generation cooperatives, such as Ranchers Renaissance, are structured so that all segments act as partners in a coordinated supply chain. This means that there should be transparency of information along the entire system, which allows for Ranchers Renaissance to verify the source, process, and genetics of all of its beef and produce a differentiated product (Butler, 2003). Through the use of formal arrangements via contracts and equity investments, the commitment of supply chain members is ensured. This differs from licensing and packer-owned programs where more loose and informal arrangements are used between supply chain partners. As will be discussed in the next chapter, the underlying reason behind this higher level of commitment is to protect the specialized investments that have been made by supply chain members to meet the more detailed production and processing requirements of cooperative based programs.

Future Beef Operations

Future Beef Operations was a comprehensive production to retail beef system with close vertical coordination along the supply chain. It was initiated in the US in 2001 (Bastian, 2001, 3). Similar to Ranchers Renaissance, it tried to bring together all members of the supply chain, but was different in that the program was neither producer nor packer driven. Instead, a new corporation was formed with major investors coming from different segments of the supply chain as well as outside of the industry.

The overall plan of Future Beef Operations was to coordinate genetics, production, and processing to deliver consistent high quality beef products tailored to a major chain of retail stores. To achieve this, investors from the industry were brought together to build a new processing and packing plant that would supply 1,700 Safeway stores in North America with branded beef products. They then partnered with feedlots and cow-calf operators using a grid pricing system to provide incentives for producing high quality cattle (Bastian, 2001). While Future Beef Operations' system of coordination was very similar to that of Ranchers Renaissance, it differed in the fact that ownership of cattle was not retained by cow-calf operators throughout the system. Further, significant investment was incurred to build a plant, whereas Ranchers Renaissance does not own any cattle or processing facilities and is merely a non-profit organization facilitating the production of branded beef products. Future Beef Operations was also different from a marketing alliance in that it was not initiated by an existing entity in the industry and instead was started as a new organization.

Less than a year after Future Beef Operations began production it filed for bankruptcy and ceased operation. There are several reasons behind the demise of Future Beef Operations, some of which are related to the structure of the branded beef program and some that are attributed to bad timing and technical failures. The biggest downfalls included the fact that Future Beef Operations had an exclusive contract with Safeway and no other customers (Ishmael, 2002). They also did not adequately address risk within their contract with

Safeway, and when Future Beef began to lose money, Safeway backed away from the risk sharing arrangements that existed (Ishmael, 2002). The failure of Future Beef Operations does not mean that this type of management structure is not viable, but issues can arise that would not arise under the alternative structures outlined above. The major mistake may have been that no retailer, processor, or cattle supplier foresaw the creation of such a firm as a potentially profitable venture and consequently did not lead the initiative. This resulted in a lack of commitment from different supply chain participants and a short-term versus long-term focus (Ishmael, 2002).

Future Beef Operations made a significant investment in the construction of a new processing plant, which was intended to process large volumes of cattle from the start. At the same time, relatively loose formal agreements were in place with their supply chain partners. As a result Future Beef Operations was vulnerable (Kovanda and Schroeder, 2003). This vulnerability became critical because Future Beef Operations had focused specifically on the production of beef for one retailer, Safeway, while not ensuring the commitment of that retailer to the project (Ishmael, 2002). Of the total US$50 million invested into the project no single investor held more than a 20 percent stake in the operation. When economic losses were incurred in the first year supply chain members began to shy away from the venture, which resulted in the system falling apart (Ishmael, 2002).

Losses are common in the first year due to unexpected problems and additional costs that may arise. Partners in the system must be committed to making the system work. Typically, due to the large investments made by members, there is a long-term commitment created. This was the case for Ranchers Renaissance where losses were incurred in the short-run, but sunk investments resulted in supply chain members having a long-term focus and a commitment to the program that enabled it to succeed. Future Beef Operations had incurred significant investments, but did not have sound relationships among its various partners through contracts or adequate equity commitments to protect these investments (Kovanda and Schroeder, 2003). This type of structure could be viable, but it requires that all supply chain members are committed to the venture via well-constructed contracts and equity investments that provide for long-term stability.

CONCLUSIONS

This chapter has provided a brief overview of North American beef industry, examining: how the industry is currently structured; the declining demand for beef; and the underlying reasons behind the decline in demand. The chapter also looked at the reasons behind the current transformation within the beef industry and its move away from the production of commodity-oriented beef products, focusing specifically on why consumers prefer branded beef products. The last two sections of the chapter discussed branded beef programs first generally and then through the use of case studies. Currently, four main types of programs have emerged with the structure of these programs varying significantly, as to their management, degree of coordination, and the types of beef products that they brand. The next chapter will further examine the structure of branded beef programs and how they have affected supply chain coordination in the industry. Transaction Cost Economics is used to explain the movement towards improved coordination in the beef industry.

Chapter 3

THE ECONOMICS OF SUPPLY CHAINS

BEEF INDUSTRY REORGANIZATION

Beef quality and consistency are important aspects of consumers' demand for beef. The beef industry should be able to garner a greater share of the consumer's meat budget by marketing branded products containing guarantees that reduce the number of unsatisfied customers. In addition, the premiums associated with branded products have the potential to increase the low or negative profits that often occur in the beef industry (Bliss and Ward, 1992).

Even though it has been determined that consumers appear willing to pay a premium for differentiated beef products, the industry may have been slow to move in this direction due to the substantial reorganization of the supply chain that would be required. The supply chain in the beef industry is currently set up to deal with commodity production. Previously, commodity agriculture was regarded as an efficient method of organizing production and distribution due to economies of scale advantages (Hayes et al., 2003). With the increased movement towards product differentiation, however, the co-mingling that occurs with bulk handling in a commodity agriculture systems means that demand signals for specific attributes cannot be sent from consumers along the supply chain (Hayes et al., 2003).

For example, consumers desire tender and consistent beef products for which they are willing to pay a premium, but the farmer does not get this price signal due to co-mingling of the output of many suppliers. As a result of this system, there is little incentive to improve production methods, as the same price will be received regardless of the final quality.

Price is an important signal for encouraging the production of consumer-oriented beef products and commodity production results in a failure of this incentive. The price system is supposed to transfer information on consumer preferences back to cattle suppliers to ensure that the livestock produced correspond with what consumers are willing to pay for. For the price system to work well to ensure quality and consistency, there must be a set of quality standards that identify all the attributes that are important to consumers. Prices must mesh with those standards in order to provide rewards for the production of particular attributes (Purcell, 2002; Barkema, 1994).

The development of a grading system that isolates all of the attributes being demanded by consumers has not occurred for several reasons. Firstly, the numbers of attributes demanded by consumers are numerous and vary from consumer to consumer, overwhelming the ability of the traditional marketing system to classify and identify all important attributes (Barkema, 1994). Secondly, the ability to accurately monitor and measure the presence or absence of particular characteristics such as specific production processes, welfare practices, inputs, and safety attributes can be constrained due to high costs. These costs arise because production practices must be monitored and finished products must be tested when the presence or absence of a particular attribute is not easily verifiable by inspecting live animals or meat products (Kovanda and Schroeder, 2003).

Purcell (2002) compares the beef industry to a firm and states that if the beef sector was a firm managed by a central control center, the first job would be to make sure livestock being produced were consistent with quality controlled products at the consumer level (Purcell, 2002). Clearly, the beef sector is not a firm, there is no single control center, and therefore beef supply chains often lack the necessary coordination to achieve the goals of quality and consistency. The result is an industry that is disconnected, with poor communication of price and quality signals across market interfaces. An industry that is not very adept in producing value-added, branded products.

SUPPLY CHAIN COORDINATION

The failure of the traditional market structure to provide the "right" signal to supply chain participants has resulted in an increased movement to develop more coordinated supply chains to produce branded beef products. The production and marketing channel for beef is segmented and complex, with numerous product ownership exchanges occurring throughout the supply chain. These impede the flow of information (Ward, 2001a). In general, increased coordination improves information flow along the supply chain and enhances the ability of the beef industry to identify and adjust to changing consumer demands (Boehlje et al., 1999). Increased coordination also typically results in the ability to gain enhanced control over the production and processing of beef products to ensure a certain standard of quality and consistency.

Vertical coordination is defined as all the ways of facilitating the movement of goods and information along the different stages of the production-marketing channel (Hobbs et al., 1996). Coordination results in the alignment and control of various factors including price, quantity, quality, and terms of exchange. The different methods for achieving vertical coordination have been conceptualized as a continuum that ranges from spot markets to complete vertical integration (Peterson and Wysocki, 1998). Most theoretical work has focused on the two ends of the continuum (spot markets and vertical integration), while the middle of the continuum has been explored less thoroughly because it is a blend of the two extremes and no single theory completely explains the many different structures that can emerge.

Increased coordination in the beef industry has been characterized by a movement away from the traditional spot market system toward the expanding use of a variety of alternative market structures. The five dominant market structures that currently exist or are emerging in the beef industry include spot markets, production and marketing contracts, informal strategic alliances, formal strategic alliances, and vertical integration. With spot markets the intensity of coordination is low. In a spot market, relatively homogenous goods with easily measurable characteristics are traded between multiple buyers and sellers, with the sole determinant of the final transaction being price (Hobbs, 1996b). Due to the nature of spot market transactions, marketing commitments are made only after the production process in a particular industry segment is complete (Unterschultz, 2000).

Production And Marketing Contracts

Production and marketing contracts are one way to overcome some of the limitations of the spot market system, as they allow for the transfer of more detailed information and the measurement of quality attributes other than price. Market specification contracts typically stipulate price or a method of determining price, as well as when the product will be sold and delivered (Hobbs, 1996b). Production contracts give even more control to the buyer of a product, with the buyer actually participating in the production process through the inspection of the production process and/or specification of the inputs to be used (Hobbs, 1996b).

In both cases, contracts are a method to legally enforce specific and detailed conditions of exchange other than price. Parties in a contract can exercise control through the ex ante negotiation of contract specifications and incentives for meeting those specifications. Ex post, parties can exert control through monitoring the contract as it is carried out to ensure all parties perform as stipulated, with third party enforcement being used to penalize any parties that violate the agreement (Peterson and Wysocki, 1998).

Contracts have typically been used between packers and feedlots, while their emergence has been less apparent between cow-calf operators and feedlots. Several motivations can be identified as to why feedlots and packers have increasingly used contracts. In a survey by Lawrence et al. (2001), packers were queried regarding the importance of specific reasons for entering into marketing contracts with feedlots. Packers used contracts mainly to secure higher quality cattle and more consistent quality cattle (Lawrence et al., 2001). Being guaranteed a specific quality and supply of beef enables packers to establish supply contracts with retailers and other end users that are demanding beef with specific attributes.

Another potential benefit that packers realize from the use of contracts is reduced operation costs that result from the improved supply and quality of inputs. Many large packing plants involve extensive investments and they must establish a constant flow of uniform inputs to manage operating costs. When plants are operating near capacity, significant cost savings are realized. It has been estimated that increasing plant utilization from 70 percent to 90 percent reduces operating costs by US$16/head (Hayenga et al., 2000). Such sizeable cost savings serve as a major motivation for beef packers to develop closer relationships with their input suppliers. Ensuring a constant flow of cattle into the plant is important and can be difficult when operating in the spot market, especially if inadequate supplies exist. In these situations, higher prices must be paid to ensure the plant is operating at an efficient level. Increased coordination reduces this concern through the assurance of a constant flow of cattle at, presumably, a more consistent price.

A feedlot's primary incentive to enter into contracts is to secure quality premiums and obtain a higher price for cattle. Also important is the receipt of detailed carcass data when a grid-based pricing system is used in the contract arrangement (Lawrence et al., 2001). Under the grid pricing systems typical of many branded beef programs, packers return slaughter summaries and other carcass performance data to feedlots to provide them with information on how their cattle performed. This information allows feedlots to identify problem areas and make appropriate adjustments to better suit grid specifications and capture premiums. Feedlots that enter into contracts also benefit from having a guaranteed market outlet and in some cases a guaranteed price that increases revenue stability and allows them to concentrate their management efforts on the production process instead of market and price discovery functions (Hayenga et al., 2000).

Strategic Alliances

Strategic alliances are similar to contracts in that they reduce the segmentation in the production and marketing channel for beef by linking production stages more closely together (Ward, 2001a). Strategic alliances are agreements between or among firms to cooperate in an effort to accomplish some strategic purpose and work jointly for mutual benefits (Sporleder, 1994). It is an exchange relationship in which firms share the risks and benefits emanating from mutually identified objectives, with joint control being exerted both ex ante and ex post. Ex ante, the control process involves building the relationship to help ensure that mutual interests are in fact present. Ex post, monitoring the relationship and performance is essential. If performance is sub-optimal, mutual resolution of concerns or a mutual decision to dissolve the relationship can occur under a strategic alliance (Peterson and Wysocki, 1998).

Strategic alliances allow supply chain participants to maintain their independence while increasing supply chain coordination to improve the flow of information and the production of beef products tailored to consumer demands. By sharing information about products and markets, in addition to market prices, information flow is more efficient and alliance participants are able to respond more quickly to market signals (Ward, 2001a). Alliances also allow for the participation of several phases of the beef production and processing sectors, whereas contracts typically organize transactions between only two participants in the supply chain. The involvement of multiple supply chain participants further improves coordination, as participants such as cow-calf operators that typically do not receive information about consumers' demands have the opportunity to respond to these market signals (Beshear and Lamb, 1998). The increased level of coordination also improves the ability to trace products throughout the supply chain and ensure that any segregation and production requirements are met.

Several alliance structures currently exist within the beef industry and they vary considerably with respect to their degree of coordination, commitment, and use of supplementary agreements to sustain the alliance. Generally, alliances have taken two paths in design structure, equity-based and non-equity based. Equity-based alliances, also known as formal alliances, typically require a contractual obligation and a financial investment to participate. Non-equity alliances, also known as informal alliances, may or may not require the use of a contract and do not require an initial financial investment to participate (Kovanda and Schroeder, 2003). While informal alliances rely heavily on trust, more formal alliances typically have joint assets, which result in participants having an obligation to each other that leads to an ongoing relationship (Kovanda and Schroeder, 2003). In some informal alliances and most formal alliances there is also the presence of an organization that has an identity distinct from the individual participants and is designed to be their joint agent in transactions (Peterson and Wysocki, 1998). For example, Ranchers Renaissance is a cooperative under which cow-calf operators, feedlots, a packer, and retailers work together, while still operating as separate entities.

Based on the discussion in the previous chapter, informal alliances can be further broken down into brand licensing organizations and marketing alliances. Similarly, formal alliances can be associated with new generation cooperatives comprised of cow-calf operators that have emerged within the beef industry. For the vast majority of alliances, pricing via grids has become the most common method of determining cattle value, as grid pricing sends clearer signals. Informal alliances typically rely on the sole use of such grids, with the Decatur Beef Alliance discussed in the previous chapter, being a good example of an informal alliance. More formal alliances rely on the organization of a new generation cooperative that mixes price incentives with non-price controls to produce cattle with particular traits (Beshear and Lamb, 1998). An example of such an alliance is the Ranchers Renaissance cooperative.

Supply chain participants are motivated to become involved in an alliance for several reasons. In addition to the motivations discussed above, alliances allow for more control of the supply chain, with the degree of control depending on whether their structure is informal or formal. In both cases, alliances allow for improved traceability and the ability to transfer more detailed information among participants, with the degree of traceability and information transfer depending on the level of coordination involved. In turn, this improves the ability of participants to produce beef with the specific quality characteristics that are desired by consumers and to respond quickly to any market changes (Kovanda and Schroeder, 2003). The restricted membership of formal alliances also provides increased stability for farmers who are guaranteed a given level of market access and are more likely to receive premium prices given the limited market size (Boland and Katz, 2000).

A significant difference between contracts, informal alliances and formal alliances is that the joint investment, which occurs in a cooperative situation, provides additional assurances that supply chain participants are committed to the quality of their product. This type of arrangement also typically works to provide downstream users with a more consistent and guaranteed supply of cattle to reduce inefficiencies associated with fluctuations in supply (Boland and Katz, 2000). The commitment of supply chain members becomes especially important when the goal of a branded program is to provide a beef product with many detailed specifications or attributes that cannot easily be detected or controlled for along the supply chain. High levels of communication and trust between all segments of the supply chain are required in this scenario to ensure consumer preferences are conveyed and that all production and process specifications are met along the entire supply chain.

Vertical Integration

Vertical integration represents the most closely coordinated supply chain structure, with all stages of the supply chain owned and controlled by one firm (Kovanda and Schroeder, 2003). Instead of independent supply chain participants using a price discovery process to transact with other participants, products move between various stages of the supply chain as a result of within-firm managerial orders (Hobbs, 1996b). Vertical integration further improves traceability and the transfer of information along the supply chain to reduce quantity and quality risk, generates efficiencies in moving a product through the system, and potentially captures profits from all levels of the supply chain (Hayenga et al., 2000).

The benefits of increased supply chain coordination in the beef industry are clear: to produce branded beef products with more detailed specifications and numerous attributes, a more coordinated system is required in order to ensure information is passed along the supply chain and to reduce the relative costs incurred to assure product quality. The movement towards full integration of the beef industry, however, has been limited for several reasons. Firstly, combining various stages of production can be problematic in that the varying scale of operation that each stage requires to function efficiently may result in cost disadvantages (Den Ouden at al., 1996). Cow-calf operations are found to typically operate on a relatively small scale and, as a result, tend to expend minimal resources to increase herd size and reduce variations in cattle quality. It is also thought that to increase operation size in order to supply adequate volumes of animals into an integrated production and processing system would result in an increase in costs. These costs arise because cow-calf production is land intensive and in order to produce the volumes that would be required by an integrated system, production would likely have to be dispersed over a large geographical area. Consequently, high monitoring costs would be incurred, as it is difficult to manage cow-calf production when it is dispersed over a large geographical area. These high costs may discourage vertical integration.

Vertical integration also consumes a large amount of capital resources. For vertical integration to be practical large capital investments need to be offset by substantial cost savings, or returns greater than an integrated firm's cost of capital (Den Ouden et al., 1996). The increase in monitoring costs in the cow-calf sector when the scale of cow-calf operations is increased to facilitate integration may offset any cost savings from integration. As a result, there is little incentive for individuals within the beef industry to vertically integrate all facets of a supply chain.

LIMITATIONS TO INCREASED SUPPLY CHAIN COORDINATION

Why has coordination in the beef industry been slow to emerge? Based on the previous discussion it is clear why the industry has not moved towards complete integration, but the movement away from spot markets towards other methods of coordination has also been slow to occur. The use of contracts and alliances may be the most effective way to coordinate production and market activities given the limitations to vertical integration in the beef industry. At the same time, the beef industry faces several challenges in moving away from the traditional marketing system towards contracts and alliances and improving vertical coordination. These challenges have limited its ability to become more competitive with the pork and poultry industries which did not encounter similar challenges.

One of the primary differences with pork and poultry supply chains on one side and beef supply chains on the other involves the speed with which biological changes such as genetic improvement are possible. While the biological process to produce changes is twenty-four months for beef cattle, it is twelve months for pork, and five months for poultry (Ward,

2001b). Shorter biological processes mean cost-reducing genetic improvements can be accomplished at a faster pace and more rapid progress towards improved consistency is possible. This reduces the costs associated with monitoring production to ensure consistency and consequently reduces the costs associated with vertical integration. Also, while the genetic bases of poultry and pork are narrow and becoming narrower, the beef genetic base is actually widening due to the lower degree of vertical coordination and a wider geographic dispersion. A widening genetic base reduces consistency of production and means that it is more difficult to recognize desirable genetic traits and separate them to breed for those specific traits (Ward, 2001b).

The number of industry stages has also affected the degree of vertical coordination. Pork and poultry have two key production stages (farrowing/finishing and hatching/growing) while beef often has three stages (seedstock/cow-calf, background feeders, and finishing feeders). Each stage has different resources and management needs and thus it is more difficult to manage a vertically integrated beef production unit (Ward, 2001b). Consequently, the number of differentiated value-added products has been limited in beef due to reduced coordination and less control over the quality and quantity of beef supplies.

Geographic concentration has also affected the emergence of vertical coordination. Beef production is dispersed, while the pork and poultry industries in the US are concentrated within specific regions. This dispersion of production may in part be due to the substantially larger land requirements for beef production. Dispersed production results in a wide variation in the production and management practices used, genetics, and overall profitability across environments. As well, the geographic dispersion combined with an added production stage means that the beef industry incurs costs as animals are moved from dispersed cow-calf operations to more concentrated backgrounding areas and to still more concentrated cattle feeding areas (Ward, 2001b).

While the majority of pork and poultry operations are relatively large, intensely managed operations, the beef industry has been limited in its ability to adopt a similar structure. This is partly a result of the high management and monitoring costs in the cow-calf sector. It is difficult to organize and manage a large number of small production units. Consequently, improved coordination between the cow-calf sector and other industry segments has been limited. This in turn has reduced the ability of the beef industry to exert control over the supply chain and ensure quality and consistency (Ward, 2001b). Based on the current limitations to integration in the beef industry, it is expected that the industry will continue to rely on the use of contracts and alliances. Contracts and alliances will probably be refined to improve coordination and substitute for vertical integration where it is not attractive.

The use of contracts is likely to be limited to coordinating transactions at the feedlot-packer interface. This limited use of contracts is where the developments within the beef industry will likely have to diverge from the current pork and poultry models, which are dominated by the use of production contracts and vertical integration. A different system is necessary to align consumers' demands with industry production and to facilitate the unique transaction interface between the cow-calf sector and the rest of the industry. The issue of improving coordination between the cow-calf sector and the rest of the industry will be examined in Chapter 5 where conjoint analysis is used to identify cow-calf operators' preferences for different transaction characteristics

DEGREE OF COORDINATION: EVIDENCE

Currently, in the US beef industry the use of cash markets, marketing agreements and informal alliances dominate transactions. In 2001, a survey of feedlots was conducted in the largest cattle feeding states (Iowa, Kansas, Nebraska, and Texas) to examine changes in marketing methods for fed cattle. The percentage of fed cattle sold under different types of contracts and alliances has increased over time, from 23 percent in 1996 to 52 percent in 2001. This trend was expected to continue (Schroeder et al., 2002). The survey does not identify the specific types of contracts and alliances included under this classification, but it likely includes market contracts, production contracts, and both informal and formal alliances.

The survey identified three distinct trends regarding the use of contracts and alliances within the beef industry. Firstly, the participation in alliances (formal and informal) has increased, with 45 percent of respondents indicating that in 2001 they marketed at least some cattle under an alliance as compared to only 11 percent in 1996. These transactions represent an estimated eight percent of total fed cattle sales in 1996 and 27 percent in 2001. Secondly, it was found that larger operations were more likely to participate in a marketing agreement than smaller operations. Thirdly, the survey identified that a shift in the price system has occurred, with the industry shifting away from pricing cattle on a live weight basis towards grid-based pricing that focuses on carcass quality. Between 1996 and 2001 the use of grid-based pricing had increased 16 percent to 45 percent with the trend expected to continue (Schroeder et al., 2002). Similar research has also found that pork and beef packers have increased the output that they have committed to retailers and other end-users under long term arrangements, with current commitments being around 40 percent of total output (Hayenga et al., 2002).

Similar data regarding changes in the marketing of fed cattle in Canada was not available, but data from the three largest packers in Alberta suggest that cash sales are still the predominant means of marketing slaughter cattle. In 2002, 60 percent of fed cattle were procured on a cash (live weight) basis, 22 percent were procured through some type of marketing agreement, and 18 percent were packer owned (Canfax Research Services, 2003). Data was also not available for the US or Canada on the marketing methods used between cow-calf operators and feeders, but it is expected that cash sales remain as the predominant means of marketing feeder cattle given the minimal consolidation and coordination in the cow-calf sector.

The statistics described above reveal that, despite limitations to coordination, a transformation is slowly occurring in the beef industry. The traditional divisions between the market segments are becoming less distinct and the prior pricing system is being replaced with other devices that improve coordination and information transfer among supply chain segments. In a sense, the beef industry is currently in disequilibrium; consumer demands have changed and the market is adjusting to supply the products being demanded, but has not fully transformed from the existing system. It is not yet clear where equilibrium will be reached in terms of the optimal vertical coordination mechanism.

Ultimately, it is likely the beef industry will operate through several different coordination mechanisms. This is because of the many different attributes that are demanded by consumers and that different levels of coordination are required to guarantee these attributes. In addition, different strengths of guarantee can be provided for a single attribute, which will affect the degree of coordination required and the cost of production. Some programs have more detailed production and processing requirements, requiring greater coordination and increased costs, but also facilitating increased assurance of tenderness and other quality attributes. These programs will charge a higher price and some consumers may not be willing to pay for that extra assurance and will therefore buy product from a different type of program with lower prices.

The key question is why one method of coordination will be preferred over another to accomplish the goals of producing a beef product with particular attributes? Transaction Cost Economics provides insights into questions pertaining to supply chain coordination in the beef industry.

TRANSACTION COST ECONOMICS

In economics, the predominant neoclassical paradigm has provided for only a limited understanding of market organization and the operation of supply chains due to its key assumptions. Neoclassical theory is based on the concept of a single product firm that operates in a perfectly competitive industry with a large number of other firms that produce the same product in a stable or near equilibrium market environment (Hobbs, 1996a). Transactions that move products between separable stages in the production, processing, and distribution chain involve the transfer of homogenous products, which means there are no costs to measuring the value of a given product, as there is no variation in the quality of products. It is also assumed that economic agents possess perfect information, which results in no price uncertainty, or other uncertainty associated with product characteristics and the behaviour of other individuals (Hobbs, 1996a). Along with its underlying assumptions, neoclassical economics fails to provide a rationale for the existence of firms and, instead, simply accepts them as an artifact of production.

Nobel prize winner Ronald Coase's (1937) seminal paper "On the Nature of the Firm" created a new approach to understanding market organization. Instead of accepting the underlying assumptions of neoclassical economics and the existence of firms, Coase questioned why firms arose as a method of coordinating transactions. He proposed that firms and markets were alternative means of economic organization, with the mode (firm or market) being chosen depending on the costs incurred under each structure (Williamson, 1986b). In doing so, Coase recognized that there are costs to using the price mechanism, which may be reduced by forming an organization to direct resources internally. Costs of using the price mechanism include costs associated with discovering what the relevant prices may be and costs associated with negotiating separate contracts for every transaction that occurs (Coase, 1937). The ideas that Coase put forth became the basis for New Institutional Economics and the costs that he referred to became know as transaction costs (Hobbs and Kerr, 1999).

New Institutional Economics views a firm as a way of organizing transactions internally and avoiding the costs of using the market to organize these same transactions. Firms will become larger as additional transactions are organized internally (Coase, 1937). As firms get larger, however, the administrative costs of internally organizing transactions may increase, which will result in there coming a point where the costs of organizing an extra transaction within the firm are equal to the costs involved in carrying out the transaction in the market. At this point, a firm will no longer expand to organize an additional transaction within the firm, as the costs of doing so are equal to the costs of carrying out the transaction in the open market (Coase, 1937).

Coase's initial contribution has since been extended with one of the major contributors to transaction cost theory being Oliver E. Williamson. Transaction cost theory has been used to advance the current understanding of how transactions are carried out along supply chains and why different types of supply chain coordination structures emerge. A transaction occurs whenever a product must move between separable stages in production, processing, or distribution (Hobbs et al., 1996). Transaction costs are the costs of carrying out a transaction, with the nature and size of these costs determining the optimum method of vertical coordination. Economic activity will be organized in such a way as to minimize these costs in the long run (Hobbs, 1998; Martinez et al., 1998).

In order to identify particular transaction costs and how they affect the optimal method of vertical coordination it is useful to separate these costs into three main categories: information costs, negotiation costs, and monitoring costs. Information costs are the costs that individuals and firms face in the search for information about prices, inputs, and buyers or sellers. Negotiation costs are the costs associated with the actual transaction that, for example, are incurred while negotiating and writing contracts. Negotiation costs also arise when a third party or intermediary is required to facilitate a transaction. After an exchange has been negotiated a transaction may require that a firm or an individual monitor the quality of goods from a supplier, monitor the behaviour of either party to ensure that all the conditions of the transaction are met, or monitor the activities of employees to ensure managerial orders have been carried out. The costs associated with these activities are known as monitoring costs and will also include any costs incurred if it is necessary to legally enforce an agreement (enforcement costs) (Hobbs, 1996a).

Key Concepts of Transaction Cost Economics

Transaction cost economics recognizes that markets do not always operate in situations where neoclassical assumptions can be comfortably applied. Agents to a transaction do not always possess perfect information, which results in uncertainty associated with prices, product quality, and the actions of other individuals in the market. Transaction cost economics maintains that economic agents are characterized by bounded rationality and opportunism. It also maintains that many transactions are characterized by imperfect information, either incomplete information or asymmetric information, and conditions of asset specificity are widespread (Williamson, 1986b). These four underlying concepts are important in examining how transaction costs affect vertical coordination in a particular supply chain.

Bounded rationality means that people's capacity to accurately evaluate all possible decision alternatives is limited even if they intend to make a rational decision. Bounded rationality becomes a problem in situations where transactions are complex and a degree of uncertainty exists, as the ability of an individual to make an accurate and all encompassing decision on how to best carry out a transaction is limited (Hobbs, 1996b). This means that agreements made between individuals in a supply chain may be incomplete and subject to opportunism.

Opportunism means that firms and individuals operating in the market are often placed in situations where it is possible to exploit others to their own advantage (self-interest seeking with guile). Certain market situations can increase the ability of one transacting party to alter the terms of an agreement ex post to their own advantage. Market circumstances that encourage or support opportunistic behaviour include situations where there are few alternative suppliers for a particular input, or the reverse where there are few alternative buyers for a particular output. This is known as a small numbers bargaining situation (Williamson, 1986a). Restricted market size may result in one party demanding a different price than was previously agreed, as the other party is limited in its ability to locate new buyers or suppliers after committing resources (Hobbs, 1996). Opportunistic behaviour associated with restricted market size is more likely when asset specificity is present.

Asset specificity occurs when one partner in an exchange invests in assets that are specialized to the needs of that particular exchange and have little or no value in an alternative use (Hobbs, 1996a). Investment in specific assets generates quasi-rents, which are defined as the value of an asset in excess of its salvage value or the value in its next best use (Martinez et al., 1998). If the quasi-rents generated are high, other partners in an exchange may try to act opportunistically and extract some of the rent from this investment. Extraction of quasi-rents by other firms will occur up to the point that the investing firm's operating costs are just covered, as they will have little choice but to accept the new arrangements given their investment has little or no value in an alternative use (Hobbs, 1996a).

The fourth concept underlying transaction cost analysis is information asymmetry. Neoclassical economic theory assumes that all parties in an exchange possess perfect information. The concept of information asymmetry recognizes that, while some information is public and available to all parties in a transaction, other information is only available to selected parties. Opportunistic behaviour can arise as information that may result in adverse selection by buyers can be hidden prior to a transaction. For example, hidden information may prevent buyers from detecting a sub-standard product and, as a result, suppliers may cheat and supply sub-standard products while being the paid for the higher quality product (Hobbs, 1998). Problems associated with information asymmetry can also arise after a transaction has occurred, as an individual's actions after a transaction may not be readily observable to others – moral hazard (Hobbs, 1996b).

Vertical Coordination and Transaction Cost Economics

Vertical coordination can be viewed as a continuum of different organizational forms. Spot markets lie at one extreme and operate in circumstances where homogenous goods are exchanged, with price being the sole determinant of the transaction. Moving along the continuum, contracts, informal alliances, formal alliances, and vertical integration provide for the increased coordination and control of transactions between supply chain participants (Hobbs, 1996a). Transaction cost economics suggests that the type of vertical coordination and supply chain structures that emerge within the beef industry will depend both on the production costs and the transaction costs incurred to produce a particular product.

Williamson proposed that the three main characteristics that determine the nature and level of transaction costs are the degree of uncertainty surrounding a particular transaction, the frequency with which transactions occur, and the degree to which transaction specific investments are made (Williamson, 1986a). Consequently, the likelihood of observing a particular supply chain structure is a function of the transaction characteristics, with organizational form being the dependent variable and asset specificity, uncertainty, and transaction frequency being the independent variables (Shelanski and Klein, 1995).

Some assets are specific to the production of specific goods in closed supply chains with bilateral trading relationships. In the beef sector, such investments can include improved herd genetics, specialized inputs related to the production process, computer chips to maintain the identity of individual animals during production and processing, new processing technologies, and investments related to specialized human capital. Those who invest in specific assets have an incentive to protect themselves against opportunistic behaviour by trading partners that could try to appropriate any quasi-rents that exist. Consequently, as asset specificity rises it is expected that the degree of vertical coordination will increase to create safeguards that protect the specific investments. Therefore, the probability of observing a more integrated governance structure will depend positively on the value of the transaction specific investments involved. Where significant levels of assets are involved, the optimal governance structure will depend on the degree of uncertainty surrounding transactions and the frequency of trade (Shelanski and Klein, 1995).

For example, as consumers' tastes become less homogenous, a variety of animal types with a different but specific set of characteristics are required. This means that producers and feedlots must tailor their output to the needs of individual production programs, which may result in increased average production costs for these supply chain participants. Ideally, the increased costs should be more than offset by premium prices received for the production of the desired attributes, but the production of a specialized product has two effects. Firstly, it removes the producer from the competitive market where prices are determined by market forces and into a smaller market with fewer buyers. In this situation a small numbers bargaining problem arises. Prices must be negotiated on an individual basis with the buyer and upon investment the buyer may act opportunistically and want to renegotiate a lower price in order to capture any quasi-rents. Secondly, it leaves the producer with a specialized product that could be heavily discounted by other buyers with different production requirements (Hobbs et al., 1996).

Cow-calf operators and feedlots are vulnerable if they produce specialized animals using only the existing commodity market mechanism to transact with buyers, as they have a perishable product and few if any alternative buyers. Buyers also become vulnerable to opportunistic behaviour by sellers. If buyers have product commitments to meet further down the supply chain, spot markets may not provide them with a sufficient assurance that their demands for specialized inputs will be filled without incurring high information/search costs (Hobbs, 1996c). To curb the tendency to act opportunistically and ensure adequate volumes of inputs, buyers and sellers will likely choose to move up the vertical coordination continuum when transaction specific investments are involved and use contracts or alliances as an alternative to carrying out transactions on the spot market.

The degree of uncertainty surrounding a transaction is a result of several factors, including the length of the relationship among transaction partners, market conditions, incomplete information, and information asymmetry. As a rule, uncertain demand and supply conditions cause firms to rely on non-market coordination methods. When transactions are conducted under uncertainty it can become very costly or impossible to anticipate all future contingencies. In this situation, alternative means of coordination that reduce uncertainty may be more desirable (Frank and Henderson, 1992). Similarly, where specialized assets are involved, uncertainty as to the longevity of a relationship will increase the reliance on non-market coordination methods to ensure that ongoing returns are sufficient to cover the cost of the initial investment.

Incomplete information about the product generates uncertainty. The degree of uncertainty depends on the attributes being produced and how easily they can be measured. Cow-calf operators and feedlots producing cattle with specific attributes that are not easily measured should prefer methods of improved coordination that move transactions away from the spot market. Currently, cattle in the spot market system are priced based on the average quality of a lot (group) of cattle, but the quality of individual animals can vary significantly within a lot of cattle. Increased coordination allows supply chain participants to move away from pricing based on average lot quality, and allows for pricing based on the identification of product attributes that are not easily measured under the existing system (Hudson and Purcell, 2003).

Processors will also prefer increased coordination in situations where uncertainty arises as a result of information asymmetry about product attributes. The presence of information asymmetry may result in processors purchasing sub-standard products at a premium price (Hobbs, 1998). For example, in the absence of credible third party monitoring, producers have the incentive to identify their product as organic even if it is conventionally produced in order to obtain premium prices. Given that it is difficult to detect this practice processors may unknowingly purchase a non-organic product. Increased coordination, allowing processors increased control over and monitoring of the production process, reduces the uncertainty associated with information asymmetry.

The frequency of transactions also affects vertical coordination. Transactions that are repeated frequently may require less vertical coordination, as firms do not wish to tarnish their reputation by acting opportunistically. Frequent transactions also allow for the increased transfer of information between transacting parties, which reduces information asymmetry and thus the need for higher levels of coordination. The incentive to act opportunistically and exploit any information asymmetry that may be present will increase as transactions occur less frequently and will result in transacting parties choosing to operate under increased levels of coordination (Hobbs, 1996).

DETERMINING THE OPTIMAL METHOD OF VERTICAL COORDINATION

The complexity of a particular transaction is dependent on all of the transaction characteristics including asset specificity, transaction uncertainty, and transaction frequency and how they combine to affect a particular transaction. According to Transaction Cost Economics, the methods of vertical coordination that emerge will minimize the sum of transaction and production costs. Transaction costs are dependent on the transaction characteristics, which are influenced by the underlying product attributes. Minimizing transaction costs essentially reduces to minimizing the effects of bounded rationality and transaction uncertainty while simultaneously safeguarding the transactions in question against the hazards of opportunism that are associated with asset specificity (Williamson, 1986a). At the same time it is important to understand that different methods of coordination may also affect production costs and therefore the optimal method of coordination must minimize the total of production and transactions costs[1].

Where transactions involve products with easily identifiable and measurable characteristics, spot markets are likely the most efficient and cost minimizing mechanism. Transactions are highly standardized and information costs are minimized because neither buyers nor sellers face uncertainties with respect to the quality of the product, which can be determined through visual inspection and existing grading schemes. Information costs associated with discovering price are also low, as prices initially determined on the spot market become a representative price and serve to reduce information costs for other buyers and sellers. Negotiation costs are also minimal. Everything but price is standardized or pre-determined, so there is little negotiation in the true sense of the word (Hobbs, 1998). Transactions in the spot market also result in low monitoring costs. When transactions involve relatively homogenous products whose quality is easily determined it is not usually necessary to monitor quality ex ante or ex post to the transaction occurring (Hobbs, 1998).

While spot markets are a feasible and cost minimizing solution for standardized transactions, they can result in extremely high transaction costs when investments in specific assets are required to produce differentiated products. Required investments may result in an increased risk of opportunistic behaviour and higher transaction costs must be incurred to protect investments. Otherwise there will be limited incentive to invest in specific assets. This is becoming apparent in the beef industry. There is an increasing demand for more complex and differentiated products, with characteristics that cannot easily be determined by visual inspection and that may require investments in specific assets. Without a long-term commitment and assurance of a continuing relationship to prevent opportunistic behaviour, there is little incentive to produce specialized beef products.

Increased vertical coordination reduces opportunism through the use of more sophisticated mechanisms that realign incentives. These typically involves the use of a reward/penalty mechanism for early termination. Similar mechanisms are also put in place to provide incentives for ensuring the production of particular attributes, such as the implementation of grid-based pricing systems that allow for more specific price signals and information to be transferred back along the supply chain. The move towards increased vertical coordination encourages the use of specialized conflict resolution mechanisms that minimize enforcement costs and ensure the commitment of partners in a transaction. Information and monitoring costs are also reduced, as it is easier to obtain information on product quality and monitor production under structures where different supply chain segments are more closely linked (Williamson, 1986b).

As asset specificity increases and the attributes being guaranteed under branded beef programs become more difficult to measure, supply chains will become more closely coordinated. From a transaction cost perspective, contracts are one alternative that have the potential to reduce costs for both producers and processors. Specified pricing formulas that

---

[1] Production costs are the fixed and variable costs incurred to produce a product. Costs are incurred to purchase physical inputs, wages for employees, management costs, and capital requirements. They are considered distinct from transaction costs.

are included in contracts reduce the information costs associated with daily price discovery for producers. These costs include time spent collecting, analyzing, and monitoring feeder cattle and fed cattle market conditions and prices (Hayenga et al., 2000). Time spent negotiating prices, delivery terms, and quality specifications are also expected to be reduced with the increased use of contracts (Hayenga et al., 2000).

Processors also benefit from the use of marketing agreements. In their absence, processors are often not willing to invest in new facilities, processing technologies, or other branded product developments, as the supply of beef in the spot market is highly variable and product attributes may be difficult to measure (Purcell, 2002). A processor's information costs are also reduced when contracts are used to procure beef with specialized attributes. Processors face lower procurement and search costs as they deal with the same suppliers on a constant basis instead of dealing with many different firms. Monitoring costs are also reduced, as contracts allow for the implementation of incentives based systems and protocols that make it easier to monitor the production process.

It is less clear whether negotiation costs will be reduced with the increased use of contracts. Although negotiations will be less frequent and processors will deal with fewer suppliers, the complexity of negotiating long-term contracts can be costly. Long-term contracts are typically incomplete given the difficulty in specifying both anticipated and unanticipated events in the future (Sporleder, 1994). Even if it were feasible to specify all possible future events that could affect a contract, it would be prohibitively costly to do so. Due to this incompleteness, parties who invest in transaction specific assets are left exposed to opportunistic behaviour if circumstances change and trading partners are able to circumvent the contract and expropriate any quasi-rents that exist (Shelanski and Klein, 1995)

Short-term contracts reduce the risks associated with incomplete contracts, but can be problematic if asset specific investments are quite significant and have a long amortization period. High levels of asset specificity favour the use of long-term contracts that ensure the returns to transaction specific investments are adequate (Williamson, 1971). Long-term contracts are problematic due to bounded rationality. Contracts are also problematic when information asymmetries are high because buyers would still incur high information costs prior to a transaction in order to determine the quality of a product. They would also incur ongoing monitoring and enforcement costs after the initial contract is in place to ensure that sellers adhere to the quality standards stipulated in the contract (Hobbs, 1998).

Contracts are also not ideal when coordination needs to occur between more than two parties in the supply chain, as such contracts are often more complex and result in increased information, negotiation, and monitoring costs due to the larger number of participants involved in a particular transaction. Consequently, in situations where high levels of asset specificity, bounded rationality, and/or numerous participants are involved, it is likely that closer coordination will occur.

In this situation, it is expected that supply chain participants would want a vertical coordination method with increased controls to monitor quality. Informal alliances that use grid-pricing initiatives result in low negotiation costs. Price and quality specifications are laid out in the grid and the only issue to be determined between supply chain partners is delivery. Information costs are also reduced for processors involved in an alliance. The incentives created under a grid pricing system result in producers that can provide the attributes self-selecting an alliance, as they will be paid premiums. Thus, processors will not have to search for suppliers. Meanwhile, those producers that do not comply with the specifications and would be penalized under the grid will not want to be involved in the alliance and sorting costs will be lower. It is less clear as to whether information costs for the producer will be lower. Initial search costs will be high to find an appropriate alliance in which to participate, but over the long-term price discovery costs will likely be considerably reduced.

For an informal alliance to be beneficial, the reduction in information and negotiation costs must be lower than the increase in monitoring costs. Processors under a grid-based alliance will still have to monitor production practices if the attributes demanded cannot easily be detected or tested. They will still have to test for other quality attributes in order to identify how an individual animal grades on the grid. If the monitoring costs incurred as a result of information asymmetries are higher than the reduction in information and negotiation costs under an informal alliance, it not likely that this type of structure would be used to coordination transactions.

Another consideration is that producers' costs may increase because they may have a greater interest in monitoring the transfer of their cattle to the processor to ensure that carcass quality is not reduced through poor handling. This activity is expected to only have a small effect on monitoring costs; packers have an incentive to ensure that beef quality is not diminished and an incentive to maintain a good reputation with suppliers in order to have the assured supply that is needed for branded programs.

Informal alliances are not ideal when high levels of asset specific investments are involved, as they are loose informal arrangements that do not require any long-term commitment. When transaction specific investments are large or high levels of information asymmetry exist, resulting in a higher risk of opportunistic behaviour, a move to a more formal alliance structure is predicted. A more formal alliance structure is particularly beneficial when it is costly to detect the presence/absence of particular attributes and/or monitor the production process. When both parties to a transaction invest equity into a new venture, the shared equity becomes a "hostage asset". Each firm has effectively posted a bond, which would be lost or only partially redeemable if operations ceased because one partner chose to act opportunistically or did not comply with the conditions of the alliance (Oxley, 1997).

The returns from a formal alliance also depend on the profits of the venture as a whole and, because of this, the interests of different supply chain members should be aligned (Oxley, 1997). The potential short-run gains from opportunistic behaviour may be more than offset by the potential long-term gains from maintaining the alliance and obtaining the benefits from improved coordination. Formal alliances are better able to minimize the costs associated with monitoring the production process and to eliminate the need for negotiating all-encompassing contracts. They also improve information flow along the supply chain, as participants now have harmonized interests and are working to maximize joint profits.

At the same time, the use of a formal alliance can result in higher initial negotiation and information costs. Given the commitment required to join a formal alliance, prospective members typically will invest more time searching and obtaining information on different organizations prior to committing to a particular one. More detailed information on an organization's reputation, longevity, requirements, and pricing structure will be sought out given the barriers to exit once participants have made a long-term commitment. Contracts are typically used between a formal alliance and its participants. This can result in higher initial negotiation costs than would otherwise be incurred under a more informal alliance structure. These costs can become quite high for the same reasons as in the case of long-term contracts.

As a result, a formal alliance is only beneficial if the one-time negotiation and information costs are offset by ongoing reductions in information and monitoring costs.

Aside from formal strategic alliances, complete vertical integration will eliminate opportunistic behaviour and harmonize incentives along the supply chain through the integration of different industry stages under one firm. While transaction costs will be internalized under such a structure, this is not likely to be the dominant vertical coordination method given that the costs associated with internalizing different industry stages may be prohibitively high for the reasons discussed above. The greatest limitation to integration is probably the large monitoring and managerial costs that must be incurred when cow-calf production is integrated with other stages of the beef supply chain. These costs arise as a result of the large land base required and geographical dispersion of this sector.

CONCLUSIONS

This chapter provided a discussion of the current reorganization of the beef industry and why the beef industry has been slow to move in the direction of branded beef programs. The existing vertical coordination continuum was described with a focus on the different types of supply chain coordination structures and the characteristics of these structures. It was concluded that Transaction Cost Economics is useful for explaining vertical coordination in the beef industry. The next chapter will develop the transaction cost model further. It will discuss on how different attributes affect transaction characteristics, namely asset specificity and informational asymmetry, and consequently how attributes affect transaction costs. This analysis will be used to identify why different supply chain structures are chosen to produce branded beef products with particular attributes.

Chapter 4

A FRAMEWORK FOR ASSESSING SUPPLY CHAIN RELATIONSHIPS

PREDICTING SUPPLY CHAIN RELATIONSHIPS

Is it possible to predict the type of supply chain structure that is likely to emerge based on the attributes guaranteed by different branded beef programs? The influence of attributes on transaction characteristics and costs and subsequently on supply chain structures forms the basis of a predictive model developed in this chapter. Supply chain structure is the "dependent variable" and transaction characteristics are the "independent variables" in this approach. Using these variables the model focuses on the number and types of coordinated links in the supply chain that are required to brand a beef product that guarantees specific attributes. Particular attention is paid to identifying those supply chain members who have a direct impact on the presence/absence of a specific attribute. Identifying the key players necessary in branding a particular beef attribute sheds further light on the key transaction characteristics and related costs.

It should be noted that the predictive model does not encompass seedstock producers and backgrounding feedlots. It was felt that the influence of these sectors was similar to that of cow-calf operators and finishing feedlots. Therefore, cow-calf operators and seedstock producers are grouped together and background and finishing feedlots are grouped together to simplify the model.

THE ATTRIBUTES OF BRANDED BEEF

A wide variety of attributes are currently being provided in branded beef products. These attributes vary in terms of how they are produced and how they are guaranteed. The production of different attributes often involves making changes to production practices, using specialized inputs, and/or using specialized processing systems and technologies. In the end, the production and bundling of these different attributes into branded beef products is supposed to provide consumers with a higher quality product, with product quality being described as a bundle of characteristics (attributes) (Caswell and Mojduszka, 1996).

The market for food quality is not perfect; the agents involved in the production of food are often better informed about quality attributes than consumers (Caswell and Mojduszka, 1996). The information available to consumers depends on the particular attribute being branded and whether it is a credence, experience, or search attribute, with the amount of information increasing as an attribute moves along the continuum from credence goods to search goods. Search attributes are characterized by plentiful and easily obtainable consumer information (Caswell and Mojduszka, 1996). Search attributes can normally be evaluated prior to purchase through visual examination, touch, or smell (Hobbs, 1998).

Several search attributes were considered in this research, including appearance, convenience and product presentation, United States Department of Agriculture (USDA) or Canadian Food Inspection Agency (CFIA) grade, and leanness. After some consideration, all but convenience and leanness were excluded from the model. Attributes such as government grades and appearance are relatively standard across all branded programs that are attempting to produce a high quality beef product. Instead, they appear to act as proxy variables for other attributes such as tenderness, freshness, and flavour. Leanness is an important attribute to include, as consumers are increasingly health-conscious and demand products with lower levels of fat. Further, the leanness of a beef product is controlled for primarily in the production process through both the genetics chosen and feed protocols implemented. Consequently, the production of leanness is expected to affect the type of supply chain structure chosen to coordinate production and processing.

Convenience is also an important search attribute. Increasing participation of women in the labor force means that there is reduced time available to prepare meals and, as a result, consumers are looking for convenient meal solutions. Convenience is interesting because it is typically provided through processing of beef into further value-added products at a processing facility and is not as dependent on other segments of the supply chain. This has implications for the coordination of the supply chain that differs from other attributes and will be discussed later in this chapter.

Experience attributes are those whose quality can only be determined after purchase when the product is consumed. Information problems are limited in situations where consumers make repeated purchases of a product, as their choices will be based on prior experience with product quality or on communication with other consumers. Firms rely on having a good reputation with consumers to obtain repeat purchases. As a result, they have a stronger incentive to disclose product quality and continually provide that quality (Caswell and Mojduszka, 1996).

The most common experience attributes that are branded include freshness, consistency, and tenderness. Freshness and consistency have been excluded from the model, as a high quality brand typically implies that a product will be fresh. Similarly, quality, however it is defined, is assumed to be consistent in order to fulfill the guarantees provided. Tenderness is the most common attribute currently being branded. Some consumers have not been satisfied with the tenderness provided under the existing grading system and have turned to purchasing brands that provide a guarantee of tenderness. A tender beef product is a result of both production and processing practices. Tenderness is affected by genetics, feeding and production practices, and the techniques and technologies used during processing. Consequently, in order to produce a tender product several different stages of the supply chain must be involved.

Credence attributes are those attributes whose quality cannot be determined by a buyer even after they have purchased a product (Hobbs, 1998). This means that access to information about product quality by consumers is limited. Typically this occurs when branded attributes are process attributes, which do not alter the physical attributes of the product. As a result, it is difficult to predict their presence through the use of search or experience related cues. Hence, the branding of credence attributes typically requires labelling and disclosure of information to consumers. A certification or verification process may also be necessary to ensure firms are providing the quality they have guaranteed consumers.

Common credence attributes that are provided in branded beef products include no hormones and antibiotics (natural), organic, free of genetically-modified organisms, grass fed, enhanced food safety, animal welfare friendly, environmentally friendly, source verification, and process verification. These attributes have emerged due to increasing consumer concern over the safety of the food they consume, environmental awareness, and heightened interest in farm animal welfare. Source verification and process verification are unique in that they are not a tangible attribute, but enable individuals to confirm the presence of credence attributes. They are included in the model, as increasingly they are being branded and promoted in concert with other credence and experience attributes. Breed and product origin, other commonly branded credence attributes, arise from consumers' association of superior quality with particular breeds of cattle or specific production regions. Both of these attributes are unique in that along the supply chain up to the processing level they could be classified as search attributes. The identification of a specific breed or region from which cattle are produced is relatively easy to verify up to the processing sector. Upon processing and at the consumer level, breed and product origin become indistinguishable and cannot be easily detected, resulting in their classification as credence attributes.

Table 4.1 displays all of the attributes that will be discussed in the predictive transaction cost model. The method used to classify these attributes is significant for two reasons. First, an attribute that is classified as being either a credence, experience, or search attribute remains as such along the entire supply chain, with the exception of breed and product origin. This provides a level of uniformity to the model. Secondly, the transaction characteristics, as will be discussed below, are often similar for attributes within the same category allowing for a more general comparison across the three categories.

COMMONLY BRANDED BEEF PRODUCTS

It is not typically the case that a branded product only provides one of the attributes mentioned above. Instead, these attributes are often provided in specific combinations in an effort to meet consumers' demands. Based on information compiled from the U.S. Livestock Marketing Information Center (LMIC) and Beef Magazine, Kovanda and Schroeder (2003) created a chart identifying the largest U.S. branded beef alliances. These alliances vary in their structures and are either producing a branded product themselves or they are producing for a separate branded beef program. The alliances identified by Kovanda and Schroeder were reviewed so as to identify key attribute combinations that are currently being branded.

Many different attribute combinations were identified and Table 4.2 displays the most common combinations.

Table 4.1 – Beef Attributes Included in the Predictive Transaction Cost Model

Credence Attributes	Experience Attributes	Search Attributes
No Hormones/Antibiotics	Tenderness	Lean
Grass Fed		Convenience
Organic & GM Free		
Animal Welfare Friendly		
Environmentally Friendly		
Enhanced Food Safety		
Product Origin		
Breed		
Source Verification		
Process Verification		

Table 4.2 indicates that natural, organic, and tenderness are three core underlying attributes of branded beef programs[1]. Natural and organic programs are provided in response to consumer concerns over health, with additional attributes being provided in some programs to also meet demands for higher food quality, animal and environmental welfare concerns, and further confirmation of how a product is produced. Tenderness programs are a response to consumers' demand for increased consistency in the palatability and eating quality of beef. Additional attributes often included in tenderness-based programs include grass fed, enhanced food safety, leanness, product origin, breed, convenience, and source and process verification. Breed and product origin are often provided in addition to tenderness, as they are frequently proxy indicators of eating quality. In the case of enhanced food safety, lean or grass fed beef, the programs are focusing on niche markets of health-conscious consumers and in the case of convenience; programs are catering to the on-the-go consumer lifestyle.

The identification of three major market directions of branded beef programs: natural, organic, and tenderness will be used in describing differences between transaction characteristics to predict the organizational form of supply chains. Similar to classifying attributes as being credence, experience, or search attributes, this narrows down the focus of the model and allows for a more detailed analysis of specific programs.

---

[1] Natural products are guaranteed to contain no hormones or antibiotics. Organic products are guaranteed to be produced using no synthetic chemicals (i.e. pesticides, fertilizers, genetically modified organisms, and other growing aids) and, in the case of livestock, use organic feed.

Table 4.2 - Key Branded Beef Attribute Combinations

	Attributes
1	Natural
2	Natural, Grass Fed, Enhanced Food Safety, Process & Source Verified
3	Natural, Grass Fed, Animal Welfare & Environmentally Friendly, Enhanced Food Safety
4	Natural, Tender
5	Organic, GM Free, Process & Source Verified
6	Organic, GM Free, Animal Welfare & Environmentally Friendly
7	Tender
8	Tender, Enhanced Food Safety, Process & Source Verified
9	Tender, Grass Fed
10	Tender, Product Origin
11	Tender, Lean
12	Tender, Breed
13	Tender, Lean, Breed
14	Tender, Convenience

Source: Adapted from Kovanda and Schroeder (2003)

ASSET SPECIFICITY

Transaction Cost Economics recognizes that conditions of asset specificity are widespread, that economic agents do not always possess perfect information, and are characterized by bounded rationality and opportunistic behaviour. Based on these four underlying concepts, three key transaction characteristics can be identified: asset specificity, transaction uncertainty, and transaction frequency. The degree to which these transaction characteristics affect transaction costs is dependent on the type of attribute being guaranteed and how they affect overall transaction complexity.

Asset specificity is one of the key variables of interest in determining how an attribute will affect transaction complexity and costs. As defined by Williamson (1986a), three different types of asset specificity exist. The first is site specificity, in which agents in a supply chain are in a fixed relationship to minimize transportation costs or produce a region specific product and assets are immobile due to program restrictions or high costs. Site specific investments are apparent when the attribute being branded is product origin or environmental preservation. In the case of product origin, a producer and processor must be located in a specific region to use a region specific brand name that consumers associate with high-quality products. Examples of this type of branded program include Alberta Beef and Nebraska Corn-fed Beef, which are promoting their province/state as the origin of high-quality beef products. The branding of environmental sustainability often requires that transportation distances are minimized and production does not occur in regions that are environmentally sensitive. This results in investment in specific sites that are located near other supply chain participants and in compliance with environmental preservation requirements. Industry participants are vulnerable when site specific investments are made because they cannot easily switch production once investments have been made in resources specific to a regional brand.

The second type of asset specificity is physical asset specificity, which refers to relationship specific investments in physical assets such as feed and health protocols, genetics, capital improvements, and technologies associated with food safety and the testing, grading, and processing of beef. Credence beef products, such as natural beef, typically requires that cow-calf operators, backgrounders, and feedlots invest in specialized feed and health protocols that eliminate the use of certain inputs, such as growth hormones and antibiotics. Instead, other regimes are substituted that are often more expensive and require a longer production period. The provision of credence attributes in branded products may also require that processors invest in technologies to test for the presence/absence of particular inputs in order to reduce the incentive to cheat. For those products that provide additional assurances of animal welfare and environmental preservation, cow-calf operators, feedlots, and processors may be required to make physical improvements to their operations in order to upgrade and comply with animal welfare and environmental guidelines.

A specific investment in physical assets is also required when producing experience and search attributes associated with high-quality tender products. Producers often invest in specific breeds and genetic lines, as some breeds have been associated with producing more tender beef and some branded beef programs are based on a specific breed. It is important to note that a producer will probably only participate in a breed-based program if they already produce a particular breed. As a result, investments in breed are often smaller, as it is unlikely that a producer will adopt a completely new production system. Instead they will be more focused on making ongoing improvements in their herd genetics.

Often, tenderness-based branded programs also require producers and feedlots to invest in specific feed and production protocols to improve meat quality and consistency. Technology associated with testing, grading, and processing beef is also used in tenderness programs at the processor level to sort incoming cattle, measure tenderness and consistency, and improve overall product quality.

The third type of asset specificity is human asset specificity. This term is used to describe transaction specific knowledge or human capital with specialized training or experience that performs functions specific to the production of a particular attribute (Shelanksi and Klein, 1995). Certain production and processing knowledge is standard across all beef products and does not require specialized human capital, but other knowledge is specialized to the attribute being produced. This is the case with certain production and management protocols, record keeping, and certification processes.

The production of credence attributes implies that attributes cannot be easily tested for along the supply chain. As a result, other methods must be used to ensure that consumers are provided with a product that fulfills the guarantees provided by a branded program. The implementation of a certification process and record keeping is typically the best way to manage credence attributes along the supply chain, but adoption of these systems sometimes requires a large investment of time, specialized management skills, and in some cases specific technologies. Different supply chain participants must be monitored and a large amount of information must be managed within different segments of the supply chain in order to guarantee an attribute.

If an attribute is either an experience or search attribute, this type of compliance mechanism is typically not required. However, the production of attributes such as tenderness and leanness do require supply chain participants to invest time and knowledge to create detailed production and management plans. These plans typically outline a purchasing protocol and how animals will be managed during the production process to maximize performance and quality, which can vary significantly if a proper management plan is not used in combination with suitable levels of physical investment. Investment into human resources may also be required to develop management plans that ensure proper procedures are in place to provide animal welfare and environmental preservation attributes.

Table 4.3 provides a summary of the asset specific investments required to produce different attributes. This table is intended as an outline; types of investments required may be more or less for a particular attribute depending on the level of consistency and guarantee a particular program is providing to consumers. From the table it is apparent that certain attributes require common specific investments, which may make it conducive to provide these attributes in combination under a branded beef program. Several of the combinations listed in Table 4.2 support this idea. Many of the attributes that are commonly combined require similar specific investments. While consumers often desire different combinations of attributes in order to maximize their own utility, common specific investment implies that the cost of providing an additional attribute may be minimal. In determining the benefit received from increasing the number of attributes provided, it is expected that another attribute will only be added if the additional costs incurred, as a result of the increase in asset specificity, are less than the increase in consumers' willingness to pay.

Table 4.3 - Asset Specific Investments Incurred to Produce Particular Attributes

Attributes	Site	Physical	Human
Natural (C)		Feed/Health Protocol	Records/Certification
Organic & GM Free (C)		Feed/Health Protocol	Records/Certification
Grass Fed (C)		Feed Protocol	Records/Certification
Enhanced Food Safety (C)		Feed/Health Protocol, Testing/Grading/Processing Tech	Records/Certification Prod/Mgmt Protocol
Animal Welfare (C)	Yes	Physical Improvements	Records/Certification Prod/Mgmt Protocol
Environmental Preservation (C)	Yes	Physical Improvements	Records/Certification Prod/Mgmt Protocol
Source & Process Verification (C)			Records/Certification
Product Origin (C)	Yes		Records/Certification
Breed (C)		Genetics	Records/Certification
Tender (E)		Genetics, Feed Protocol, & Testing/Grading/Processing Tech	Production/Management Protocol
Lean (S)		Genetics, Feed Protocol, & Testing/Grading/Processing Tech	Production/Management Protocol
Convenience (S)		Processing Technology	

C – Credence Attribute E – Experience Attribute S – Search Attribute

The total transaction costs incurred as a result of different supply chain participants investing in transaction specific assets varies significantly and depends on the investment necessary to produce a particular attribute. As the degree of transaction specific assets required for producing a particular attribute increases, negotiation costs are expected to increase. Participants will move away from transacting in the spot market towards increased vertical coordination and more long-term relationships. This will be done in order to protect asset specific investments, reduce the risk of opportunistic behavior, and minimize negotiation costs. As firms use more detailed and coordinated arrangements to reduce opportunistic behaviour, it is expected that negotiation costs will increase. Often such arrangements require large amounts of time, exhaustive stipulation, the hiring of lawyers, and other third party involvement. Increased coordination and higher negotiation costs will also arise when the number of attributes that are provided under a branded program increases, as it is expected that this will increase the overall level of asset specificity.

Transaction Uncertainty

The second main transaction characteristic that affects the type of supply chain coordination that emerges is transaction uncertainty. Uncertainty surrounding transactions can be broken down into four main categories: information asymmetry, incomplete information, price uncertainty associated with quality variability, and price uncertainty associated with the number of buyers in a market.

Information Asymmetry

The verification of different production and processing practices in a branded beef program may be difficult due to information asymmetries between different supply chain participants. Problems associated with information asymmetry exist with all of the credence attributes branded, as shown in Table 4.4. Table 4.4 shows those industry sectors where information asymmetries can occur when transacting with other segments of the supply chain.

The overall level of information asymmetry that exists for a particular attribute does vary. For example, with the branding of natural beef, production practices have to be closely monitored to ensure that the final product is in fact "natural". Cow-calf operators and feedlots have an incentive to cheat and use growth-hormones and antibiotics in order to capture the premium associated with an increased consumer willingness to pay for natural products without incurring the costs. This is not to suggest that all, or any, cattle producers will act on the incentive (Hobbs and Kerr, 1999). The potential, however, is there and must be dealt with in the design of a program.

In the case where attributes such as enhanced food safety, environmental preservation and animal welfare are branded, cow-calf operators, feedlots, and processors must be monitored. This is because there is an incentive to cheat in all stages of production and processing. Cow-calf operators, backgrounders, finishing feedlots, and processors could cheat. They could use prohibited feeds or avoid incurring the initial investments and ongoing costs associated with complying with higher environmental and welfare standards, while capturing the premiums associated with these higher standards. In these scenarios monitoring is required, with the degree of monitoring being dependent on the number of stages involved.

Table 4.4 - Relationship between Attributes and Information Asymmetry

	Information Asymmetry		
Attribute	Cow-Calf Operators	Feedlots	Processors
Natural (C)	Yes	Yes	
Organic & GM Free (C)	Yes	Yes	
Grass Fed (C)	Yes	Yes	
Animal Welfare (C)	Yes	Yes	Yes
Environmental Preservation (C)	Yes	Yes	Yes
Product Origin (C)	Yes	Yes	
Food Safety (C)	Yes	Yes	Yes
Breed (C)			Yes
Tender (E)			
Lean (S)			
Convenience (S)			

C – Credence Attribute   E – Experience Attribute   S – Search Attribute

The presence of credence attributes and information asymmetries requires that a traceability or identity preservation system be in place in order to ensure that particular production and processing practices are implemented. Otherwise, end-products that contain credence attributes are indistinguishable from products without these attributes. Obtaining sufficient information about production and processing practices when branding credence attributes involves increased transaction costs; more specifically information and monitoring costs.

Increased information costs arise when supply chain participants cannot determine the presence of a particular attribute and consequently focus on trying to determine the reputation of other supply chain partners in order to minimize the risk of cheating. Information costs associated with determining the reputation of a supply chain partner are expected to increase as the degree of measurability for a particular attribute decreases and monitoring for the attribute along the supply chain becomes more difficult. As such, information costs are expected to be highest for credence attributes and lowest for search attributes, which are more easily measured. The costs associated with determining reputation are also expected to be low for experience attributes, as participants rely on having a good reputation if they wish to maintain an ongoing relationship.

As information costs increase, the cost of transacting through the spot market will rise and supply chains become more closely coordinated. Similarly, closer vertical coordination may emerge to reduce monitoring costs that arise from monitoring the activities of different supply chain participants to ensure that stated standards are adhered to and to facilitate the transfer of product quality information. Monitoring costs are also expected to increase with an increase in the number of supply chain segments where information asymmetries exist. For example, producing natural beef requires that only cow-calf operators and feedlots are monitored, while producing environmentally friendly beef requires monitoring of the cow-calf, feedlot, and processing stages.

The implementation of certification institutions for monitoring the production and processing of particular credence attributes may reduce monitoring costs. These institutions typically focus on developing a common set of industry-wide standards and, as a result, monitoring costs are lowered. The presence of organic certification institutions is quite common in Canada and other countries. These institutions act as a neutral third-party that supervises production and processing to ensure that organic standards are complied with at various stages of the supply chain. If these institutions were not in place, buyers would have to implement their own systems to monitor sellers. This would likely be more costly as industry-wide standards would be replaced with numerous different individual sets of standards.

To summarize, information asymmetries result in an increase in information and monitoring costs, with these costs increasing as the degree of measurability and ease of monitoring decreases. The presence of certification institutions can aid in reducing monitoring costs, but they have not been established for many of the credence attributes currently being provided in the beef industry. Instead, internal monitoring and certification processes must be developed for individual programs. As a result, monitoring costs are expected to be high due to the inefficiencies created when many smaller non-uniform mechanisms are used. Information and monitoring costs are also highly dependent on the number of attributes being branded. As the number of attributes increases it is expected that monitoring and information costs will also increase.

Incomplete Information

With the provision of certain branded beef attributes, problems associated with incomplete information can exist as neither party to a transaction may have perfect information about the presence of a particular attribute. While credence attributes are typically either present or absent, and there is less uncertainty with respect to their quality, other attributes can vary widely in terms of quality. Incomplete information on quality is readily apparent in the production stages, when the attributes being produced are leanness and tenderness. The level of leanness or tenderness cannot easily be measured until livestock is processed.

When animals are being transferred between cow-calf operators, feedlots, and processors, it is difficult to obtain precise measures of the level of tenderness or leanness and payment is typically made on a live weight basis instead of on a quality basis. Although proxy variables for the attributes are often used in a live weight pricing system, they are often poor indicators of actual quality. As a result, incomplete information regarding attribute quality exists. The presence of incomplete information has one main effect. Producers and feedlots that are paid on a live weight basis are not penalized for producing lower quality products and are not rewarded for producing higher quality products. Consequently, there is little incentive for them to follow program guidelines put in place to reduce variability and improve product quality. Hence, in order to obtain the desired attributes increased transactions costs will be incurred.

Technologies exist to measure for tenderness and leanness when the animal is still alive. The problem is that these technologies are relatively new and expensive, which has resulted in their limited use. Instead, monitoring and the transfer of product quality information along the supply chain are relied upon to reduce variability and increase product quality when tenderness or leanness is being provided.

As with information asymmetry, information costs will be incurred to determine the reputation of other participants in the supply chain. In this case packers (feedlots) will focus on determining whether or not feedlots (cow-calf operators) provide a product that is of the right quality. For transactions between the packer and feedlot, a packer can measure tenderness and leanness qualities to some extent upon purchase. This means that feedlots have an incentive to maintain a positive reputation with packers. If quality is low, packers will choose not to purchase from them again. The effect of reputation on transactions between packers and feedlots suggests that information costs will be lower between feedlots and packers than between cow-calf operators and feedlots. In the latter interface, information regarding reputation is more difficult to obtain because quality cannot be determined even at purchase. Transactions are also more numerous and infrequent due to the large number of small scale cow-calf operators.

Monitoring costs will also arise in programs that brand tenderness. This is because, even after processing, the actual level of tenderness cannot be completely guaranteed, as measurements are often based on proxy variables. Technologies exist to measure tenderness at processing, but thus far they have not been implemented on a commercial basis due the high costs of implementation and operational problems that need to be overcome. Another reason for monitoring production and processing is that the identity of an individual product cannot be easily traced back from the consumer to the feedlot or cow-calf operator. If consumers dislike a product they may switch away from the brand entirely, and demand signals will fail to differentiate between high and low quality. Therefore, production and processing standards are often implemented that reduce quality variability and raise tenderness levels to ensure consumer satisfaction. These standards must be monitored in order to ensure compliance as there is an incentive to cheat given the limited ability to track tenderness throughout the supply chain.

The monitoring costs associated with obtaining product quality information along the supply chain are expected to increase as production and processing guidelines become increasingly detailed and stringent to ensure quality. As a result, transactions between supply chain participants may move away from the spot market, with vertical coordination increasing to offset increased transaction costs. The implementation of more detailed standards will also result in increased negotiation costs, as agreements between transaction partners become more complex in order to ensure compliance with program requirements.

As with information asymmetry, institutions exist that reduce the level of incomplete information and improve the transfer of product quality information along the supply chain. Branded beef programs have begun to focus on the use of grid pricing initiatives. Grid pricing allows for the transfer of product quality information back to both cow-calf operators and feedlots. This results in a realignment of incentives, as cow-calf operators and feedlots are penalized for the production of poor cattle and rewarded for the production of high quality cattle. Consequently, less monitoring is required.

Grid pricing institutions also have an effect on information and negotiation costs. The benefit of reduced monitoring costs must be considered against the increase in these costs when a grid pricing structure is used. Information costs associated with searching for price information may initially increase under a grid pricing system, as participants must search out detailed information on how the grid works and also identify a grid that best suits their existing operation to maximize returns. There are also information costs in gathering carcass quality information at the time of processing and transferring this information back along the supply chain. In the long run, the costs associated with searching are expected to be lower, as individuals commit production to one grid and receive information on the quality of cattle produced on an ongoing basis. Increased coordination may be considered if the information costs associated with transferring quality information back along the supply chain are high.

Negotiation costs may also increase, as negotiations will take place around determining the structure of the grid pricing system instead. Costs will also be incurred because under a grid pricing system there is typically a delay between the times when a transaction occurs and when payment is actually received. This is because quality cannot be determined until the product has actually been processed. The costs associated with payment delay are expected to be larger for cow-calf operators, which retain ownership, than feedlots because the delay in payment will be longer. These costs will also depend on the payment system used. Various payment systems exist, including a single payment at the time of processing or for cow-calf operators a partial payment can be made at the time calves are sold to the feedlot, which is then followed by a final payment upon processing.

The reduction in monitoring costs by buyers, as a result of a grid pricing initiative, may also be offset by an increase in monitoring costs for feedlots and cow-calf operators. Due to the nature of grid pricing systems the final price received by feedlots and/or cow-calf operators is dependent on the end quality measurement. There is a risk that processors will under-grade carcasses (Hobbs et al., 1998). As a result, feedlots and cow-calf operators may have an incentive to monitor the grading process. The risk of processors actually doing this is considered to be small given that it is to their benefit not to damage relationships with well managed feedlots and cow-calf operators that retain ownership, who can supply them with high quality product on an ongoing basis.

In order to determine whether a grid-pricing system will be used, the increase in information and negotiation costs must be less than the decrease in monitoring costs. Whether or not a grid-pricing institution is implemented, supply chain participants may move towards increased vertical coordination when problems associated with incomplete information arise. Increased vertical coordination will offset the overall rise in transaction costs and eliminate some of the costs involved when a grid-pricing system is implemented. It is difficult to determine the optimal degree of coordination. It is not easy to value the tradeoff between increased information costs associated with transferring information back along the supply chain against reduced long run information costs that arise because production segments have easier access to quality information.

The role of other institutions also needs to be considered as they will have an impact on the use of grid pricing and the degree of coordination required to implement a grid-based system. For example, with the establishment of programs such as the Canadian Cattle Identification Agency and its associated national standardized tagging program, increased numbers of database tracking systems are being developed and provided at a lower cost. This should make it easier to track production and transfer information along the supply chain. Systems like this could reduce the degree of coordination required to facilitate information transfer and traceability and allow increased flexibility in terms of the nature of beef industry coordination programs. They could also reduce the costs associated with current information transfers.

Price Uncertainty – Quality Variability

Price uncertainty can arise as a result of the variability in quality for different experience and search attributes (i.e. tenderness and leanness). The price received by a seller is uncertain when tenderness and/or leanness attributes are provided and grid-based pricing systems are used. Although price discovery activities can help to determine general market prices, the actual price that will be received cannot be readily predicted given uncertainty over final quality until after final processing is complete.

Uncertainty as to the price received makes it difficult to plan and market appropriately in order to obtain a specific reserve price. Price is more difficult to establish when quality cannot be determined prior to a transaction and, as a result, sellers face an increased risk that they will obtain a lower than expected price. In situations where price uncertainty exists, transaction costs are expected to be similar to those in the previous discussion regarding imperfect information. Information costs are a key cost incurred by sellers in an effort to reduce price uncertainty associated with incomplete information on quality. Negotiation costs also arise in establishing agreements that minimize price uncertainty and reduce the risk of a seller not obtaining their reserve price. It is predicted that as price uncertainty increases, and consequently price discovery and negotiation costs increase, supply chain participants will move towards increased vertical coordination in an effort to reduce this uncertainty and minimize the associated transaction costs.

Price Uncertainty – Number of Buyers

The size of a market for a particular attribute can be defined in two different ways. First, the number of consumers and market share of a particular attribute can be identified. Second, the number of buyers at different transaction points in the supply chain can be used to define the market size for a particular seller. The latter definition of market size seems to be more important when considering the impact that market size will have on price uncertainty and supply chain structure. This is because the number of buyers available to sellers will affect the risk of sellers not obtaining their reserve price. It is expected that the risk of selling at a reduced price increases when there are a smaller number of buyers. A reduction in sellers' bargaining power is the result – a small numbers bargaining problem.

Determining the actual number of buyers at different points along the supply chain is difficult as limited public information is available on the numbers and types of branded beef programs that currently exist. The limited information is, in part, a result of the relative newness of branded beef products in North America. Branded beef programs have been increasing in the US market over the last ten years and have more recently emerged in the Canadian market. The lag in their development in the Canadian market will be discussed in Chapter 6. Only general approximations regarding the number of buyers can be made based on information pertaining to the largest branded beef alliances currently operating in the US

This information, which was compiled by Kovanda and Schroeder (2003), was used to determine the most common combinations of attributes currently being branded.

Kovanda and Schroeder (2003) do not identify the number of buyers for each particular attribute. Instead, the information provided by Kovanda and Schroeder (2003) is used as a proxy to estimate the expected number of buyers. The branded beef programs identified by Kovanda and Schroeder (2003) were examined with respect to the attributes they provided. Twenty-five programs out of a total of thirty-two identified by Kovanda and Schroeder (2003) were examined, as information on the other seven programs could not be found. The number of branded programs identifying a particular attribute was divided by twenty-five to obtain a percentage value. This value is an approximation of the proportion of branded beef programs that include a particular attribute.

Although this method does not identify the number of buyers, it does provide an insight into the presence of certain attributes in the market. Consequently, it provides a rough approximation of the market size for certain attributes. Using this method, it is assumed that market size is correlated with the number of buyers. A smaller market size is assumed to result in a smaller number of buyers and a larger market size implies that a larger number of buyers exist in the market. Clearly, this method only establishes a proxy variable. In certain cases the market for a particular attribute could be large, but a monopoly or monopsony situation is present. In this situation, price uncertainty will remain considerable even though the market is large. The absence of direct information on the actual number of buyers in a market limits the ability to make accurate predictions regarding the organization of supply chains in the beef industry.

Table 4.5 identifies the branded attributes and the percentage of programs that include these attributes. Percentage values range from zero to eighty-eight percent. Those attributes with zero percent do not mean that programs containing these attributes do not exist. Instead, it means that programs with these attributes have a very small market share and, as such, were not considered in the identification of the largest US branded beef programs by Kovanda and Schroeder. Predicted market size in terms of the number of buyers in a market was categorized as being either small (0-30% of branded beef programs), medium (30-60% of branded beef programs), or large (60-100% of branded beef programs). Small markets, with few downstream buyers, are niche markets that exist on a small-scale in the North American beef industry. Medium sized markets are those that have several buyers along the supply chain. They produce branded beef products that are growing in demand, but still only capture a small portion of beef's total market share. Large markets are those that produce branded beef products with attributes that appear to be the most highly demanded by consumers. Consequently, there are a large number of buyers in these markets.

Table 4.5 indicates that the number of buyers for the majority of attributes is expected to be small. Breed and natural attributes are the exception; the number along the supply chain is expected to be in the middle range. Also, for tenderness the number of buyers is expected to be large. When measuring the number of buyers, the transaction interface (cow-calf operator/feedlot or feedlot/processor) is not considered. Instead, it is assumed that if a small number of buyers exist at the feedlot/packer interface, a small number of buyers will also exist at the cow-calf/feedlot interface. Similarly if a large number of buyers exist at the feedlot/packer interface a large number of buyers are also assumed to exist at the cow-calf/feedlot interface.

Table 4.5 - Predicted Market Size in Terms of Number of Buyers

Attribute	Branded Programs	Percentage*	Number of Buyers	Price Uncertainty
Natural	8	32	Medium	Medium
Organic & GM Free	0	0	Small	High
Grass Fed	1	4	Small	High
Enhanced Food Safety	0	0	Small	High
Animal Welfare	3	12	Small	High
Environmental Preservation	2	8	Small	High
Product Origin	2	8	Small	High
Source Verification	0	0	Small	High
Process Verification	0	0	Small	High
Breed	12	48	Medium	Medium
Tender	22	88	Large	Low
Lean	5	20	Small	High
Convenience	0	0	Small	High

*Percentages were calculated by dividing the number of branded beef programs that provide a particular attribute by the total number of programs identified (25) in Kovanda and Schroeder's paper.
Source: Adapted from information in Kovanda and Schroeder (2003)

The method used to determine the estimated number of buyers is arbitrary, but it allows for the provision of a general comparison of the types of markets that exist for different branded beef attributes. The above analysis can be used to identify the transaction costs associated with both the number of buyers and price uncertainty. It is expected that as market size decreases, and the number of buyers available for a specialized product decreases, the information costs incurred by a seller will increase. Sellers operating in a market with a small number of buyers will have to spend more time searching out buyers, identifying their specifications, and obtaining price information. This information may not be readily available when only a small number of buyers exist in a market. In a smaller market, with fewer buyers, increased costs will also be incurred to determine a buyer's reputation and whether or not they are likely to act opportunistically and pay a lower price than was initially agreed.

When a small number of buyers exist, negotiation costs will also be incurred to reduce the risk of opportunistic of behaviour and to reduce the risk of price uncertainty. Price uncertainty is expected to increase as the number of buyers in a market decreases. With fewer buyers there is a higher risk that sellers will not be able to obtain the price they expected for their product. In an effort to protect themselves against the risks associated with opportunistic behaviour and price uncertainty, sellers will spend increased time and expense negotiating with buyers to establish an agreement that minimizes their risk.

An additional issue is the relationship between price uncertainty arising from the number of buyers and asset specific investments. With a smaller number of buyers in the market, there is an increased risk that buyers will act opportunistically and attempt to capture the available quasi-rents associated with any asset specific investments made by sellers. Consequently, if asset specific investments are low, less emphasis will be placed on the number of buyers because there is less incentive for them to act opportunistically. As a result, when asset specificity is low it is expected that transaction costs incurred as a result of fewer buyers in the market will be lower.

Number of Sellers

The number of sellers available also has an impact on the degree of supply chain coordination. With fewer sellers for a particular attribute, processors face increased risks that they will not be able to procure a constant supply of product. This limits their ability to establish supply agreements with retailers and other end-users for a specialized product. As a result, the number of sellers in a market also has an influence on transaction costs and the optimal degree of vertical coordination.

When the number of sellers in a market decreases it is expected that information costs will increase, given that buyers will spend more time searching out suppliers and will also incur costs in an effort to determine a supplier's reputation. A seller's reputation becomes important if there is a risk that they could act opportunistically and request a higher price than was initially arranged, knowing that the buyer needs the product to fulfill its downstream commitments. Negotiation and enforcement costs will also be higher, as there will be increased incentive to establish and enforce agreements that reduce the risk of opportunistic behaviour and minimize a buyer's price uncertainty.

It is apparent that both the number of buyers and sellers in a market can significantly impact transactions costs, with transaction costs increasing as the number of buyers and sellers decrease. Hence, it is likely that as market size becomes smaller and transaction costs increase, supply chain participants will choose to increase coordination to minimize transaction costs. The level of asset specificity required to produce a particular attribute will affect the degree of coordination. Smaller market size and the associated higher transaction costs are relatively less important in situations where the degree of asset specific investments is low.

Under conditions of asset specificity and transaction uncertainty, enforcement costs may also arise to ensure compliance with agreements negotiated between supply chain partners. Enforcement costs may not actually be incurred every time an agreement is made, but the possibility exists that an agreement between supply chain participants will be breached. Then partners to an agreement would have to incur enforcement costs, for example, to cover court or arbitration costs. It is expected that as the degree of asset specificity and transaction uncertainty increases, the risk of opportunistic behaviour and, as a result, the risk of breaching an agreement will increase. In order to minimize these higher transaction costs, beef industry participants may choose to increase supply chain coordination.

TRANSACTION FREQUENCY

The frequency with which transactions occur between supply chain participants is another transaction characteristic that will affect vertical coordination. The probable number of transactions between different industry segments is outlined in Table 4.6. Typically, cow-calf operators are on a one-year cycle. They calve once a year and sell their total production over a brief period later in the year. Larger cow-calf operators may switch their production plan so that they have cows calving at two or three different times during the year, which will result in the sale of their production being staggered into two or three transactions per year. Such changes in production are difficult to adopt in Canada and parts of the U.S., however, due to the increased costs of wintering calves born in the fall. As a result, transactions between cow-calf operators and feedlots are limited to one or two per year, with most cow-calf operators focusing on only making small adjustments in their marketing schedules to provide cattle to feedlots at alternate times of the year.

Feedlots, which often operate on a significantly larger scale than cow-calf operators, typically have a continuous flow of cattle going through their operations to packers. This is done in order to cover fixed costs year round and to maximize operational efficiency in both feedlots and packing plants.

Table 4.6 - Transaction Frequency

Transacting Parties	Transactions/Year
Cow-Calf Producers – Feedlots	1 to 2
Feedlots - Packers/Processors	Multiple

As transactions become more frequent there is increased reliance on trust. It is in the best interest for participants that transact frequently to not hide information or act opportunistically in ways that could jeopardize their ongoing relationship. When transactions are more frequent and reputation and trust are increasingly relied upon, the transaction costs incurred to reduce information asymmetries, incomplete information, and price uncertainty are reduced. Consequently, a lower degree of vertical coordination is expected when transactions occur on a more frequent basis.

Transaction frequency differs from other transaction characteristics in that, while frequency varies between different segments of the supply chain, this variation is essentially constant across all attributes. Differences are more a result of variation in concentration across industry sectors. Therefore, the effect of frequency on transactions costs, as a result of the production of different attributes, is expected to be minimal and has not been included in the model. Instead, consideration needs to be given to how transaction frequency affects coordination between different industry participants. It is expected that more coordination will be required at the cow-calf/feedlot interface than at the feedlot/processor or processor/retailer interfaces where transactions occur on an ongoing basis. When transactions occur on a more frequent basis between supply chain participants, negotiation costs will be lower as participants will have a greater incentive to maintain ongoing relationships by not acting opportunistically.

ADDITIONAL FACTORS THAT AFFECT VERTICAL COORDINATION

Additional transaction characteristics may also affect the transaction costs and degree of vertical coordination required to produce a particular attribute. The number and types of links required to provide an attribute and the implementation of source/process verification systems also need to be considered when examining transaction costs and the optimal degree of vertical coordination.

Number of Links

It is important to identify the number of links or stages in the vertical supply chain that have an influence on the provision of a particular attribute. As more links are required, there are an increased number of transactions where information other than the price of a product must be transferred between participants. Downstream users of products require information on the quality of inputs, and in some cases upstream suppliers also need to obtain information on end-product quality. The ease with which information is transferred depends on the type of attribute being produced, with the costs being highest for credence attributes and lowest for search attributes. The costs associated with experience attributes are expected to lie somewhere in between. In the case of experience attributes, information may flow back to the production stages when attributes such as tenderness are being produced where quality cannot be determined until after processing. In this situation, information may be relayed back to cow-calf operators and feedlots in the form of price premiums/discounts, as well actual carcass quality data that provides cow-calf operators and feedlots with more detailed demand signals and price incentives to better align their production with consumer demands.

Table 4.7 identifies the different branded beef attributes and the supply chain participants that influence these attributes. For example, natural beef requires that no hormones or antibiotics are used, which only occurs in the production stages. Therefore cow-calf operators and feedlots are the critical participants. As another example, tenderness can be affected by genetics, feed, other factors in the production process, and the processing techniques used. Therefore, when providing a guaranteed tender product, all of these stages (cow-calf operator, feedlot, and processor) need to be involved with information being transferred as to the required production and processing practices and the quality of finished products.

Similar to previous tables, it should be noted that Table 4.7 excludes seedstock producers, background feedlots, and the retailer. These participants have been excluded in order to simplify the model. In the production stages, finishing feedlots and background feedlots have a very similar influence on the production of particular attributes. Seedstock producers and commercial cow-calf operators also have a similar influence on the production of particular attributes. Therefore, it is easier to group commercial cow-calf operators and seedstock producers into one group and background and finishing feedlots into another group.

Retailers have been excluded from the model, as it has been assumed that their impact on the production of particular attributes is minimal, with the exception of certain processing and value-added practices. The retailer's involvement in these processes has also diminished significantly. Increased processing and value-added production is being undertaken by packers, where retail case-ready products are produced for supermarkets effectively replacing in-store butchers. This increases product consistency and captures the economies of scale available in large processing plants versus small-scale in-store product preparation.

Table 4.7 - Supply Chain Participants that Affect the Presence of an Attribute

Attribute	Cow-Calf	Feedlot	Processor
Natural (C)	X	X	
Organic & GM Free (C)	X	X	
Grass Fed (C)	X	X	
Food Safety (C)	X	X	X
Animal Welfare (C)	X	X	X
Environmental Preservation (C)	X	X	X
Source Verification (C)	X	X	X
Process Verification (C)	X	X	X
Product Origin (C)	X	X	
Breed (C)	X		
Tender (E)	X	X	X
Lean (S)	X	X	
Convenience (S)			X

C – Credence Attribute E – Experience Attribute S – Search Attribute

Of course, coordination with the retailer is essential in selling a branded beef product. Retailers and other end users are the link between production and processing stages and consumers. They facilitate the transfer of consumer demands, in the form of price signals, back along the supply chain. Retailers also have reputations to maintain with their customers so they have a vested interest in ensuring consistency and quality.

Source and Process Verification

Source and process verification have previously been included in some branded beef programs. This has occurred in response to increasing demand by consumers that the production of attributes can be verified along the supply chain. New source verification and traceability systems are being brought into place that require investments into specialized I.D. technologies (tags, microchips, etc.), scanners, and data management systems. The investments made by supply chain participants must be protected from opportunistic behaviour, which may result in transactions becoming more complex. At the same time these systems often facilitate easier monitoring and tracking along the supply chain, which can offset the increase in transaction costs associated with opportunistic behaviour. Also, in the long run, the implementation of a traceability system is expected to reduce information costs. The creation of a comprehensive information management system increases the ease with which information can be transferred between supply chain participants.

OVERVIEW OF TRANSACTION CHARACTERISTICS

Linking together supply chain participants in order to facilitate the provision of differentiated attributes implies that supply chain participants will be working more closely together to transfer increasingly detailed information. This results in transactions being moved away from spot markets and towards increased vertical coordination. The actual level of vertical coordination chosen depends on all of the transaction characteristics combined and how they affect costs. The method chosen will be that which minimizes the total transaction and operating costs.

Table 4.8 provides an overview of transaction characteristics and their relationship with different branded beef attributes. Several conclusions can be drawn from the table. Firstly, the transaction characteristics associated with all credence attributes are very similar. Information asymmetry exists when producing any credence attribute. Consequently, the branding of any credence attribute implies that some sort of traceability or identity preservation system will be required. The structure of such a system will depend on whether external institutions already exist for monitoring the production and processing of a particular attribute or whether a new traceability system has to be developed that is specific to an individual supply chain. In addition, the number of buyers and/or sellers along a supply chain providing credence attributes typically ranges between small to medium. This means that price uncertainty is higher and, as a result, transaction costs are higher.

The biggest variance for different credence attributes is the level and type of asset specific investments required. For example, beef products that brand product origin require supply chain participants to be located in a specific region. It is most likely that instead of new investors coming into the region, existing operations located in the region will take part in the program and therefore site specific investments will actually be quite low. Investment will only become high if new investors enter a region in order to participate in a program. At the opposite extreme, as animal welfare and environmental preservation program standards become more stringent, the physical improvements required may be quite large and result in high levels of physical asset specificity and, consequently, higher transaction costs. Human asset specific investments also vary between attributes and will result in differences in the transaction costs incurred when producing particular attributes.

Incomplete information on the production of particular attributes can result in transaction uncertainty when experience and search attributes are concerned, which will affect the transaction costs incurred to provide these attributes. The number of buyers and/or sellers for experience and search attributes is often much larger than for credence attributes. As a result, the risk of price uncertainty is lower for experience and search attributes and the transaction costs incurred to reduce the risk of opportunistic behaviour will be lower. Asset specific investments also vary, with investment at the processor level increasing for experience and search attributes such as tenderness, leanness, and convenience. Investment is required into both human capital and physical assets used in the production of these attributes. For credence attributes, investments are often required in the cow-calf or feedlot sectors related to particular production processes.

Table 4.8 – Overview of Transaction Characteristics

Attribute	Source Verification /Traceability	Asset Specificity	Information Asymmetry	Price Uncertainty (Quality*)	#of Buyers /Sellers	Price Uncertainty (Buyers /Sellers)**	Links Required
Natural (C)	Yes	Physical, Human	Yes	No	Medium	Medium	Cow–Calf Operators Feedlots
Organic & GM Free (C)	Yes	Physical, Human	Yes	No	Small	High	Cow–Calf Operators Feedlots
Grass Fed (C)	Yes	Physical, Human	Yes	No	Small	High	Cow–Calf Operators Feedlots
Enhanced Food Safety (C)	Yes	Physical, Human	Yes	No	Small	High	Cow–Calf Operators Feedlots, Processors
Animal Welfare (C)	Yes	Physical, Human	Yes	No	Small	High	Cow–Calf Operators Feedlots, Processors
Environmental Preservation (C)	Yes	Physical, Human, Site	Yes	No	Small	High	Cow–Calf Operators Feedlots, Processors
Source Verification (C)	Yes	Human	Yes	No	Small	High	Cow–Calf Operators Feedlots, Processors
Process Verification (C)	Yes	Human	Yes	No	Small	High	Cow–Calf Operators Feedlots, Processors
Product Origin (C)	Yes	Site, Human	Yes	No	Small	High	Cow–Calf Operators Feedlots
Breed (C)	Yes	Physical, Human	Yes	No	Medium	Medium	Cow–Calf Operators
Tender (E)	Varies	Physical, Human	No	Yes	Large	Low	Cow–Calf Operators Feedlots, Processors
Lean (S)	Varies	Physical, Human	No	Yes	Small	High	Cow–Calf Operators Feedlots
Convenience (S)	No	Physical	No	No	Large*	Low	Processors

*Price uncertainty arising as a result of variability in quality (e.g. If quality varies prices vary).
**Price uncertainty arising as a result of the number of buyers/sellers (e.g. If the number of buyers/sellers is small, price uncertainty will be high).

Shared asset specific investments and other transaction characteristics may help to explain the types of attributes that are commonly grouped together, as outlined in Table 4.2. Although consumers ultimately guide the production of different combinations of attributes, the increase in transaction and operating costs must also be considered. For example, providing a natural grass-fed beef product versus just a natural product does not require much more investment aside from minor alterations to the feed protocol and certification/record keeping systems. Consequently, the marginal increase in costs will be small. It is expected that for attributes to be provided in combination with others, the marginal increase in consumers' willingness to pay for the two attributes combined has to outweigh the willingness to pay for each attribute individually. It is also expected that for an additional attribute to be produced in combination with other attributes, the marginal cost of producing that attribute must be less than the marginal increase in consumers' willingness to pay.

The approach of comparing the marginal increase in consumers' willingness to pay for additional attributes with the marginal increase in costs associated with providing these attributes can be applied to any of the attribute combinations in Table 4.2. As long as consumers are willing to pay more for an additional attribute than the marginal increase in transaction and operating costs, supply chain participants should be willing to provide those attribute bundles. It is likely that the marginal increase in costs for an additional attribute will be small due to common transaction characteristics. This explains why branded beef programs often bundle several attributes.

A PREDICTIVE MODEL

It is important to understand the relationship between transaction complexity and the supply chain structures emerging in the branded beef industry. As discussed in the previous chapter, five main structures exist: spot markets, informal alliances, contracts, formal alliances, and vertical integration. Informal alliances can be further broken down into brand licensing organizations and marketing alliances. Contracts can be broken down into marketing and production contracts. Each supply chain structure is distinct in how it manages, or in some cases does not manage, various transaction characteristics. Table 4.9 presents a model that predicts the type of supply structure that is expected to emerge based on the previously identified transaction characteristics.

Each supply chain structure is examined with respect to whether it allows for the presence of a particular transaction characteristic. In some cases, such as with asset specificity, the model identifies the level of a characteristic that can be managed within a particular structure. The model presented in Table 4.9 is based on the analysis of supply chain structures presented in Chapter 3. Consistent with the predictions of Transaction Cost Economics, supply chain structures are expected to emerge to minimize the production and transaction costs associated with different transaction characteristics. For example, when information asymmetry exists for a particular attribute, supply chain participants will choose between carrying out transactions via production contracts, formal alliances, or vertical integration. The transaction costs associated with information asymmetry will be minimized under these structures given the increased ability to monitor other firms in the supply chain, and to ensure compliance.

Table 4.9 Predictive Model

	Spot Market	Informal Alliances		Contracts		Formal Alliances	Vertical Integration
		Brand Licensing Organizations	Marketing Alliances	Marketing	Production		
	⇑⇑	⇑	⇑	⇑	⇑	⇑	⇑
Overall Transaction Complexity	Low	Low	Low/Medium	Low	Medium/High	High	High
	⇑⇑	⇑	⇑	⇑	⇑	⇑	⇑
Asset Specificity	None	Low	Low/Medium	Medium/High	Medium/High	High	High
Information Asymmetry	No	No	No	No	Yes	Yes	Yes
Price Uncertainty (Quality Variability)	No	Yes	Yes	Yes	Yes	Yes	Yes
Price Uncertainty # of Buyers/Sellers	Large Market	Large Market	Market Size Varies	Market Size Varies	Medium/Small Market	Small Market	Small Market
Number of Participants	2	>2	>2	2	2	>2	>2
Traceability System	No	No	Yes	Yes	Yes	Yes	Yes

The optimal supply chain structure depends on the combination of transaction characteristics when producing a particular attribute. For example, information asymmetry may exist when providing an attribute, but this attribute may also require high levels of asset specificity. This will limit the optimal structure to using production contracts, a formal alliance or vertical integration. Production contracts are unlikely to be used if agreements need to be established between cow-calf operators and other sectors. This is because negotiation costs will be high due to the large number of small cow-calf operators with which individual agreements would have to be negotiated. Given the high capital costs associated with vertical integration in the beef industry, it is most likely that a formal alliance will be used to produce an attribute characterized by information asymmetry and a high degree of asset specificity.

The price uncertainty associated with quality variability and the number of buyers/sellers does not appear to limit the type of coordination that will occur as much as other transaction characteristics. This is expected because of the reciprocal nature of interactions between supply chain participants. Buyers need a constant supply of a differentiated product on an ongoing basis to meet their commitments and suppliers also need access to a market that will accept the differentiated product they produce. It is likely that price uncertainty will result in production being coordinated outside the spot market; the outcome will be dependent on the combination of other characteristics. In terms of quality variability, any system that can implement a grid-based pricing initiative will result in improved information transfer and reduced quality variability. At the same time, it is expected that the number of buyers and sellers will be closely linked to the degree of asset specificity. Thus, as asset specificity increases and the number of buyers and sellers decreases, supply chain coordination will increase

The number of participants that are involved with the production of a particular attribute is also important. In situations where cow-calf operators, feedlots, and processors are involved in the production of a particular attribute they will likely choose an informal or formal alliance structure. These structures are expected to be preferred over the use of contracts because feedlots will likely be transacting with many cow-calf operators, resulting in high negotiation costs if contracts must be negotiated with each individual. Contracts are also typically limited to coordinating transactions between two parties. When more than two parties are involved in the production of a particular attribute, contracts become complex and negotiation costs increase.

The need for a traceability system to ensure the presence of a particular attribute does not appear to limit the type of coordination that will occur to any great extent. Traceability systems can vary significantly in terms the types of information being transferred between supply chain segments. It is expected that as the information required to be transferred along the supply chain becomes greater or more detailed the optimal supply chain structure will exhibit a higher degree of vertical coordination.

Levels Of Standards

From the discussion of branded beef programs in Chapter 2, it was clear that programs differ in the stringency of their standards. While two different programs may guarantee the same attribute, one will require a higher level of coordination due to its more stringent production standards, traceability systems, and other program requirements. The most common example is the production of tenderness. Both Certified Angus Beef and Ranchers Renaissance are promoting the production of a consistently tender product. Yet under the Ranchers Renaissance program, participants must comply with very detailed production, processing, and management protocols. The focus is also to provide precise information back along the supply chain. Given the high level of investment required to comply with the program's physical and human capital demands, as well as detailed information, Ranchers Renaissance operates under a formal alliance structure. Typically, this type of organizational structure is referred to as a new generation cooperative. The cooperative uses membership fees and contracts to ensure participants make a long-term commitment and supply high quality cattle into the program.

In contrast, the Certified Angus Beef program also guarantees tenderness, but has minimal production requirements. It focuses on the use of specific and narrow grading standards along with a grid-based pricing system as its key method of transferring information back along the supply chain. This type of system requires a lower level of coordination and operates under a brand licensing organization which lies on the opposite end of the coordination continuum. Why are there two different structures that, in essence, are branding the same attribute? The key variant is the method used in achieving the attributes being guaranteed by their programs. It appears that each method results in a different level of transaction costs. Higher levels of standards and more detailed program requirements result in higher investments. This will increase the transaction costs incurred by supply chain participants and coordination will increase in order to minimize these costs.

More detailed program requirements typically require higher levels of investment in physical, human, or site specific capital. Examples are human capital investments in time, management, and the implementation of record/certification systems to guarantee compliance. The type of asset specific investments required to produce different attributes varies depending both on the attribute and the stringency of program standards. As a result, in order to understand the degree to which asset specificity contributes to overall transaction complexity, individual programs need to be examined based on the combination of the attributes they produce and the level of standards implemented.

Attribute Combinations

The second issue that arises is the combination of attributes in a differentiated product. The predictive model is essentially looking at the production of one attribute. Therefore, the vertical coordination outcome that emerges will be the one that facilitates the production of all of the attributes. It is expected that as the number of attributes provided in a differentiated product increases, coordination will increase.

Managing Differences in Frequency of Transactions

With the production of different beef attributes, the management of supply becomes crucial to the success of the program. In order to successfully market a brand to consumers, it needs to be made available to them on an ongoing and consistent basis. One of the greatest challenges in developing a branded beef program is maintaining a consistent and adequate volume of production. In the cow/calf sector, production occurs during specific months of the year, which results in inconsistent flows into the remainder of the supply chain. As a result, information costs have to be incurred to search for adequate supplies of suitable cattle. Improving supply chain coordination is often used to ensure the consistent delivery of cattle on an ongoing basis, while minimizing the information costs incurred.

The actual supply chain structure that emerges will depend on the attributes being branded. If attributes are readily available due to a larger number of sellers, a lower level of coordination is expected. As branded programs become more detailed, with a focus on higher levels of standards, multiple attributes, or attributes with a small number of sellers, it is expected that coordination will increase to reduce search costs. Coordinating the supply of beef has also allowed large processors to maintain a consistent supply of inputs for the production of convenience and value-added products. Producing convenience varies significantly from other attributes in that the majority of value is added in the processing segment. This relatively new segment in the beef industry is consuming a large volume of beef. In order to ensure a constant flow of supply into the plants and to reduce their procurement costs, processors have focused on increasing coordination.

Role of Institutions

Institutions can result in transaction costs being lowered and consequently can affect the degree of coordination required to produce a particular attribute. Whether an institution is a grid-based pricing system, a third-party certification body or a standardized tracking and traceability system, it is likely to impact the degree of coordination required. Processes that were previously implemented through a program become external. This results in increased flexibility in terms of the coordination of a particular program. The presence/absence of market institutions needs to be considered in terms of their impact on the optimal degree of supply chain coordination. Although the role of institutions was not encompassed in the predictive model, it is expected that when institutions exist the degree of coordination required to produce an attribute will be lower. The role of institutions will be further investigated in Chapter 6.

CONCLUSIONS

The objective of this chapter was to explore the relationship between Transaction Cost Economics and supply chain coordination in the beef industry. A predictive transaction cost model was developed that can be used to identify how different beef attributes affect transaction characteristics and consequently transaction costs. The model was then extended to identify why different supply chain structures have emerged to produce differentiated beef products with particular attributes. Several issues including the stringency of program standards, combinations of attributes under branded beef programs, ensuring adequate supply flow, and market institutions were then discussed in terms of how they can also affect the optimal method of coordination when producing a particular attribute.

It is important to extend the theoretical model and empirically examine the links between transaction characteristics, transaction costs, and supply chain coordination. Currently, no data on transaction costs in the beef industry is available and these costs are difficult to measure. The next chapter develops a survey that identifies the impact of different transaction characteristics on a cow-calf operator's decision to become involved in different types of supply chain coordination.

Chapter 5

COW-CALF OPERATORS AND CHANGING SUPPLY CHAINS

COW-CALF OPERATIONS IN THE BEEF SUPPLY CHAIN

It is apparent that significant benefits can be derived from increased coordination in meat supply chains. At the same time, coordination and the production of differentiated beef products can result in increased transaction costs. Transaction costs arise as a result of the increased risks associated with participating in a more coordinated program and must be traded off against any cost savings in order to determine the optimal degree of coordination.

Currently, the degree of coordination between the cow-calf sector and the rest of the value chain is lower than the degree of coordination between other segments of the beef industry. At the same time, cow-calf operators' participation in the production of differentiated products is necessary. Better linkages are needed between this sector and the rest of the supply chain to improve both information and product flow. The question arises as to why coordination has been limited between the cow-calf sector and the rest of the supply chain. It is expected that limited coordination at this transaction interface may be a result of the transaction characteristics arising when differentiated branded beef products are produced. In determining what has limited participation of cow-calf operators in different supply chain structures, it is necessary to evaluate the importance of different transaction characteristics to cow-calf operators. It is also important to examine the degree to which transaction characteristics affect their decision to participate in a particular supply chain relationship.

This chapter empirically evaluates the importance of different transaction characteristics to cow-calf operators when they are choosing to participate in a range of beef supply chain coordination programs. In particular, the chapter discusses the use of conjoint analysis as a methodology for studying the importance of different transaction characteristics to cow-calf operators and develops a conjoint analysis experiment.

USING CONJOINT ANALYSIS TO EXAMINE SUPPLY CHAIN COORDINATION

Conjoint analysis was used to evaluate cow-calf operator preferences for different supply chain structures based on the transaction characteristics that they may face. From a family of stated preference methods, conjoint analysis is the appropriate technique in this case, as it allows the researcher to evaluate preferences for a range of hypothetical supply chain structures based on their underlying characteristics, etc. Conjoint analysis assumes that products can be defined as a set of characteristics and respondents evaluate the utility of a combination of characteristic levels when making decisions (Ness and Gerhardy, 1994)). As conjoint analysis focuses on utility as the dependent variable instead of price, it is an appropriate framework to use when attempting to evaluate existing or hypothetical products, services, or programs.

Conjoint analysis, therefore, can be used to evaluate the utility derived by beef industry participants entering into different supply chain structures. Alliances and other methods of vertical coordination in the beef industry offer participants different combinations and levels of transaction characteristics. Conjoint analysis can be used to measure the relative importance of the transaction characteristics that were discussed in Chapter 4. It is expected that cow-calf operators will seek to maximize their utility and minimize transaction costs when making their decision to join a beef supply chain coordination program.

CONJOINT MEASUREMENT

Conjoint measurement was developed primarily by mathematical psychologists and was introduced into the marketing literature by Green and Rao in 1971. Conjoint analysis is consistent with Lancaster's (1971) notion of consumer utility being a function of preferences for the characteristics inherent in a good. Lancaster argued that utility is not derived from goods directly, but from their characteristics. As a result, goods are ranked according to utility only indirectly through the values assigned to levels of the characteristics that they are perceived to possess (Green and Wind, 1973).

Conjoint measurement involves examining respondents' overall judgments about a set of product alternatives and breaking those judgments down into the contribution of each product/program characteristic and characteristic level (Steenkamp, 1987). This process is used frequently in market research, as researchers are often concerned with finding out which characteristics of a product or a service are most important. Conjoint analysis is able to determine the contribution of each characteristic to a respondent's total utility and provide insights into the relative importance of different product/program characteristics (SPSS Inc., 1997). It enables researchers to identify combinations of product/program characteristics that give the respondent the highest utility. It establishes a valid model that is useful in predicting the acceptance of any combination of product characteristics, including those not originally evaluated by survey respondents (Ness and Gerhardy, 1994). In this case, the methodology is useful in predicting the combination of branded beef program attributes preferred by cow-calf operators.

The conjoint experiment developed in this chapter involves the combination of different levels of possible branded beef program characteristics to describe hypothetical supply chain coordination programs. The hypothetical profiles are then presented to respondents who indicate their overall evaluations for each hypothetical profile through either a ranking or rating scale. This is a strength of conjoint analysis, as respondents are asked to evaluate whole products/programs, much as cow-calf operators do when making a decision to participate in a particular supply chain coordination program. They must implicitly compare program features, and based on those features, make trade-offs between different programs (SPSS Inc., 1997). Based on the respondents' choices, conjoint analysis allows for the estimation of utility scores. These utility scores measure the relative importance of each program characteristic to the respondent's overall preference for a program, as well as estimating which levels of each characteristic are most preferred (SPSS Inc., 1997).

Conjoint analysis allows elements of a product, service, or program to be evaluated through a relatively low cost and convenient method (Patterson et al., 2003). The scenarios presented to respondents do not have to describe existing products or programs. Instead, hypothetical scenarios can be presented, which allows for the measurement of characteristics or combinations of characteristics that are not currently in the market. This allows researchers to forecast preferences for different characteristics prior to the development of new products and services (Louviere, 1988). The only risk with the creation of hypothetical scenarios is that credibility problems can occur. In order to ensure credibility, characteristics must be plausible and capable of being traded off by respondents (Hobbs, 1996c). Another advantage that sets conjoint analysis apart from other multivariate methods is that it can be carried out at the individual level. Using conjoint analysis, a researcher generates a separate model for predicting preferences for each respondent in the experiment. This reveals individual preferences and allows for the segregation of respondents into different groups based on their preferences (Hair et al., 1992).

The majority of research using conjoint analysis has focused on consumer preferences for products and services. However, conjoint analysis can be useful in almost any field where there is a need to measure people's preferences or perceptions. Conjoint analysis has often been applied outside of consumer preference research. Sy et al. (1997) focused on evaluating the preferences of cow-calf operators for different cattle characteristics and used conjoint analysis to estimate the marginal contribution of specific animal characteristics to overall cow-calf operator preference ratings (Sy et al., 1997). Prentice and Benel (1992) used conjoint analysis to examine the perception of US carriers regarding the desirability of obtaining loads in Canada versus returning empty to the Northern United States. Their analysis focused on the importance of selected elements of transborder movements (Prentice and Benal, 1992).

Hobbs (1996c) undertook a study that used conjoint analysis to measure the relative importance of selected transaction costs in beef processors' procurement decisions. The study was based on the premise that each supply chain displays different characteristics, similar to how goods and services are often viewed as bundles of characteristics. A processor's preference for a particular supply chain channel is determined by the bundle of characteristics that are present in that channel. The characteristics may result in transaction costs or may offset transaction costs. The presence of these characteristics varies among supply chain channels and will affect a processor's preference for a particular channel (Hobbs, 1996c).

A second study, which ties in closely with the conjoint method developed in this chapter, was done by Stevens et al. (2002) and uses conjoint analysis to examine landowners' attitudes toward specific forestland management program characteristics and requirements. The objectives of the study were to examine the characteristics that influence private landowners' decisions to participate in forestland management programs. The study also analyzed the tradeoffs between different management program characteristics. In order to evaluate landowner response, hypothetical management programs, defined by several characteristics and levels were created. Landowners were asked to indicate their willingness to participate in the different hypothetical programs.

Conjoint analysis is a very flexible and potentially powerful tool for exploring respondents' preferences and perceptions for particular products, services, and more importantly in this case, program structures. The discussion in Chapter 4 emphasized that programs in the beef industry vary significantly in terms of the attributes being produced and the transaction characteristics emerging, and are quite heterogeneous. Many current non-market valuation techniques do not facilitate the examination of multiple characteristics with different levels. Conjoint analysis provides a potential solution to this problem (Sy et al., 1997).

The purpose of the conjoint experiment developed in this chapter is to analyze the choices made by cow-calf operators. It investigates the hypothesis that a participant's choice to operate within a particular supply chain program is influenced by the different transaction characteristics and the levels of transaction characteristics that emerge. These transaction characteristics are a result of the various beef attributes being produced to satisfy consumer demands and have been discussed in Chapter 4. In the analysis that follows, beef programs are characterized as bundles of transaction characteristics. Conjoint analysis is used to measure the relative importance of selected transaction characteristics in a respondent's decision to participate in a value chain alliance.

A conjoint experiment was chosen to evaluate the importance of different transaction characteristics for two additional reasons. First, the lack of experience with supply chain coordination and branded programs in the Canadian beef industry results in an absence of relevant data, making experimental methods like conjoint analysis the only way to evaluate participants' perceptions and preferences for different potential programs. Second, any publicly available data cannot be used, because it cannot reveal preferences for characteristics of programs. This is because when intangible transaction characteristics are to be measured it is difficult to obtain quantitative data that allows for comparison between characteristics. Conjoint analysis provides a means to measure these variables and compare them by creating a common scale that allows weights to be assigned to the various levels of each characteristic. It is then possible to analyze how respondents tradeoff between characteristics when making their decisions (Sanderson, 2001).

LIMITATIONS, RELIABILITY, AND VALIDITY

In conjoint studies the researcher is assuming that the product/program being evaluated by respondents can be defined in terms of a few important characteristics. As more characteristics and characteristic levels need to be defined due to the increased complexity of an object, an increasing number of hypothetical scenarios must be presented to respondents.

Increasing numbers of scenarios are required in order to allow for the measurement of the relative importance of all the characteristics. There is, however, a limit on the number of judgments that respondents can reasonable be expected to make, which restricts the number of characteristics and levels that can be used in the experiment. This may affect the reliability of the experiment due to the exclusion of certain characteristics that are significant to the overall valuation of a particular scenario (Louviere, 1988). In order to overcome this limitation and ensure all relevant characteristics are included, it is important to research all possibilities and pretest the survey.

Another limitation of conjoint studies is that people may not actually do what they state they will in the hypothetical situation. This is less of a concern though, as most applications, such as the one in this chapter, are intending to identify estimates of relative importance rather than absolute values. In this situation there is less of worry about under or over estimates. The over or understatement of values is not likely to affect the actual order of importance for characteristics, which is what is of interest (Kroes and Sheldon, 1988).

McCullough and Best (1979) evaluated the temporal stability and structural reliability of conjoint measurement. In examining the temporal stability of conjoint measurement, McCullough and Best were focusing on the accuracy with which respondents can replicate their judgment of scenarios at different points in time. In terms of structural reliability, the focus was on examining the degree to which preference patterns identified by conjoint measurement remained unchanged, as the scenario describing the object is altered. In their paper it was concluded that the results of conjoint measurement were both stable over time and when characteristics were measured using alternative scales (McCullough and Best, 1979).

DESIGNING STIMULI OR TREATMENTS

The framework developed by Hair et al. (1992) provides a clear and concise method to design and execute a conjoint experiment. Three main steps are involved in the research process: 1) designing the stimuli or treatments, 2) collecting data, and 3) estimating and interpreting the model. Figure 5.1 provides an outline of the design and execution of a conjoint experiment. It will be used to describe the design of the cow-calf operator conjoint experiment.

The purpose of the conjoint experiment is to identify how different transaction characteristics influence a cow-calf operator's decision to participate in different supply chain alliances. In Chapter 4 it was established that different transaction characteristics emerge as a result of the production of particular beef attributes. Based on the production of these attributes, certain supply chain coordination methods are likely to be chosen to minimize the associated transaction costs. In the following analysis, methods of supply chain coordination to produce particular beef attributes will be characterized as bundles of transaction characteristics. Conjoint analysis will be used to measure the importance of selected characteristics in a respondent's decision to participate in a particular supply chain coordination program.

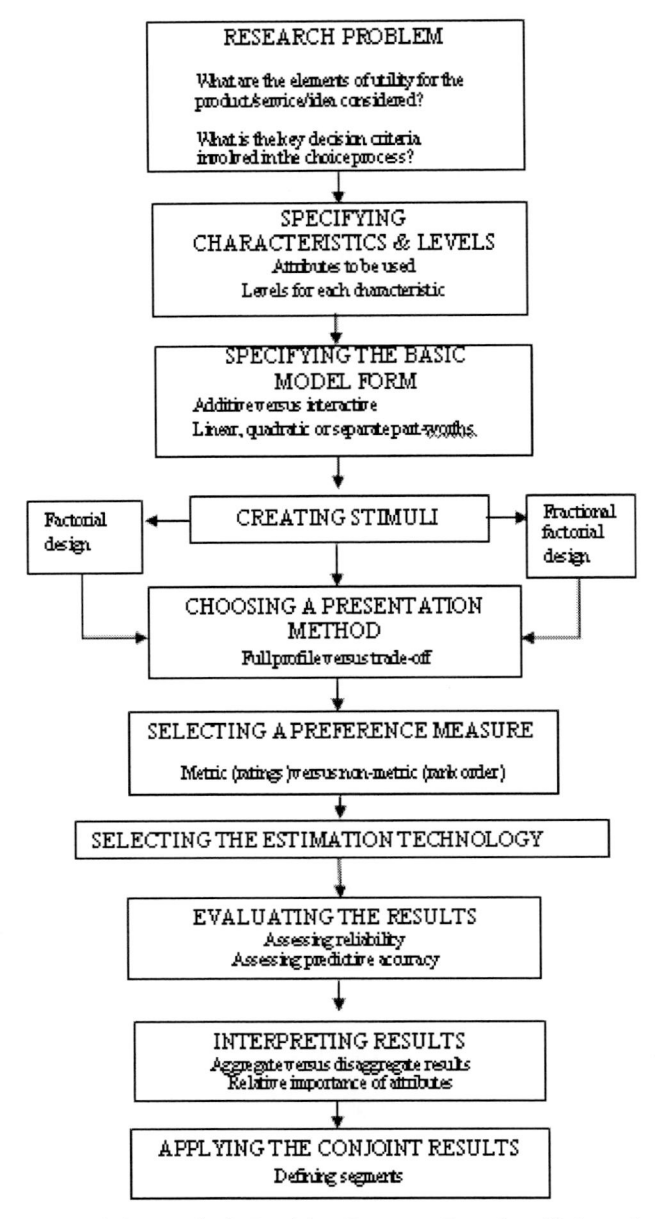

```
┌─────────────────────────────────┐
│      RESEARCH PROBLEM           │
│ What are the elements of utility│
│ for the product/service/idea    │
│ considered?                     │
│ What is the key decision criteria│
│ involved in the choice process? │
└─────────────────────────────────┘
               ↓
┌─────────────────────────────────┐
│   SPECIFYING                    │
│   CHARACTERISTICS & LEVELS      │
│   Attributes to be used         │
│   Levels for each characteristic│
└─────────────────────────────────┘
               ↓
┌─────────────────────────────────┐
│   SPECIFYING THE BASIC          │
│   MODEL FORM                    │
│   Additive versus interactive   │
│   Linear, quadratic or separate │
│   part-worths.                  │
└─────────────────────────────────┘
               ↓
┌──────────┐  ┌──────────────┐  ┌──────────┐
│Factorial │←│CREATING      │→│Fractional│
│design    │  │STIMULI       │  │factorial │
└──────────┘  └──────────────┘  │design    │
                  ↓             └──────────┘
┌─────────────────────────────────┐
│   CHOOSING A PRESENTATION       │
│   METHOD                        │
│   Full profile versus trade-off │
└─────────────────────────────────┘
               ↓
┌─────────────────────────────────┐
│   SELECTING A PREFERENCE MEASURE│
│   Metric (ratings) versus       │
│   non-metric (rank order)       │
└─────────────────────────────────┘
               ↓
┌─────────────────────────────────┐
│   SELECTING THE ESTIMATION      │
│   TECHNOLOGY                    │
└─────────────────────────────────┘
               ↓
┌─────────────────────────────────┐
│   EVALUATING THE RESULTS        │
│   Assessing reliability         │
│   Assessing predictive accuracy │
└─────────────────────────────────┘
               ↓
┌─────────────────────────────────┐
│   INTERPRETING RESULTS          │
│   Aggregate versus disaggregate │
│   results                       │
│   Relative importance of        │
│   attributes                    │
└─────────────────────────────────┘
               ↓
┌─────────────────────────────────┐
│   APPLYING THE CONJOINT RESULTS │
│   Defining segments             │
└─────────────────────────────────┘
```

Figure 5.1 - Conjoint Analysis Decision Process - Based on Hair et al. (1992)

SPECIFYING CHARACTERISTICS AND CHARACTERISTIC LEVELS

One of the most important aspects of the research design process involves the identification of appropriate characteristics and the specification of feasible levels for the characteristics (Ness and Gerhardy, 1994). It is important to identify the appropriate transaction characteristics and characteristic levels that define a particular beef supply chain. Hair et al. (1992) suggest that all characteristics that potentially create or detract from the overall worth should be included, with it being essential that both positive and negative characteristics be considered. In determining characteristics it is also important to include those characteristics and characteristic levels that best differentiate between the alternatives being studied. While many may be considered important, they do not facilitate in the decision process if they do not substantially vary between objects (Hair et al., 1992).

The characteristics and levels chosen must also be realistic in terms of whether or not they can actually be put into practice. Characteristics that are not distinct in their definition and instead are fuzzy allow for misinterpretation by respondents and lead to a lack of comparability between individual responses. The success of conjoint analysis relies on the ability of a researcher to adequately describe characteristics in order to allow accurate responses (Hair et al., 1992). To obtain accurate responses, Hair et al. (1992) suggest that each characteristic should be assigned the same number of levels. They argue that respondents may focus on the characteristics with more levels, biasing the results. It has been observed that as the number of levels increases, the relative importance of a variable increases even if the end points stay the same (Hair et al., 1992).

In choosing characteristics for this study it was necessary to select a subset of potential of transaction characteristics considered in order to limit the number of hypothetical supply chain coordination programs to avoid overcomplicating the task for respondents. Transaction characteristics were chosen based on the analysis in Chapter 4. Eight possible categories of characteristics were identified. These categories include: (1) Asset specific investments required, (2) Price uncertainty associated with quality variability, (3) Price uncertainty associated with the number of buyers, (4) Premiums received, (5) Information asymmetry, (6) Incomplete information, (7) Transaction frequency, and (8) Other benefits received. Each of these potential characteristics is discussed below.

Asset Specific Investments

The asset specific investments required to participate in a particular program was hypothesized to be a significant transaction characteristic and was included in the model. This is because there is an increased risk of opportunistic behaviour as a result of asset specificity. The seller incurs increased information and negotiation costs in order to determine a buyer's reputation and reduce the risk of opportunism. It is expected that when asset specificity is present these costs will impact a cow-calf operator's willingness to participate in a program.

Four different asset specific investments were defined based on what has typically been required of cow-calf operators in existing beef programs. The levels of investments included in the conjoint experiment were: (1) no additional investments, (2) adoption of a specific feed and health protocol, (3) capital expenditures for farm improvement, and (4) implementation of a record/certification system. Further definition of these investments was included in the survey which is provided in Appendix A. It is expected that the risk associated with opportunistic behaviour varies with each type of investment. The purpose of the conjoint experiment is to determine the relative importance of each investment and the degree to which each one limits cow-calf operator participation due to the associated risk of opportunistic behaviour.

Price Uncertainty – Quality Variability

The price uncertainty associated with quality variability was also hypothesized to influence a cow-calf operator's decision to participate in a program. As discussed in Chapter 4, quality variability has resulted in an industry shift towards grid-based pricing systems. When cow-calf operators move away from using a live weight pricing system, their short-term information costs can be higher due to the costs involved when searching out information on different quality-based pricing systems and determining a buyer's reputation. At the same time, ongoing information costs should be lower as information is transferred through the pricing system to feedlots and cow-calf operators and, as a result, they are not required to search out additional quality information. The impact on negotiation costs is indeterminate, as ongoing costs should be lower due to reduced negotiation of individual transactions, but a delay in payment can result in increased costs.

Cow-calf operators' preferences for different pricing systems will help identify the significance of different costs in the short-term and long-term and the degree to which they impact a cow-calf operator's willingness to participate in a particular program. Three different pricing methods were defined and included in the conjoint model: (1) grid-based carcass quality pricing, where price for cattle is determined based on the quality of the carcass upon processing, (2) live weight pricing, where price for cattle is determined at the time of sale based on their live weight, and (3) a combination of grid-based carcass quality pricing and live weight pricing, where an initial payment for cattle is determined at the time of sale and a final payment is made after processing when the quality of the carcass can be determined. These three pricing methods are the ones that are most commonly used in the North American beef industry. The three different pricing levels are expected to be discrete and independent of each other, with no linear relationship expected.

Price Uncertainty – Number of Buyers

The number of buyers available was also included in the model, as it is expected to have an effect on the level of transaction costs incurred. As the number of buyers for beef with a particular attribute decreases price uncertainty and the risk of opportunistic behaviour by buyers is expected to increase. Cow-calf operators will incur increased information and negotiation costs in determining a buyer's reputation to reduce the risk of opportunistic behaviour. Understanding the relative importance that different numbers of buyers will have on a cow-calf operator's transaction costs and willingness to participate in a program will be determined using three different levels where: (1) a single buyer is available, (2) a small number of buyers are available, and (3) a large number of buyers are available. A linear relationship is expected to emerge whereby as the number of buyers increases, cow-calf operator utility increases.

Premiums Received

The fourth characteristic included in the conjoint analysis was the premium paid to the cow-calf operator. This is not an actual transaction characteristic, but has been included in the analysis to determine the extent to which cow-calf operators will trade off between an increase in the transaction costs that they must incur to produce a particular beef product and the premium they receive upon the sale of their product. It is expected that if the benefits are greater than the increase in transaction costs, which arise due to different transaction characteristics, cow-calf operators will be more willing to participate in a particular program. Four different premium levels were defined, based on the amount current programs in the beef industry are paying to cow-calf operators. They include: (1) no premium, (2) 0-5% premium above current market price, (3) 5-10% premium above current market price, and (4) 10-15% premium above current market price. The relationship between different premium levels is expected to be linear, with cow-calf operator's utility increasing as the expected premium increases.

Additional Characteristics

Several other potential features of beef supply chain coordination programs could influence a cow-calf operator's participation decision. However, it was necessary to limit the analysis to four variables to avoid making the conjoint experiment too complicated. When the number of characteristics included in an experiment increases, the task of trading off between characteristics becomes difficult for respondents and can lead to inconsistent responses and a low response rate. For this reason, information asymmetry, incomplete information, and transaction frequency, while potential variables, were excluded from the conjoint experiment.

In the cattle production stages of beef supply chains the risk of information asymmetry is minimal, as compared to later industry stages where uncertainty arises over the production methods used in earlier stages of production. As a result, this characteristic was unlikely to be important to cow-calf operators. However, they may be required to implement a record/certification system by downstream industry segments that are looking to reduce information asymmetries. The costs and implications associated with this are captured within asset specific investments, where one of the options is the implementation of a record/certification system. The issues associated with incomplete information were captured under pricing method, as this characteristic ties directly in with price uncertainty arising as a result of quality variability.

Transaction frequency was also excluded from the conjoint experiment. While there is an increasing focus on getting cow-calf operators to provide cattle into programs on a more frequent basis, or to switch from spring to fall calving, this variable was felt to be relatively less important than the other four variables. Finally, other benefits received by coordination programs including carcass quality information and market access were not used in the conjoint experiment. Again, they were deemed relatively less important based on the analysis in Chapter 4 and were excluded to limit the overall complexity of the experiment. The combinations of the characteristics and characteristic levels included in the conjoint survey are presented in Table 5.1.

Table 5.1 - Characteristics and Characteristic Levels Used in the Survey

Characteristics	Characteristic Levels
Asset Specific Investments	No Additional Investment Feed & Health Protocol Record/Certification System Farm Improvement Expenditures
Pricing Method	Carcass Quality Live Weight Live Weight & Carcass Quality
Number of Buyers	Single Buyer Small Number of Buyers Large Number of Buyers
Expected Premium	No Premium 0-5% 5-10% 10-15%

While Hair et al. (1992) recommended that the number of levels of all characteristics be equal, for the purposes of this conjoint experiment levels for the characteristics varied, with each one having either three or four. Given the small variance between characteristic levels it was felt that varying levels would not have a significant influence on the relative importance of the different characteristics in the experiment. While this may not be ideal, it is not always feasible to obtain the same number of levels for each characteristic and there are several examples in the literature where different numbers of levels have been used. In a study done by Hobbs (1996c), the characteristics examined in the conjoint analysis had between two and three levels. Similarly, in a study done by Anderson and Bettencourt (1993) the number of levels for each characteristic examined ranged between 2 and 7.

SPECIFYING THE FORM OF THE BASIC MODEL

As Figure 5.1 indicates, the next step is to specify the basic form of the model. Both the composition rule and the part-worth relationship need to be specified. The composition rule specifies how characteristic levels are combined to obtain an overall preference rating for alternative programs. It may be additive or interactive (Ness and Gerhardy, 1994). In the additive model, respondents are assumed to obtain an overall preference or utility rating by implicitly adding the part-worth values for different characteristic levels in a scenario. Part-worth values are the utility scores for each characteristic level, which are calculated by conjoint analysis based on respondents' scores. They are analogous to regression coefficients, with the dependent variable in the conjoint model being total utility and the part-worth values for different characteristic levels being the independent variables. The interactive composition rule allows for the total value of certain combinations of characteristic levels to be more or less than the sum of their individual part-worths (Ness and Gerhardy, 1994).

The simplest and most commonly used composition rule, the additive model, is used in the conjoint experiment presented in this chapter. This model is the most appropriate given that no interactive relationship is expected between the different characteristics specified. It also requires fewer evaluations from the respondent, and it is easier to obtain estimates for the part-worth values (Ness and Gerhardy, 1994). The additive part-worth model assumes that the part-worth of each characteristic level is independent of other characteristic levels and as such a respondent's preference for a particular beef program can be defined as sum of the different levels of transaction characteristics (Ness and Gerhardy, 1994). The underlying model is therefore:

Preference of program =   part-worth of level i for transaction characteristic 1 +
                           part-worth of level j for transaction characteristic 2 +
                           part-worth of level k for transaction characteristic 3 +
                           part-worth of level l for transaction characteristic 4

The part-worth specifies the relationship between the levels of each characteristic. Three types of part-worth relationship exist, and include the linear or vector model, the quadratic or ideal model, and the part-worth model (Ness and Gerhardy, 1994). The linear model assumes that characteristic levels are linearly related and, as a result, overall preference changes proportionally as characteristics levels change (increase or decrease). This differs from the quadratic model, where the assumption of strict linearity is relaxed and preference is represented by a convex or concave curve. The part-worth model is the most general in that it assumes the relationship between overall preference and characteristic levels is entirely flexible and may not follow any set functional relationship (Ness and Gerhard, 1994). This type of model is used for the conjoint experiment presented in this chapter as the relationship between different asset specific investments and pricing methods is not expected to follow any specific functional form. While linear relationships are expected for different levels of buyers and premiums the part-worth model was chosen due to its ability to handle the expected relationship between the levels of the other two transaction characteristics.

CREATING STIMULI

Once the different characteristic and characteristic levels have been defined and a model form has been chosen, hypothetical beef program scenarios were created. The number of possible scenarios that can be created is dependent on the number of characteristics and the number of characteristic levels. The total number of scenarios in a full factorial design is equal to the product of the number of levels associated with each characteristic. In the experiment pertaining to cow-calf operators a full factorial design would give rise to one hundred and forty-four different scenarios depicting beef programs (4x3x3x4). Thus, even in a fairly small experiment the number of scenarios can become far too many for respondents to reasonably evaluate.

In order to avoid this problem, a fractional factorial design can be used. A fractional factorial design selects a sample of characteristic levels, while preserving the ability to evaluate the relative importance of all the different characteristics presented (Halbrendt et al.,

1992). Orthogonal arrays are the most commonly used method of constructing fractional factorial designs. This type of experimental design allows a researcher to capture the main effects that need to be estimated with fewer scenarios than the full factorial design requires. This reduces the evaluation task for respondents and reduces the risk of inconsistencies emerging due to the complexity of the task (Halbrendt et al., 1992). Using the fractional factorial design, sixteen hypothetical program scenarios were designed to capture the main effects of each transaction characteristic. The fractional factorial design was created using the SPSS Version 10.0 conjoint analysis program.

In addition, two holdout scenarios were generated in order to check the reproducibility of the model. Respondents' rate holdout scenarios, but the data obtained is not used in the computation of the part-worth values for the model. The holdout scenarios are instead used to test the validity of the conjoint model by comparing each individual's preference score for the holdout scenarios with the individual's actual preference scores (Hobbs, 1996c). The eighteen program scenarios designed are presented in the survey in Appendix A. An example of the scenarios presented in the survey is shown in Figure 5.2, which is the first scenario that was presented to respondents.

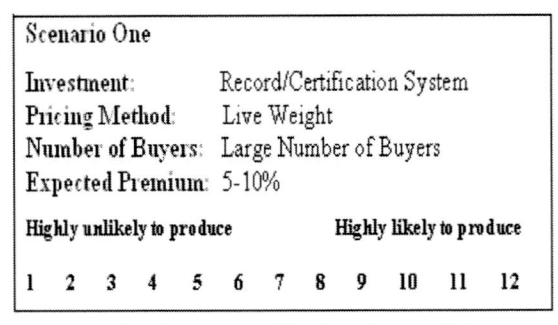

```
Scenario One

Investment:        Record/Certification System
Pricing Method:    Live Weight
Number of Buyers:  Large Number of Buyers
Expected Premium:  5-10%

Highly unlikely to produce        Highly likely to produce

1   2   3   4   5   6   7   8   9   10   11   12
```

Figure 5.2 - Example of Scenarios Used in Cow-calf Operator Survey

DATA COLLECTION

Presentation Method

When presenting the hypothetical program scenarios to respondents, two different methods of presentation are available. The first method is the trade-off method, which requires respondents to compare attributes two at a time, ranking all combinations of characteristic levels from least preferred to most preferred. This method of presentation is fairly simple to apply and reduces the information that must be taken in by a respondent. At the same time, however, it sacrifices realism, as in real situations respondents are confronted with products that are combinations of all characteristic levels and not in pairs (Ness and Gerhardy, 1994). The trade-off method cannot use fractional factorial design and, as a result, the total number of judgments a survey respondent must make can be quite large. Respondents can become confused in ranking a large number of paired characteristics or may adopt a pattern in ranking choices (Green and Srinivasan, 1978).

The alternative to the trade-off method is the full profile method, which is used in this conjoint experiment. The full profile method uses the complete set of characteristics to construct program profiles that are then presented to the respondent. This approach provides a more realistic description of scenarios and the decision process faced by respondents when they are making tradeoffs between different scenarios (Green and Srinivasan, 1978). This method also allows researchers to use a fractional factorial design to limit the number of profiles that respondents are required to evaluate. While this approach does elicit fewer judgments, each judgment is more complex and may result in respondents being overloaded with information. Respondents may be tempted to simplify the task and ignore variations in certain characteristics and focus on only a portion of the characteristics presented. As a result, the number of characteristics presented under the full profile procedure should be limited to, at most, five or six characteristics (Green and Srinivasan, 1978). Clearly in this experiment presented in this chapter, four characteristics and a fractional factorial design allow the use of the full profile method.

Preference Measure

Respondents can evaluate program scenarios under the full profile method through two different methods: non-metric (ranking) or metric (rating). With the ranking method, respondents are asked to rank different scenarios from least to most preferred. Alternatively, respondents can be asked to assign a score to each profile. This is known as the rating method, with a higher score indicating a greater preference for that particular profile (SPSS Inc., 1997).

Ranking profiles is sometimes thought to be the preferred method, as it may be easier for respondents to say which scenario they prefer more rather than expressing a magnitude for their preference. At the same time, as the number of profiles that respondents are required to rank increases it may become difficult for them to accurately rank them all. In this situation, individually rating each profile becomes the preferred method in determining respondents' preferences (Green and Srinivasan, 1979). For the purposes of the study presented in this chapter the metric rating method was used due to the large number of scenarios that respondents had to consider. Overall, the estimation methods do not seem to differ materially in their predictive powers.

The Survey

The conjoint experiment portion of the survey asked respondents to evaluate 18 different program profiles using a scale of 1 to 12 according to how likely they would be to produce under the particular program profile outlined. The profiles do not necessarily represent existing programs, but are combinations of the transaction characteristics that do typify existing beef coordination programs. This is a strength of conjoint analysis, as it allows an evaluation of program characteristics and potential programs.

In addition to the conjoint experiment, the survey contained two other sections. The first section asked questions regarding how important different beef marketing characteristics were to cow-calf operators. It also gauged cow-calf operator perceptions on the performance of existing alliances in the beef industry. Cow-calf operators were asked to explicitly rate the importance of different marketing characteristics and the performance of alliances on a scale of 1 to 5. The last section of the survey gathered socioeconomic data and information on the respondent's beef operation. This information was gathered to aid in identifying differences between cow-calf operators based on socio-economic characteristics.

The survey was conducted at the Western Stock Grower's Association Annual meetings held in Saskatoon, Saskatchewan in December 2003. The Western Stock Growers Association is a voluntary organization that works to support cow-calf operators and protect their interests. It lobbies the government and promotes education of both the general public and beef industry members. Cow-calf operators were approached during the conference and asked if they would be willing to complete the survey. Respondents were provided with a copy of the survey and a brief set of verbal instructions on how to complete the survey. Completion of the survey took an average of ten minutes and respondents were able to fill it out at any time during the conference period and then return it to a specified location.

The survey was limited to the cow-calf sector of the beef value chain for two key reasons. First, as discussed previously, closer coordination of cow-calf operators with the rest of the supply chain is not emerging to the same extent as closer coordination between other beef industry segments, limiting the ability of programs to ensure consistency and the production of branded attributes. Therefore it is important to understand what is limiting cow-calf operator involvement in emerging value chain alliances in order to work with this segment and improve supply chain coordination. Conjoint analysis allows one to gain a better understanding as to what limits their involvement in particular programs and what can be done to encourage increased involvement in new and developing beef programs.

Second, the application of conjoint analysis to other segments of the beef chain is likely less appropriate given the concentrated nature of the industry. This would make it difficult to obtain sufficient data for the analysis to be statistically significant. Detailed case studies are instead used to explore and analyze these segments of the supply chain in Chapter 6.

SURVEY RESULTS

The Respondents

The survey was administered to seventy-three respondents in December 2003 at the Western Stock Growers Association annual meeting. A comparison of the cow-calf operator survey population to the farm operator population represented in the 2001 Canadian Census of Agriculture is provided in Table 5.2. For some of the characteristics no comparable information was available through the Census of Agriculture data. The survey sample did not follow Statistics Canada's Census of Agriculture data closely. The gross revenues of survey respondents were higher than those for the general Canadian farm population. This is not surprising as typically these organizations are made up of full-time cow-calf operators. The sample also has a higher education attainment than the general population of farm operators in Canada. Younger farm operators are also over represented in the sample. Directly comparable data was not obtained for the distribution of farm operators by herd size, but the average herd size of the sample appeared to be larger than was reported in the Canadian Census of Agriculture.

Table 5.2 - Comparison of Sample and Canadian Census of Agriculture Data

	Percentage in Category	
	Census of Agriculture (2001)	Cow-calf operator Survey
Gross Revenues ('000's)		
0-10	21%	6%
10-49	29%	11%
50-99	14%	16%
100-249	20%	30%
250-499	10%	23%
500+	6%	14%
Farm Income Sources		
Other Farm Income		60%
Backgrounding Feedlot	No Comparable Data	48%
Finishing Feedlot	Available	15%
No Other Farm Income		19%
Alliance Participation		
Yes	No Comparable Data	15%
No	Available	85%
Herd Size		
0-50		20%
50-100	Avg. Canadian Herd Size: 53	18%
100-150	Head	20%
150-200	Avg. Western Canadian Herd	21%
200-300	Size: 67 head	10%
300+		11%
Education		
Less than Grade 9	14%	0%
Grade 9 – 12	48%	29%
Post Secondary (Non-University)	27%	51%
Post Secondary (University)	11%	20%
Farm Operator Age		
Less than 35	11.5%	35%
35-60	53.6%	62%
60+	34.9%	3%

Source: Adapted from Statistics Canada Internet Site (2003)

Figures 5.3, 5.4, 5.5, 5.6, 5.7 and 5.8 show the distribution of respondents by socioeconomic characteristics. Of the 73 respondents, 67% had gross farm incomes above $100,000, 23% had gross farm incomes above $250,000 and 13% had gross farm incomes above $500,000 (Figure 5.3). Approximately 60% of all respondents have other sources of farm income. Forty-eight percent of respondents' background calves and 15% have a finishing feedlot (Figure 5.4). Fifteen percent of respondents have participated in some method of further coordination. Participation ranges between the use of contracts and more formal alliances

(Figure 5.5). Herd size also varied, with 38% of respondents having cow herds of less than 100 head and 41% having herds of between 100 to 200 head (Figure 5.6). Of the individuals that completed the survey, 29% had a high school education, 51% had a college diploma or a certificate from a technical school, and 10.4% had either an undergraduate or graduate degree. Thirty-five percent of respondents were less than 35, while 62% were between 35 and 60 and 3% were older than 60 years of age.

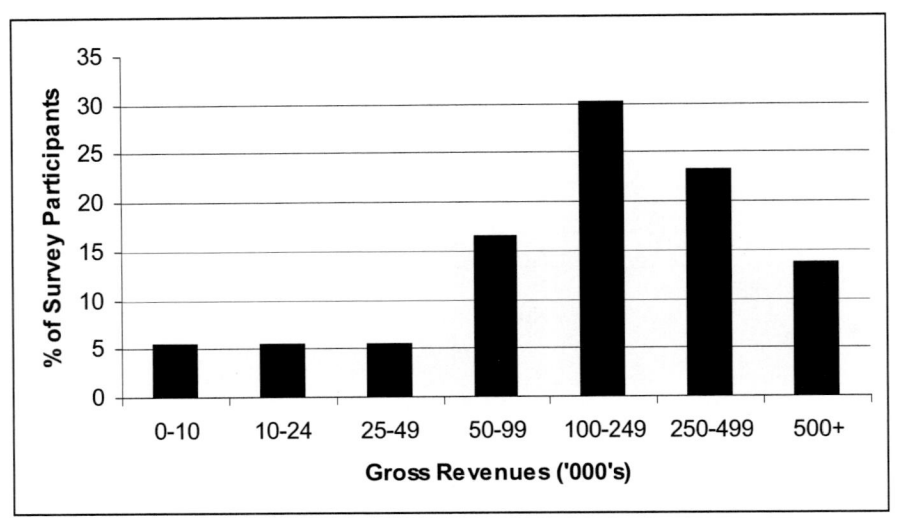

Figure 5.3 - Respondents by Gross Farm Income (n=73)

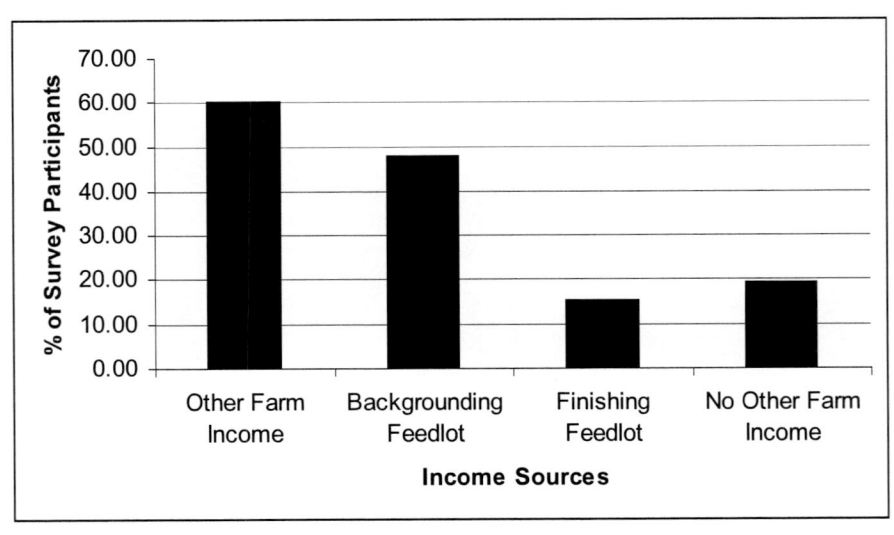

Figure 5.4 - Respondents by Farm Income Sources (n=73)

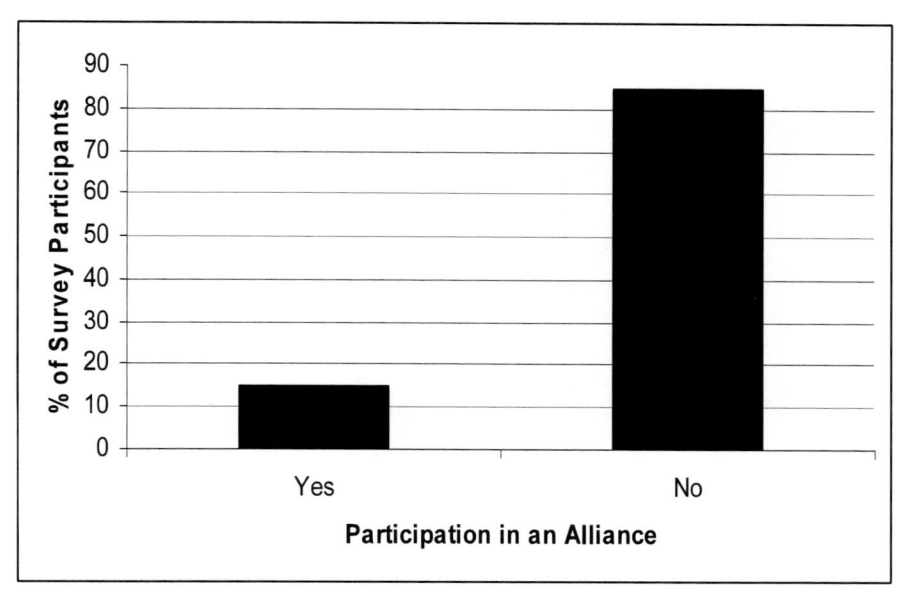

Figure 5.5 - Respondents by Participation in Alliances (n=73)

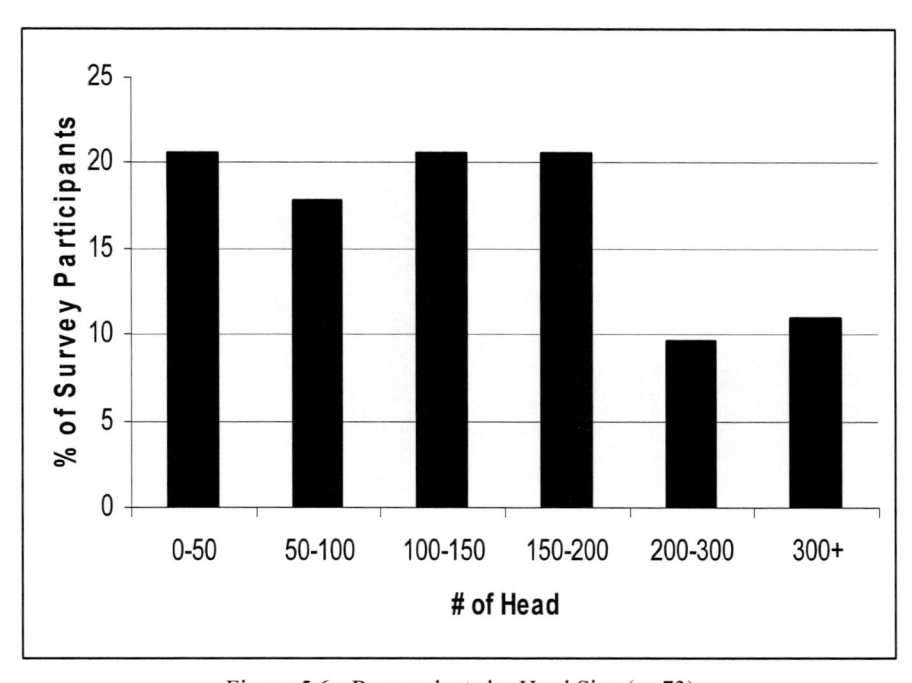

Figure 5.6 - Respondents by Herd Size (n=73)

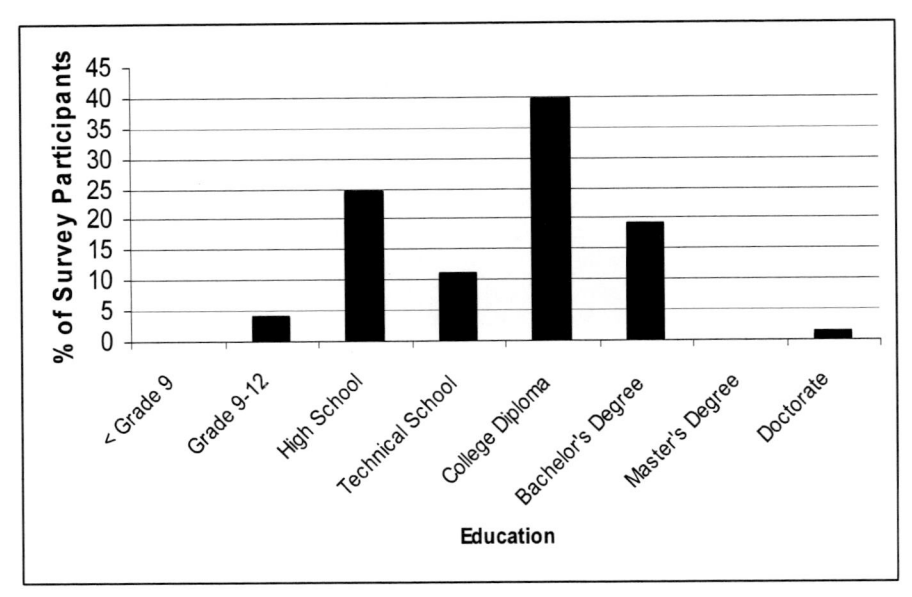

Figure 5.7 - Respondents by Level of Education (n=73)

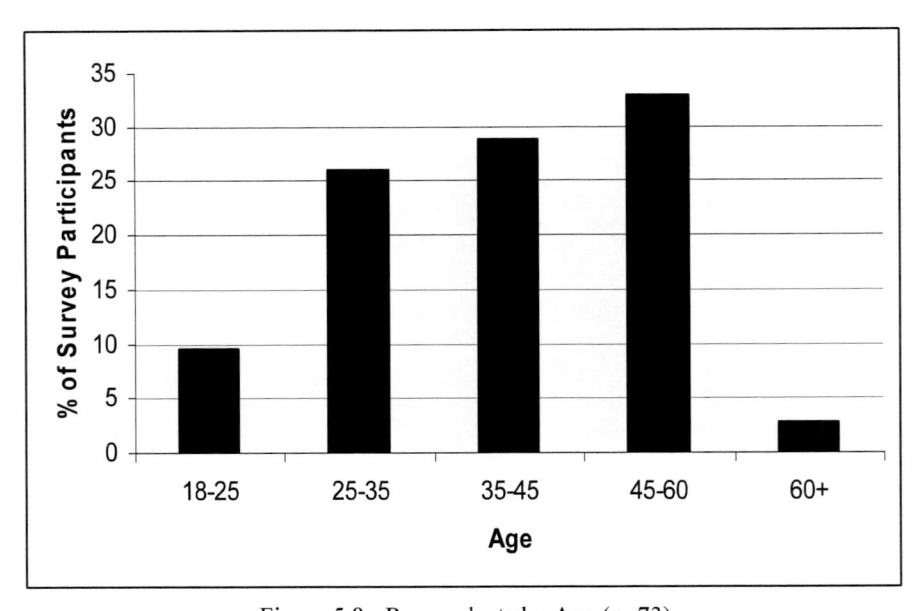

Figure 5.8 - Respondents by Age (n=73)

CONJOINT RESULTS – RELIABILITY AND VALIDITY

Having obtained the conjoint data, the objective was to estimate the different part-worth values for each different characteristic level included in the experiment. There are currently five commonly used estimation methods: Monanova, Linmap, Dummy Variable Regression, Logit analysis, and Probit analysis (Ness and Gerhardy, 1994). Given that a part-worth relationship is expected to exist between characteristic levels, a dummy variable regression model was selected. This model is used when a particular characteristic level is either present or not, and different part-worth values are expected for each level of each characteristic. The Ordinary Least Squares (OLS) procedure is the most commonly used procedure to estimate part-worth values. This method has been found to perform as well as others, and it has the advantage of being easier to use and interpret (SPSS Inc., 1997). For the purposes of the conjoint experiment presented in this chapter SPSS conjoint software using OLS was used to estimate the following model:

$$U = \beta_0 + \beta_1 I_1 + \beta_2 I_2 + \beta_3 I_3 + \beta_4 I_4 + \beta_5 P_1 + \beta_6 P_2 + \beta_7 P_3 + \beta_8 N_1 + \beta_9 N_2 + \beta_{10} N_3 \\ + \beta_{11} M_1 + \beta_{12} M_2 + \beta_{13} M_3 + \beta_{14} M_4 + \mu \quad (5.1)$$

Where:
- U = total utility
- β_0 = constant
- β_i = part-worth values. Where $i = 1....14$
- I_i = 1 if level i of Investment is present, 0 if not present. $i = 1...4$
- P_j = 1 if level j Pricing Method is present, 0 if not present. $j = 1...3$
- N_k = 1 if level k of Number of Buyers is present, 0 if not present. $k = 1...3$
- M_l = 1 if level l of Expected Premium is present, 0 if not present. $l = 1...4$
- μ = error term

It is possible that certain characteristic levels included in the study may be collinear, with an example being the number of buyers and investments required in a program. It could be argued that as the degree of investment changes, the preference for a certain number of buyers in the market will also change in order to reduce the risk of opportunistic behaviour. While recognizing that there is a possibility of correlation between these two characteristics, the additive model was nevertheless used to estimate the conjoint experiment. This is because the sample size was not felt to be sufficiently large to estimate the interactive effects along with the separate part-worth values. If there is a correlation between the two characteristics the part-worth values provided for these characteristics may be very sensitive to the addition or deletion of a few observations or the deletion of an apparently insignificant variable (Hill et al., 2001).

Using the SPSS procedure, a separate model was estimated for each respondent and these responses were averaged in order to give results for the entire sample. In addition to obtaining part-worth estimates showing the preferences for different characteristic levels, output from the conjoint analysis includes importance scores for the different characteristics. The importance scores are derived from the part-worth estimates. Output from the conjoint experiment also includes correlations relating predicted ratings from the conjoint model with observed ratings using the hold-out profiles. Two hold-out profiles were generated from a random plan. These were rated by respondents but were not included in calculating the part-worth values for different characteristic levels. Instead, they are used to determine the accuracy and validity of the calculations (SPSS Inc., 1997).

Pearson's R and Kendall's Tau statistics for each respondent were reported, based on the hold-out scenarios. The Kendall's Tau statistic represents the degree of correlation that exists between the observed and estimated preferences and confirms the validity of the model. The Pearson's R statistic measures how well the model was able to predict the respondent's preferences by comparing how the respondent rated the hold-out profiles with the ratings predicted by the model. For both statistical indicators a good model fit is signified by statistics that are close to 1.00 (Hobbs, 1996c). The Pearson's R statistic for the model was .994, indicating that the model is highly accurate in predicting respondents' preferences for the hold-out profiles. The Kendall's Tau coefficient was calculated both for the 16 program profiles and the 2 hold-out profiles and were .950 and 1.0 respectively, indicating a high degree of correlation between the observed and estimated preferences.

CONJOINT RESULTS – ESTIMATED MODEL

Using the SPSS conjoint software, part-worth values for each characteristic level were estimated (i.e. the β_i's in the estimated equation). These part-worth values are generated using a set of regressions on the ratings of the sixteen program profiles (SPSS Inc., 1997). The part-worth values calculated are expressed in a common unit and as such they can be added together to provide insights into the total utility of particular program scenarios. Importance scores are then derived by taking the utility range for a particular characteristic and dividing it by the sum of all the utility ranges (SPSS Inc., 1997). It is expected that the greater the range of utility between levels for a particular characteristic, the more important this characteristics is in the decision to join a program. The importance values for all characteristics sum to 100% for each individual respondent.

In order to better understand the importance measures, the part-worth values generated by SPSS conjoint software are used to determine the impact that each characteristic level has on a respondent's preferences. Part-worth estimates for respondents as a collective group are provided in Table 5.3. This table shows that as premium levels decrease the utility received at each premium level is reduced when compared to other premium levels. This is in line with the expectation that a linear relationship exists between premium levels where higher premiums result in higher relative levels of utility.

Similarly, when cow-calf operators are required to incur capital expenditures for farm improvement, utility is reduced relative to other levels of investments. When cow-calf operators are required to invest in a specific feed and health protocol, a record /certification system, or not required to make any investments relative utility improves. These results show that cow-calf operators are willing to make investments into specific assets in order to participate and that opportunistic behaviour is not always a concern, but as the degree of investments required increases, willingness of cow-calf operators to participate decreases as a result of an increasing risk of opportunistic behaviour. The relationship between different investments levels follows a priori expectations, with higher levels of investments resulting in lower levels of utility.

When the part-worth values for the number of buyers are examined, it is apparent that the cow-calf operators receive greater utility from having a large number of buyers available in the market, reducing the risk of opportunistic behaviour and the associated transaction costs. At the same time most supply chain coordination programs that produce differentiated beef products do sell into a market with fewer buyers, which will result in a reduction in overall utility. The importance of this attribute is smaller and the part-worth values are lower, thus it is likely that cow-calf operators will be more willing to accept a smaller number of buyers if other transaction characteristics exist in the program that increase overall utility. The relationship between the numbers of buyers is linear, as was initially expected, where relative utility decreases as the number of buyers decreases.

Table 5.3 - Aggregate Part-Worth Values for Each Characteristic Level

Characteristic Level	Relative Importance	Part-worth Value
Constant		5.9977
Expected Premium	41.99	
No Premium		-2.3887
0%-5%		-.8853
5%-10%		1.3031
10%-15%		1.9709
Asset Specific Investments	23.93	
Farm Improvements		-.7825
Record/Certification System		.1421
Feed & Health Protocol		.1798
No Asset Specific Investment		.4606
Number of Buyers	18.44	
Single Buyer		-.5936
Small Number of Buyers		-.1878
Large Number of Buyers		.7814
Pricing Method	15.64	
Carcass Quality		-.3630
Live Weight		.1678
Carcass Quality & Live Weight		.1952

Pricing method used is also of less relative importance to cow-calf operators indicating that there is relatively less concern over uncertainty associated with price. As a result, the transaction costs associated with this are likely to be lower than for other characteristics. Cow-calf operators prefer a combination live weight and carcass quality pricing. A pricing method based on carcass quality grades alone was less desirable than a live-weight pricing method. The preferences towards a quality based pricing method may provide some insights into transaction costs. The potential long term reduction in ongoing information costs may be greater than the short-term search costs that must be incurred. Similarly, the negotiation costs associated with a delay in payment may be less than the overall gain associated with reduced negotiations over the long term under such a system.

The aggregate importance measures for the survey are shown in Figure 5.9. On average the expected premium was the most important program characteristic (41.99%). Investments in specialized assets were the second most important program characteristic (23.93%). Number of buyers was third in relative importance at 18.44% and pricing method was fourth at 15.64%. These results help explain the value placed on different transaction characteristics by cow-calf operators. While pricing method was relatively less important, the premiums expected and investments required in specific assets both have an important impact on cow-calf operators' preferences for different supply chain coordination programs.

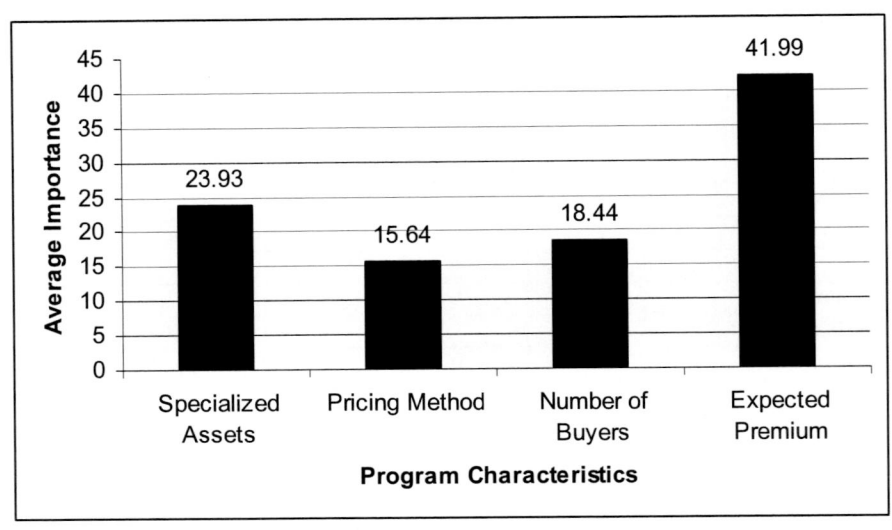

Figure 5.9 - Transaction Characteristic Importance Measures (n=73)

TRADE-OFFS BETWEEN TRANSACTION CHARACTERISTICS

In addition to the initial insights regarding each transaction characteristic and its levels, by examining the contribution of part-worth values for different characteristic levels it is possible to determine the type of program that would be most preferred and least preferred by respondents. These combinations were not evaluated by respondents but can be simulated by the part-worth values estimated by the model. The most preferred program structure, based on the results presented in Table 5.3, is a program that allows cow-calf operators to receive a 10-15% premium above current market price, while having to make no asset specific investments and being able to operate in a market with a large number of buyers using a pricing method that considers both carcass quality and live weight. The least preferred program structure would be one where no premium was expected, cow-calf operators had to make expenditures on farm improvements, a single buyer existed in the market, and pricing was based solely on carcass quality.

Using the part-worth estimates, the total utility for the most preferred and least preferred program structures can be calculated. Total utilities can also be calculated for the sixteen hypothetical program profiles provided to respondents in the survey by adding the aggregate part-worth values for each characteristic level along with the constant. Comparing the total utility values for the different program profiles provides a better understanding of how respondents implicitly trade-off between the different transaction characteristics and their associated levels. Table 5.4 presents the total utility calculations for the most preferred and least preferred program structures, along with the total utility values for the sixteen hypothetical scenarios in the survey. The two hold-out scenarios are omitted. For ease of reference, the scenarios in the table have been sorted based on their total estimated utility in a descending order.

Several conclusions can be drawn with respect to how cow-calf operators trade-off between different levels of the transaction characteristics when they make a decision to participate in a particular program. One example is with respect to the trade-offs between programs when different expected premiums exist. Expected premiums was the most important characteristic considered when cow-calf operators are choosing between different program types and yet Scenario 1, which has an expected premium of 5%-10%, is ranked higher than Scenario 4 which has an expected premium of 10%-15%. It is clear that premium alone does not determine a cow-calf operator's preference for a particular program. In fact, cow-calf operators' make trade-offs between different levels of all of the characteristics when they are determining which programs they would be willing to participate in.

Table 5.4 - Total Utility Calculations for Hypothetical Profiles

Transaction Characteristic	Characteristic Level	Utility
Most Preferred Program		
Expected Premium	10%-15% Premium	1.9709
Asset Specific Investments	No Specific Assets	0.4604
Number of Buyers	Large Number of Buyers	0.1952
Pricing Method	Carcass Quality & Live Weight	0.7814
	Constant	5.9977
	Total Utility	9.4056
Scenario 5		
Expected Premium	10%-15% Premium	1.9709
Asset Specific Investments	No Specific Assets	0.4604
Number of Buyers	Small Number of Buyers	-0.1878
Pricing Method	Live Weight	0.1678
	Constant	5.9977
	Total Utility	8.4090
Scenario 1		
Expected Premium	5% - 10% Premium	1.3031
Asset Specific Investments	Record/Certification System	0.1421
Number of Buyers	Large Number of Buyers	0.7814
Pricing Method	Live Weight	0.1678
	Constant	5.9977
	Total Utility	8.3921
Scenario 15		
Expected Premium	10%-15% Premium	1.9709
Asset Specific Investments	Feed & Health Protocol	0.1798
Number of Buyers	Single Buyer	-0.5936
Pricing Method	Carcass Quality & Live Weight	0.1952
	Constant	5.9977
	Total Utility	7.7500
Scenario 7		
Expected Premium	10%-15% Premium	1.9709
Asset Specific Investments	Farm Improvement Expenditures	-0.7825
Number of Buyers	Large Number of Buyers	0.7814
Pricing Method	Carcass Quality	-0.3630
	Constant	5.9977
	Total Utility	7.6045
Scenario 4		
Expected Premium	10%-15% Premium	1.9709
Asset Specific Investments	Record/Certification System	0.1421
Number of Buyers	Single Buyer	-0.5936
Pricing Method	Carcass Quality	-0.3630
	Constant	5.9977
	Total Utility	7.1541

Table 5.4. Continued

Transaction Characteristic	Characteristic Level	Utility
Scenario 2		
Expected Premium	5% - 10% Premium	1.3031
Asset Specific Investments	Feed & Health Protocol	0.1798
Number of Buyers	Small Number of Buyers	-0.1878
Pricing Method	Carcass Quality	-0.3630
	Constant	5.9977
	Total Utility	6.9298
Scenario 10		
Expected Premium	5%-10% Premium	1.3031
Asset Specific Investments	No Specific Assets	0.4604
Number of Buyers	Single Buyer	-0.5936
Pricing Method	Carcass Quality	-0.3630
	Constant	5.9977
	Total Utility	6.8046
Scenario 13		
Expected Premium	0%-5% Premium	-0.8853
Asset Specific Investments	No Specific Assets	0.4604
Number of Buyers	Large Number of Buyers	0.7814
Pricing Method	Carcass Quality & Live Weight	0.1952
	Constant	5.9977
	Total Utility	6.5494
Scenario 9		
Expected Premium	5%-10% Premium	1.3031
Asset Specific Investments	Farm Improvement Expenditures	-0.7825
Number of Buyers	Single Buyer	-0.5936
Pricing Method	Carcass Quality & Live Weight	0.1952
	Constant	5.9977
	Total Utility	6.1199
Scenario 16		
Expected Premium	0%-5% Premium	-0.8853
Asset Specific Investments	Feed & Health Protocol	0.1798
Number of Buyers	Single Buyer	-0.5936
Pricing Method	Live Weight	0.1678
	Constant	5.9977
	Total Utility	4.8664
Scenario 3		
Expected Premium	0%-5% Premium	-0.8853
Asset Specific Investments	Record/Certification System	0.1421
Number of Buyers	Single Buyer	-0.5936
Pricing Method	Carcass Quality	-0.3630
	Constant	5.9977
	Total Utility	4.2979
Scenario 11		
Expected Premium	No Premium	-2.3887
Asset Specific Investments	Feed & Health Protocol	0.1798
Number of Buyers	Large Number of Buyers	0.7814
Pricing Method	Carcass Quality	-0.3630
	Constant	5.9977
	Total Utility	4.2072

Transaction Characteristic	Characteristic Level	Utility
Scenario 12		
Expected Premium	0%-5% Premium	-0.8853
Asset Specific Investments	Farm Improvement Expenditures	-0.7825
Number of Buyers	Small Number of Buyers	-0.1878
Pricing Method	Carcass Quality	-0.3630
	Constant	5.9977
	Total Utility	3.7791
Scenario 8		
Expected Premium	No Premium	-2.3887
Asset Specific Investments	Record/Certification System	0.1421
Number of Buyers	Small Number of Buyers	-0.1878
Pricing Method	Carcass Quality & Live Weight	0.1952
	Constant	5.9977
	Total Utility	3.7585
Scenario 14		
Expected Premium	No Premium	-2.3887
Asset Specific Investments	No Specific Assets	0.4604
Number of Buyers	Single Buyer	-0.5936
Pricing Method	Carcass Quality	-0.3630
	Constant	5.9977
	Total Utility	3.1128
Scenario 6		
Expected Premium	No Premium	-2.3887
Asset Specific Investments	Farm Improvement Expenditures	-0.7825
Number of Buyers	Single Buyer	-0.5936
Pricing Method	Live Weight	0.1678
	Constant	5.9977
	Total Utility	2.4007
Least Preferred Program		
Expected Premium	No Premium	-2.3887
Asset Specific Investments	Farm Improvement Expenditures	-0.7825
Number of Buyers	Single Buyer	-0.5936
Pricing Method	Carcass Quality	-0.3630
	Constant	5.9977
	Total Utility	1.8699

The estimation of part-worth values using conjoint analysis also allows for the examination of hypothetical programs outside of the ones that were presented to respondents in the survey. This is done by using the part-worth values for each characteristic level to estimate a total expect 'utility' for a new program scenario. Creating alternate scenarios and using them as a comparison allows researchers to gain a further understanding of the trade-offs between certain characteristics, while other characteristics in the scenarios are held constant.

Table 5.5 presents an example of the trade-offs cow-calf operators make when they are determining which programs they are willing to participate in. Two hypothetical scenarios (A and B) were created. Both hypothetical programs presented have access to a single buyer and use a combined carcass quality and live weight pricing method. They are different in that the premiums expected in Scenario A are between 5 and 10 percent and no investment is required, while in Scenario B premiums range between 10 and 15 percent and cow-calf operators are required to make farm improvement expenditures. When utility is calculated for the two scenarios it is apparent that the preference for a lower level of investment is traded-off against the decrease in premiums. Cow-calf operators are willing to accept a lower of level of premiums in exchange for the lower level of investment provided in Scenario A.

Table 5.5 - Total Utility Calculations for Scenario A and B

	Scenario A	Scenario B
Expected Premium	1.3031 (5%-10%)	1.9709 (10-15%)
Investments	0.4604 (None)	-0.7825 (Farm Impr.)
Number of Buyers	-0.5936 (Single)	-0.5936 (Single)
Pricing Method	0.1952 (CQ & LW)	0.1952 (CQ & LW)
Constant	5.9977	5.9977
Total Utility	7.3628	6.7877

While recognizing that trade-offs are made between premiums and other characteristic levels, it is important to understand that there are limitations in the willingness of cow-calf operators to participate in programs when certain trade-offs are required. For example, Scenario B is compared with a new hypothetical scenario (Scenario C) that requires no investments and has an expected premium between 0 and 5 percent (see Table 5.6). When total utility is calculated for the two scenarios the utility in Scenario B is greater than that in C even though cow-calf operators are required to make farm improvement expenditures. In this situation for scenario C, the decrease in relative utility as a result of the reduction in expected premiums outweighed the increase in relative utility from the lower level of investments required. Cow-calf operators are unwilling to accept a decrease in premiums from 10%-15% to 0%-5% in exchange for the benefits of having to make no additional investments in their operation.

Table 5.6 - Total Utility Calculations for Scenario B and C

	Scenario B	Scenario C
Expected Premium	1.9709 (10%-15%)	-0.8853 (0%-5%)
Investments	-0.7825 (Farm Impr.)	0.4604 (None)
Number of Buyers	-0.5936 (Single)	-0.5936 (Single)
Pricing Method	0.1952 (CQ & LW)	0.1952 (CQ & LW)
Constant	5.9977	5.9977
Total Utility	6.7877	5.1744

As an additional example, a new hypothetical program scenario was created where cow-calf operators can expect a premium of 10%-15%, are required to implement a record/certification system, have access to a small number of buyers, and are paid using a grid-based carcass quality pricing system. This type of program would have a total utility value of 7.5599 (i.e. 1.9709 + 0.1421 + -0.1878 + -0.3630 + 5.9977), which is obtained by summing the constant and the part-worth values for each of the transaction characteristic levels. When the new profile is compared to Scenario 2 in Table 5.4, which has a total utility value of 6.9298, it is possible to understand the trade-off between different asset specific investments and premium levels. The number of buyers and pricing system are held constant in both scenarios. When the type of investment changes from the implementation of a feed and health protocol, as in Scenario 2, to the implementation of a record /certification system in the new scenario, and premium increases from 5%-10% to 10%-15% the total utility of the program increases. Cow-calf operators are making a trade-off between an increase in premiums and a change in investments. Based on the increase in utility it is apparent that cow-calf operators felt that the increased transaction costs incurred as a result of the change in required investments is less than the benefits received from an increase in the premiums paid.

Continuing this line of investigation, if another hypothetical program is considered where the expected premium is 10%-15%, cow-calf operators are required to incur capital expenditures for farm improvement, a small number of buyers is present, and they are paid using a grid-based carcass quality pricing system the total utility would be 6.6353 (i.e. 1.9709 + -0.7825 + -0.1878 + -0.3630 + 5.9977). When this program is compared with Scenario 2, which has a total utility value of 6.9298, it is apparent that the increase in utility, as a result of an increase in premiums, is offset by the change in required program investments. As the expected transaction costs associated with specific investments increase, cow-calf operators become more sensitive and are less willing to participate in a program even if they have access to higher premiums.

It is apparent that cow-calf operators make implicit trade-offs in their decisions to participate in different beef programs. Cow-calf operators are willing to incur increased costs (transaction and operating) for the transaction characteristics outlined in different programs. They are willing to accept higher investment requirements, smaller number of buyers, and a move towards a quality-based pricing system, but only within a limited premium range. At lower premium levels it is expected that cow-calf operators' elasticity of supply will be greater and their willingness to participate in programs will be lower than it would be with higher premium levels. This is because cow-calf operators become increasingly responsive to small changes in program requirements at lower premium levels and are less willing to participate in circumstances where their net benefit becomes quite low or even negative.

The responsiveness of cow-calf operators to changes in transaction characteristics will also vary based on the importance of the different characteristics. Survey respondents placed more importance on expected premiums and investments required, being more responsive to changes in these characteristics than to changes in the number of buyers and pricing method. This indicates that the transaction costs incurred as a result of asset specificity are larger than those incurred as a result of the other two transaction characteristics. Consequently, the investments required by a program will have a greater bearing on a cow-calf operator's decision to participate in a particular program.

Based on comparing the differences in part-worth values for certain characteristic levels, more specific conclusions can be made regarding a cow-calf operator's willingness to make trade-offs between different levels of the transaction characteristics included in the model. Most significant is the effect a change in premium has on a cow-calf operator's total utility. If the premium is reduced from 10%-15% to 5%-10% utility is reduced by .6678, but if the premium is reduced from 5%-10% to 0%-5% utility declines by 2.1884 showing that cow-calf operators become more responsive to a change in premium as it decreases.

Similarly, when cow-calf operators are required to implement a record/certification system or a feed and health protocol, their utility remains relatively constant and only declines a small amount from the scenario where no investment is required. If, on the other hand, cow-calf operators are required to make farm improvement expenditures, the decline in utility from the scenario where no investment is required is much larger, being 1.2431. This may be a result of cow-calf operators' perceptions regarding the amount of human and capital resources required for each of the levels of investments considered in the experiment. While the difference in the amount of human and capital resources required to implement either a record/certification system or a feed and health protocol was thought to be quite small, cow-calf operators perceived that a much greater amount of resources was necessary when programs required them to make farm improvements.

Cow-calf operators are also responsive to a decline in the number of buyers, with utility declining by .9692 when the number of buyers moves from large to small and less responsive as the number of buyers moves from being small to a single buyer. This again may be a result of cow-calf operators' perceptions. When cow-calf operators make the choice between a program with a small number of buyers and a program with a single buyer the difference in the number of buyers is not felt to impact their risk of opportunistic behaviour substantially. Whereas, it may be that cow-calf operators perceive that when the number of buyers increases from a small number to a larger number there is a much larger reduction in the risk of opportunistic behaviour and, as a result, a much greater change in utility.

The decrease in utility when the pricing system moves from a combined carcass and live weight pricing system to a strictly live weight pricing system is smaller than when cow-calf operators have to move from a live weight pricing system to a grid-based carcass quality system. This provides some insight into the willingness of cow-calf operators to accept the increased price uncertainty associated with variations in quality, which occurs with the use of grid-based pricing systems, in exchange for increased access to premiums and quality information. While they are willing to accept some risk that they will receive discounts due to variations in the quality of cattle they produce, they are not willing to accept a price that is completely dependent on carcass quality. Consequently, the decline in relative utility is larger when programs use a pricing system that relies strictly on carcass quality.

Understanding cow-calf operators' preferences for particular characteristic levels over others and the trade-offs that they are willing to make between different characteristics is essential when evaluating opportunities for the creation and expansion of coordinated programs to produce differentiated beef products. This research provides an initial insight into the degree to which different transaction characteristics affect cow-calf operators' willingness to participate in various types of coordination programs. Conjoint analysis makes it possible to evaluate cow-calf operator preferences and the trade-offs they make between programs based on the different transaction characteristics they contain. To ask cow-calf operators directly what their preferences are and how they would trade-off between different characteristic levels would be difficult. Cow-calf operators may not be conscious of their preferences or how they would trade-off between different characteristics and characteristic levels, but allowing them to respond to realistic program descriptions reveals this to a researcher based on preferences for comprehensive program scenarios.

SOCIO-ECONOMIC GROUPINGS

In addition to examining the conjoint results for the respondents as a group, they were also analyzed based on sub-groups using the socio-economic information gathered in the survey. This reveals whether preferences for different transaction characteristics varied based on characteristics such as operation size (number of head of cattle), current participation in a beef program, sources of farm income, and age. Results were also broken down by level of education, but no significant differences were found among education levels.

Cow-calf Operation Size (Number of cows)

It is expected that cow-calf operator preferences will vary depending on the size of their cow-calf operation, with the size of an operation affecting the importance of different characteristics as well as their ability to comply with different program requirements. When required investments are considered, the relative importance of specific investments is expected to be lower for larger operations that may have greater access to additional human and capital resources. Figure 5.10 shows that while relative importance of investments remains the second most important characteristic for all herd sizes, its relative importance was greater for smaller herd sizes (0-150 head) than for larger herd sizes (150-300+ head). The relative importance of investments in specific assets for cow-calf operators that had 0 to 150 head was approximately 26 percent, while the relative importance for larger cow-calf operators was 22 percent.

Overall, the order of importance for different characteristics did not change from the order that appeared in the aggregate data, with the exception of cow-calf operators that had a herd size of 200-300 head, for whom pricing method was more important than the number of buyers. It is not clear why the relative importance of pricing method was higher than the number of buyers for this group. It could be because when herd sizes are larger, cow-calf production is more likely to be the primary source of income for these operations and, thus, the method of determining returns becomes more important due to the effect pricing method can have on an operation's net returns.

The importance scores associated with the number of buyers did not appear to vary across different herd sizes. While the number of buyers available is relatively important to all cow-calf operators, the size of the operation does not seem to affect the relative importance. The largest difference in importance scores occurred for expected premiums. Premiums remained important throughout, but their relative importance ranged from 35.45% to 48.50%, with the most emphasis being placed on premium by those cow-calf operators with 150-200 head. The relative importance of premiums for cow-calf operators with larger herd sizes (150-300+ head) was 43%, while for smaller herds (0-150 head) it was around 40%. The difference in relative importance may be attributed to the fact that farms with larger herd sizes may derive a greater portion of their income from cow-calf production. Consequently, the level of premiums they receive has a greater effect on farm returns and, as a result is of greater importance.

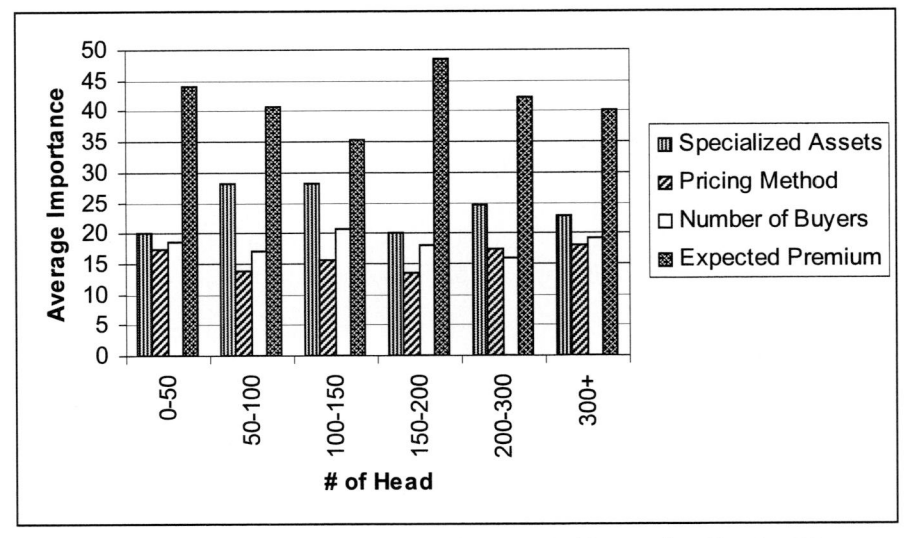

Figure 5.10 - Importance Measures by Cow-Calf Operation Size (n=73)

Alliance Participation

Figure 5.11 summarizes the results of the conjoint analysis grouped by participation in an alliance. Respondents were asked if they had ever participated in some sort of an alliance and were able to choose whether it was a marketing contract, production contract, brand licensing program, marketing alliance, new-generation cooperative, or some other structure. Of the total 73 respondents, 11 answered yes to having participated in some sort of alliance. These eleven respondents were compared to all of the other respondents to see if the relative importance of program characteristics varied according to experience with alliances. Given the low number of respondents that had participated in programs, the analysis was not further divided to evaluate the variance in importance scores for different program structures.

Figure 5.11 shows that respondents who have previously participated in an alliance place less importance on premiums (36.27%) than those who have not previously participated in an alliance (43%). Alliance participants may place less value on premiums given their improved understanding of the other benefits that can be derived from participation. These benefits include improved market access and detailed production and quality information. The additional benefits aid in offsetting any increase in production and transaction costs and, as a result, less importance is placed on the level of premiums received to offset these costs.

Other variations across the two groups are minimal, with very little difference emerging in the relative importance of other characteristics. The low level of variation for other characteristics may imply that cow-calf operator knowledge of these program characteristics is similar whether or not they have previously participated. Consequently, being involved in an alliance has not brought any additional insights to these cow-calf operators that have led them to change their preferences, with the exception of expected premiums.

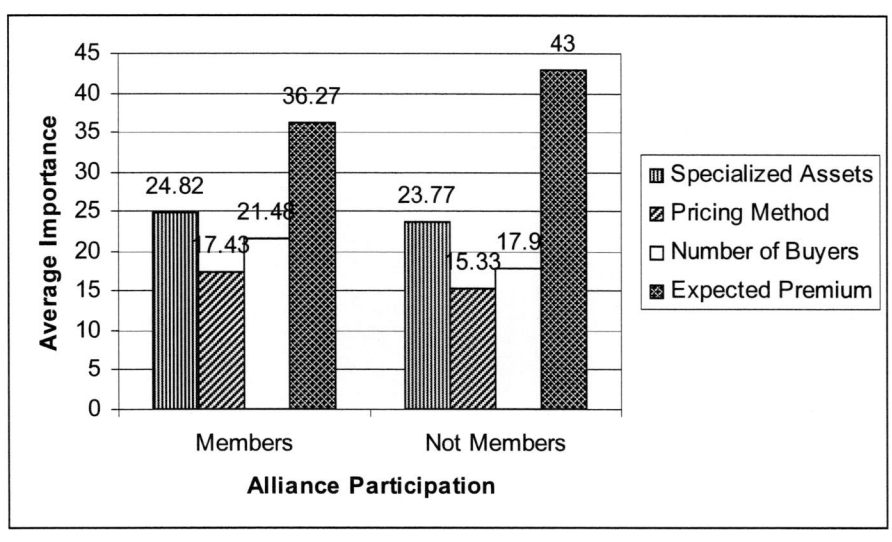

Figure 5.11 - Importance Measures by Alliance Participation

Farm Income Sources

The results from the conjoint analysis were also evaluated based on the other sources of income a cow-calf operator derives from his farming operation. The structure of producer operations varies considerably and may affect their willingness to participate in beef programs and their preferences for particular characteristics. Four major farm income categories were used to group data, which include income from background feeding, finishing feeding, other farm ventures, and no other farm income. It is expected that those cow-calf operators that are also involved in further segments of the beef industry will place greater emphasis on the relative importance of premiums. This is because their involvement in more than one segment of the beef industry results in their overall farm returns being highly dependent on their ability to capture premiums. Figure 5.12 presents the relative importance of different characteristics for these sub-groupings.

Respondents that indicated they also ran a finishing operation placed less importance (16.70%) on the investment in specific assets than all other categories, with the relative importance being significantly lower than the aggregate importance for investment in specific assets, which was 23.93%. In fact, the relative importance for the number of buyers (16.55%) for this group of respondents was almost equivalent to that for investment in specific assets. The relative importance of pricing method and number of buyers did not, however, vary significantly from the aggregate average. The lower importance of investments in specific assets for cow-calf operators with finishing operations may arise because these operations already have greater access to existing human and physical capital. This may result in their costs being lower when programs require investment into assets that they already have or can more easily implement due to their existing degree of vertical coordination.

Cow-calf operators that operated either backgrounding or finishing feedlots placed a higher relative importance on premium levels with importance scores being 44.76% and 47.47% respectively, whereas the other two segments importance scores were both around 41%. The emphasis on premiums for those cow-calf operators that run feedlots may be a result of their ability to have greater control over the quality of production, as they manage more than one production segment. As a result of the increased control over quality, cow-calf operators may be more focused on capturing a premium for their cattle.

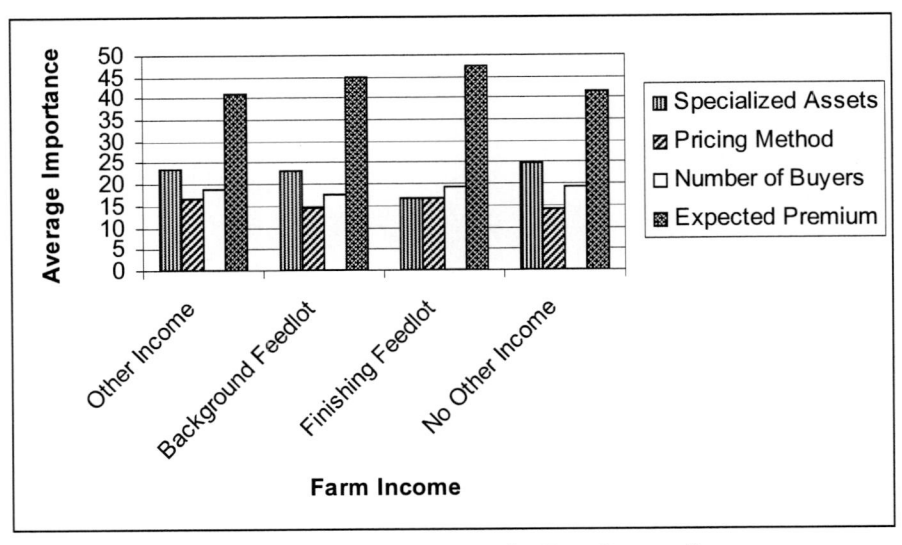

Figure 5.12 - Importance Measures by Farm Income Sources

Age

The results of the conjoint analysis broken down by age are provided in Figure 5.13. The importance of both pricing method and number of buyers remains relatively constant across all of the different age categories. Expected premium becomes increasingly important as age increases, rising from an importance level of 36.63 percent to 44.72 percent when age increases from 18-25 to 45-60. At the same time, the relative importance for investments in specialized assets decreases as age increases (from 18-25 to 35-45) falling from 29.87 percent to 21.75 percent. Between the ages 45 and 60 the importance of investments in specialized assets rises again to 24.06 percent, which could be a result of a shorter expected time horizon in which individuals in this age group have to recover the investments they incur prior to retirement.

While none of the differences in relative importance values show a distinct trend when examined based on different socio-economic groupings, the range in values does show that cow-calf operators' preferences vary considerably. When developing new programs in the industry, it is important to understand the differences among cow-calf operations. In order to encourage the participation of cow-calf operators in a program, their preferences and limitations need to be taken into account and managed for within a program's structure.

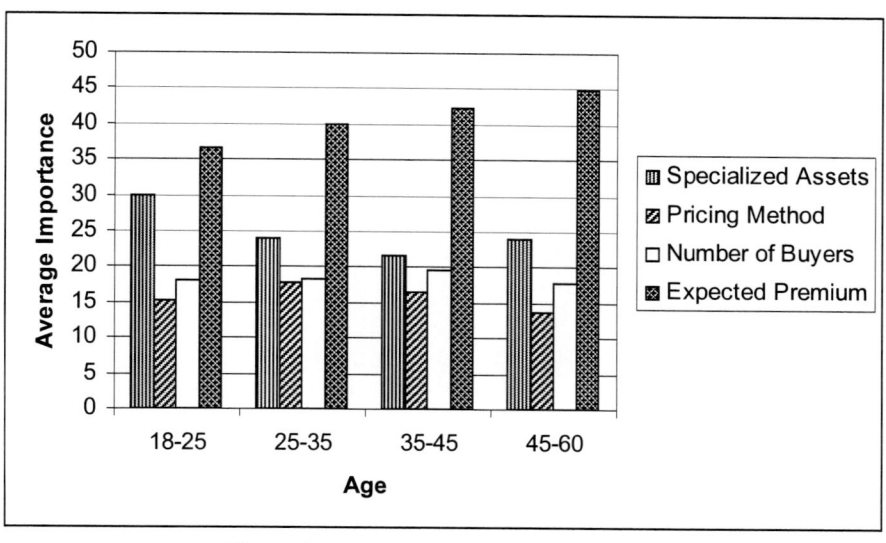

Figure 5.13 - Importance Measures by Age

ADDITIONAL DATA ANALYSIS

Importance of Different Marketing Characteristics

Additional transaction characteristics could have been included in the conjoint analysis, but were excluded in order to reduce the number of profiles respondents were required to rate and to limit the overall complexity of the task. In order to gather further information on the importance of different transaction characteristics, cow-calf operators were asked to explicitly rate the importance of four marketing characteristics on a 5-point scale where 1 was "not very important" and 5 was "very important". Respondents were also asked to explicitly rate how well they think alliances manage different marketing characteristics on a 5-point scale where 1 was "not very good" and 5 was "very good". The mean of respondents' explicit ratings is presented in Figure 5.14, where perceived importance of the marketing characteristics is on the horizontal axis and the perceived ability of alliances to provide these features is on the vertical axis.

Respondents felt that it was important to be able to receive a premium price for their animals and detailed data about the quality of animals they sold. Relatively less importance was placed on having a secure buyer and locking in a price for animals a considerable time before they are sold. At the same time, alliances are perceived by respondents to be a good method for securing a buyer for cattle, obtaining a premium price, locking in a certain price, and obtaining carcass quality information on the cattle sold.

Besides analyzing the relative importance respondents place on different characteristics as an aggregate group, they were also analyzed based on the socio-economic information gathered in the survey. This was done in order to determine if perceived importance ratings were different based on farm income sources, herd size, education, or age. Variances found when data was analyzed using farm income sources, herd size, education, and age categories were small and as a result are not included in the discussion. Participation in alliances did not seem to result in a significant difference in the importance ratings respondents assigned to the different marketing characteristics, with the exception of securing a premium price. Securing a premium price was more important to non-alliance participants than alliance participants. This is consistent with the results of the conjoint analysis.

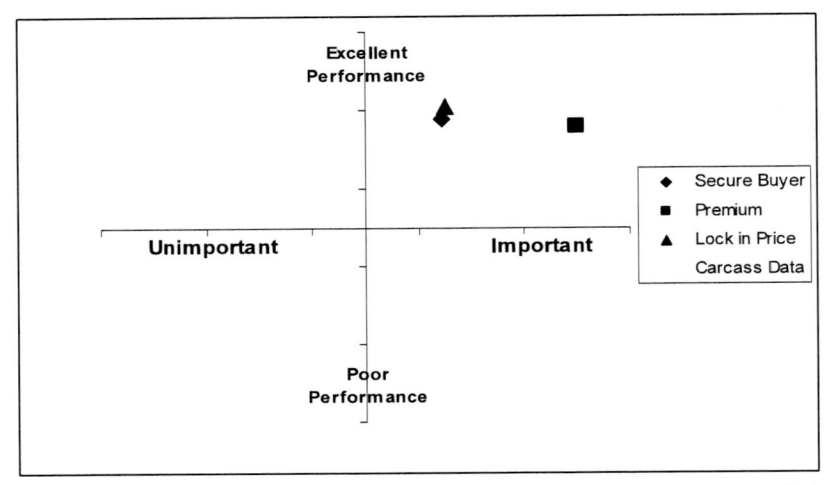

Figure 5.14 - Importance and Performance for Different Marketing Characteristics

The perceived performance of alliances did, however, vary. Most obvious was the difference in the perceived ability of alliances to provide carcass quality information, with respondents that have been involved in an alliance rating the ability of alliances to provide this information lower than those not currently involved in some sort of alliance. This is surprising, as alliances are typically thought to aid in providing cow-calf operators with data on carcass quality and may indicate the failure of previous alliances to provide this benefit. The small number of respondents who had participated in an alliance could have an effect on perceived importance. If any of the alliance participants have been dissatisfied with an alliance's ability to provide them with carcass information, the average could be lower than expected due to the small sample.

The perceived ability of alliances to secure a buyer also varies, with alliance participants rating their performance higher than non-alliance participants. This could be attributed to the greater knowledge that alliance participants have regarding the benefits of an alliance. Again, however, these results are based on a small number of producers having participated in alliances.

PERCEIVED MARKET SIZE

Participating cow-calf operators were also asked their perceptions regarding the attributes demanded by consumers. This is of interest to discern whether the predictions cow-calf operators made corresponded with the market sizes that were estimated in chapter four for different attributes. Cow-calf operators were asked to rate several different attributes that are currently being branded in terms of whether they thought consumer demand for each attribute was large, medium, or small. The results from the survey were then compared to the market sizes estimated in chapter four where the number of buyers and sellers was examined. It was assumed that the number of buyers and sellers is directly correlated with level of consumer demand. In examining the results of this analysis, it is important to understand that the type of measurement used can be ambiguous in the sense that cow-calf operators may vary in their evaluation of what constitutes a small, medium, or large market. At the same time, this analysis does provide general insights into cow-calf operators' perceptions of demand and new market opportunities.

Figure 5.15 illustrates the difference between the market sizes estimated in the previous chapter and consumer demand as perceived by respondents. Respondents recognize the large demand for tender products. They also are aware of the emerging market for natural and breed-oriented products. With the exception of grass-fed products, respondents appear to overestimate the market size for other attributes such as leanness, product origin, and organic.

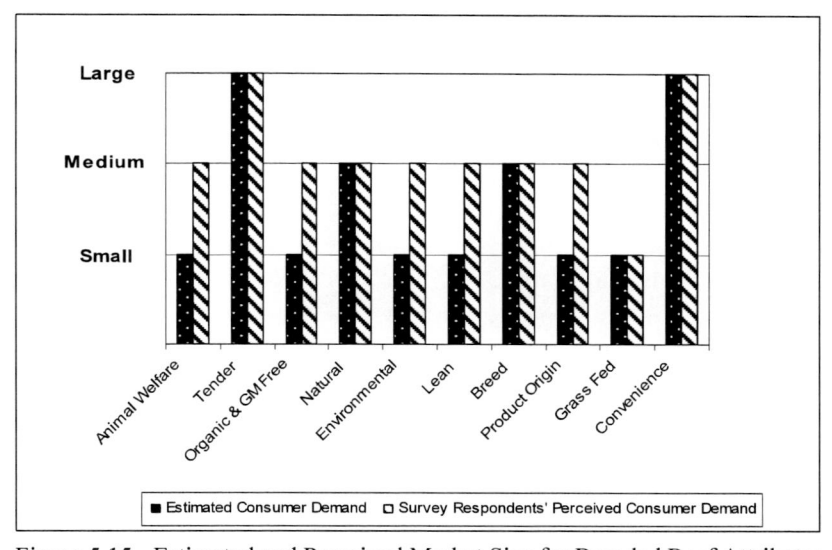

Figure 5.15 - Estimated and Perceived Market Size for Branded Beef Attributes

MEMBERSHIP FEES

Many of the different supply chain structures require that members pay fees in order to participate. Programs vary in terms of what types of fees they require participants to pay and the actual amount of fees. Two main fee structures occur within programs. Programs may require a one-time entrance fee and a yearly fee per animal marketed through the program or they may just require a yearly fee per animal. Typically, one-time entrance fees are required to ensure a participant's commitment to the program, while yearly per animal fees are paid in order to cover program administration and management costs. Different membership fee scenarios and values could have been analyzed through the conjoint experiment, but were not included due to the limited number of variables that can be considered using conjoint.

In order to gain insight into the effect different fee structures and fees have on a respondent's willingness to participate in a program, the survey included three different program scenarios that varied in terms of the fees participants were required to pay (Appendix

A). Respondents were asked to select the minimum premium that they would be willing to accept in order to enter into a program with a particular fee structure from a range of premiums provided. In Scenario A, participants were required to pay a one-time fee of $15,000 and then a yearly per head fee of $5. In Scenario B, participants were required to pay a one-time fee of $2,500 to enter into the program and then a yearly per head fee of $5. Participants in Scenario C did not have to pay a one-time entrance fee, but were still required to pay a yearly per head fee of $5. The values of fees were chosen based on examining the fees required within existing programs. The range of premiums that respondents selected from was also representative of the premiums available in existing alliances.

Figure 5.16 illustrates the premiums that respondents expect for them to be willing to participate in each of the program scenarios. When one-time fees are quite high, as in Scenario A, 83% of respondents required a premium of at least 10% above current market price and 49% required premiums to be 15% to 20% above current market price in order to participate. In Scenario B, where there was a lower one-time fee, 80% of respondents required a premium in the range of 5% to 15% in order to participate and 44% expected a premium between 5% and 10% in order to participate. In Scenario C, where no one-time fee is charged, 82% of respondents were willing to accept a premium of less than 10% in order to participate and 48% of respondents were willing to accept a premium that ranged between 5% and 10% in order to participate.

Understanding the effect different fees have on the willingness of cow-calf operators to participate in a program is tied in directly with cow-calf operators' willingness to invest in specific assets, as when cow-calf operators pay fees they are committing capital to a program. From the perspective of the program, higher fees ensure a cow-calf operator's commitment to the program as they have a vested interest in its success. At the same time, the willingness of cow-calf operators to make these investments decreases and the capital required increases due to the increased risk of opportunistic behaviour. Cow-calf operators required to commit to a program become locked into a specific supply relationship, with fewer buyers and increased costs associated with transferring out of the program. Therefore, in order to pay the fees required, the benefits associated with entering into program must offset the transaction costs arising from the increased commitment required.

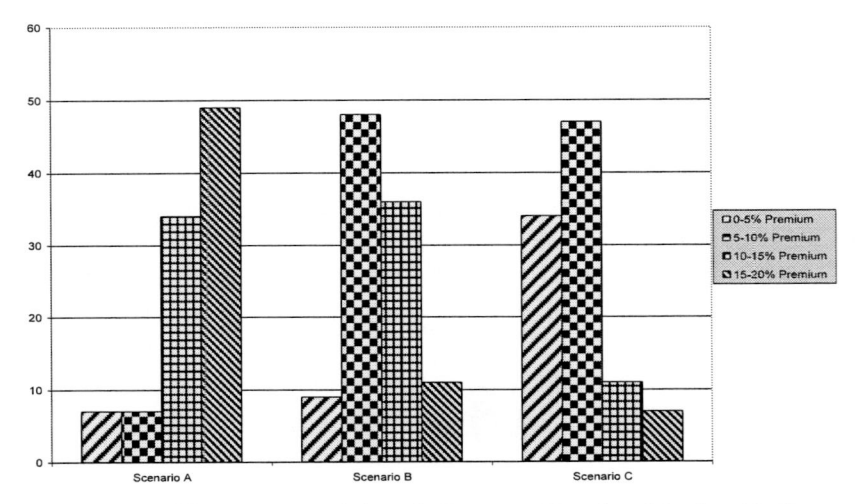

Figure 5.16 - Willingness to Participate in Programs Based on Membership Fees

CONCLUSIONS

When beef industry participants are developing programs to improve coordination and produce different beef attributes, cow-calf producer attitudes need to be kept in mind. Cow-calf operators can have a significant impact on the production of different attributes, whether it is through the genetics they use, their production protocols, or the management systems they have in place. Currently, coordination between this sector and other segments of the supply chain is not occurring to any significant scale. As a result, information and incentives are not being transferred to cow-calf operators to improve coordination and provide consumers with the products they demand on a consistent basis.

To improve coordination between cow-calf operators and other supply chain participants, those developing branding programs need to work with cow-calf producers and consider the trade-offs producers make between different program characteristics and requirements. The values cow-calf operators place on reduced transaction costs and the premiums they can receive has to be greater than the increase in transaction costs incurred as a result of the production of different beef attributes. This chapter has provided some insights into the trade-offs cow-calf operators are willing or are not willing to make. At the same time, the analysis is limited in its approach as several program characteristics could not be included in the conjoint experiment in order to manage the overall task complexity for survey respondents. Additional conjoint analysis would be beneficial in order to consider the trade-offs made when other benefits, membership fees, and program characteristics are included.

It is also important to consider other variables. Operation and management characteristics at the cow-calf operator level may also limit or encourage participation in different programs and need to be considered in order to create suitable and successful programs that are able to work effectively in the cow-calf operator environment, as well as within the rest of the industry. This segment of the beef supply chain faces significant challenges associated with individual cow-calf operator size and industry concentration that are not present and do not limit coordination between other segments of the beef industry. Further discussion regarding these characteristics is provided in the next chapter.

This chapter discussed the importance and degree to which certain transaction characteristics affect a cow-calf operator's willingness to produce different beef attributes. It did not discuss to any great extent the actual method of coordination chosen by beef industry segments to coordinate production, as was outlined in the predictive model presented in Chapter 4. The choice of whether to use contracts, informal alliances, or more formal alliances is discussed further in the next chapter. The types of supply chain coordination programs emerging within the beef industry and the challenges, limitations, and opportunities associated with these different programs are the subject of Chapter 6. Key to the discussion will be an examination of the opportunities and constraints associated with different characteristics of the beef industry and alliances within the industry.

Chapter 6

SUPPLY CHAIN ALLIANCES

AN IN DEPTH LOOK AT BEEF INDUSTRY ALLIANCES

In the previous chapter, cow-calf operators' preferences for different transaction characteristics were examined through the use of survey questions and conjoint analysis. This chapter provides an in-depth look at the structure of alliances within the North American beef industry using case studies. Information was gathered from interviews with key managers and directors of different beef value chain alliances in both the US and Canada. The information obtained from these interviews is used to identify the critical success factors and challenges to improving coordination in the North American beef industry.

Seventeen interviews were conducted with individuals who were either managers or directors of an existing alliance or involved in developing and managing information technology for the beef industry. The alliances and companies interviewed are located in Kansas, Nebraska, Missouri, Saskatchewan, and Alberta. The three US states were selected because they have some of the largest breeding herds and feeding operations in the US. Similarly, Alberta and Saskatchewan are Canada's largest beef producing provinces. Ten interviews were completed in the US and seven were completed in Canada during February and March 2004.

Individuals were first contacted by phone and/or email and their willingness to participate in a personal interview was established. The interviews took approximately one hour and an outline of interview questions was developed in order to guide the discussion. The interview guide is presented in Appendix B. After the completion of the interviews, an interview transcript and a transcript release form were sent to each participant so that they could review the contents and release the transcript for use in the study.

The interview focused on the organizational characteristics of the alliance and structure of the program and/or company. Questions were also asked about the pricing method used, average premiums, additional benefits received, and other issues surrounding pricing structure and market access. In the last part of the interview, interviewees were queried regarding the current limitations and barriers their alliances had faced, expected growth, and the value of standardized traceability systems. Table 6.1 provides a list of the organizations interviewed, their location, and approximate size of alliances in terms of the number of animals marketed through each program per year.

Table 6.1 - Organizations Interviewed Regarding Supply Chain Alliances

Organizations	Location	Size (# animals/year)
PM Beef Group	United States	65,000*
Heartland Premium Beef Alliance	United States	35,000
Cow Camp Beef Alliance	United States	1,500
GeneNet	United States	100,000
Nebraska Corn Fed Beef	United States	40,000
Laura's Lean Beef	United States	85,000
Ward Feed Yard/ILS	United States	90,000
Beef Marketing Group	United States	450,000
Decatur Beef Alliance	United States	50,000
U.S. Premium Beef	United States	692,000
Highland Premium Alberta Beef Alliance	Canada	2,000
Tee Creek Premium Meats	Canada	300
Ranchers Renaissance	Canada/United States	260,000
Excel Meats/Cargill	Canada/United States	Not specified
Sunterra Farms	Canada	Not specified
Ranchers' Beef	Canada	Not specified
XL Foods Inc.	Canada	Not specified
ComputerAid Professional Services Ltd.	Canada	N/A
Viewtrak Technologies Inc.	Canada	N/A

* Process approximately 200,000 head annually, with 65,000 being processed through their Ranch to Retail process/source verified system

OVERVIEW OF THE ALLIANCES

The Structure Of Alliances In The Beef Supply Chain

Tables 6.2 and 6.3 provide a synopsis of the different program structures, requirements, and benefits. The programs listed in the tables are limited to those that can be classified as being either an informal or formal alliance. Excel Meats, XL Foods Inc., and Ranchers' Beef were excluded from Tables 6.2 and 6.3. Ranchers' Beef was an industry initiative to develop a mid-size producer owned processing plant in Alberta, however it ceased trading and filed for bankruptcy in 2007. Individuals at both XL Foods Inc. and Excel Meats were interviewed, but did not provide sufficiently detailed information that could be used to derive a meaningful comparison between the alliances they are involved in and the other alliances for which interviews were conducted.

The alliances varied significantly, ranging from very informal and loosely coordinated alliances to very formal and highly integrated arrangements. The volume of cattle marketed annually through each alliance is included in Table 6.1 and ranges from 300 head to over 650,000 head. Alliances also varied in terms of who was driving the alliance and its ownership structure. The sector of the industry that drives an alliance seems to be important in determining the organizational and ownership structure of an alliance.

Table 6.2 – Key Features of Alliances in the Beef Supply Chain

Alliance	Initiating Party/ Ownership	Packer/End User Involvement	Attributes	Branded Program	Commitmnt	Fees	Pricing Method
PM Beef Group (U.S)	Packer Private Company	- PM Beef - 2 mid-size retailers	High Quality Process-verified	Retail Brand Labels	Annual Contract Per Head Fee	$3/head	Quality Grid (Futures) + $3/cwt (live)
Heartland Premium Beef (U.S)	External (Service) Private Company	- IBP - Smithfield Foods - No retailer	Holstein High Quality	No	Verbal		Base Price + % of Profits
Cow Camp Beef Alliance (U.S)	Feedlot Private Company	- US Premium Beef - IBP - No retailer	High Quality	No	Verbal	↑ Custom Charges & Lease USPB Shares	IBP Grid or USPB Grid
GeneNet (U.S)	External (Service) Private Company	- Swift & Co. - No retailer	Different Breeds High Quality	No	Per Head Fee Verbal	$3 to $7 per head based on data type	Quality Grid
Nebraska Corn Fed Beef (NCFB) (U.S)	External (Markets EndProduct) Non-profit Licensing Org	- Swift & Co. - 1 mid-size retailer & other end-users	High Quality Nebraska Corn Fed	Nebraska Corn Fed Beef	Per Head Fee Verbal	$3 to $4 per head & $1 tag fee	Swift & Co. Quality Grid Or Cash Market
Laura's Lean Beef (LLB) (U.S)	External (Markets EndProduct) Private Company	- Multiple packers - Multiple large & mid-size retailers	High Quality Lean Natural	Laura's Lean Beef	Annual Contract		Lean/Quality Focused Grid
Ward Feed Yard/ ILS (U.S)	Feedlot Private Company	- IBP - Other packers - No retailer	High Quality	No	Annual Feeding Agreement	Fees to use different services	Packer Grids Or Cash Market
Beef Marketing Group (U.S)	Group of Feedlots (Closed)	- IBP (excl. agrmt.) - No specific retailer	High Quality Volume	No	No Producers Feedlots own shares	None	Exclusive Deal: IBP Grid or Bid
Decatur Beef Alliance (U.S)	Feedlot Private Company	- Excel - No specific retailer	High Quality	No	Annual Contract Per Head Fee	$5/head + $0.02/head/ day on feed	Quality Grid
U.S. Premium Beef (U.S)	Producer Cooperative (Closed)	- National Beef (USPB majority owner) - Supplies several large retailers	High Quality	Nat'l Beef Brand Programs	Buy/Lease Shares (Cost is $138/share/ animal) Lease rate varies	Member Fee: Lifetime $500 Annual $100	Quality Grid

Table 6.2 – Continued

Alliance	Initiating Party/ Ownership	Packer/End User Involvement	Attributes	Branded Program	Commitment	Fees	Pricing Method
Highland Premium Alberta Beef Alliance (Cdn)	Feedlot Private Company	-XL Foods (Natural) - Cargill (Non-natural) - 1 mid-size retailer - 1 internet based co.	High Quality Natural Alberta Origin	Highland Premium Alberta Beef, Blue LabelBeef	Annual Feeding Agreement Per Head Fees	$5/head	Live-weight Pricing System (Natural) Quality Grid (Non-natural)
Tee Creek Premium Meats (Cdn)	Producers Private Company	-Custom processed @ Northwest Foods - 1 small retailer	High Quality Natural	Tee Creek Premium Beef	Participants are all shareholders in the company	None	Live-weight Pricing System
Ranchers Renaissance (U.S)	Producer Cooperative (Closed)	- Excel - Multiple large retailers	High Quality	Retail Brand Labels	Membership Fee Between $2,500 and $25,000 (Class A & Bmember)	$3/head	Price based off of boxed beef price

Table 6.3 – Requirements and Benefits Received from Participation in Alliances

Alliance	Program Requirements				Average Premiums	Other Benefits
	# of Head	Ownership	Protocols/ Certification	Traceability		
PMBeef Group (U.S)	40	- Sell Calves -Partner w/Feedlot Retainownership	-Feed Protocol -Health Protocol - Certified Feedlots -USDA Verified	Animal Passports Electronic identification	$40-$60 per head	-Ind. Carcass Data
Heartland Premium Beef (U.S)	Not specified	-Retain ownership	-Feed Protocol -Health Protocol	Electronic identification	↓ Discount in beef market	
Cow Camp Beef Alliance (U.S)	50	-Retain ownership -Partner w/Feedlot	- No Specific Protocols	-Electronic identification	Grid Premiums	-Ind. Carcass Data(USPB) -Group Carcass Data(IBP)
Gene Net (U.S)	40	- Sell Calves -Partner w/Feedlot -Retain ownership	- No Specific Protocols	Optional: - Tags -Electronic identification	$20-$40per head	-Ind.Or Group Carcass Data -Cost of Data Varies

Supply Chain Alliances

Alliance	Program Requirements				Average Premiums	Other Benefits
	# of Head	Ownership	Protocols/ Certification	Traceability		
Nebraska Corn Fed Beef (NCFB) (U.S)	40	- Sell Calves -Partner w/Feedlot -Retain ownership	- Produced in Nebraska -Feed Protocol -Health Protocol -Beef Quality Assurance Certification -Affidavits & Internal Audits	-Required to keep records	Slotting Premiums: $1-$3/cwt + Grid Premiums	-Group Carcass Data
Laura's Lean Beef (LLB) (U.S)	No Minimum	- Sell Calves -Retain ownership	-Exotic Breeds -Feed Protocol -Health Protocol - Affidavits & Internal Audits - USDA Cert.	- Program specific tags	Cow/Calf Bonus Fdlt Bonus Grid Premiums	-Ind. Carcass Data
Ward Feed Yard/ILS (U.S)	Not specified	- Sell Calves -Retain ownership	- No Specific Protocols		$5-$20 per head	-Ind. Or Group Carcass Data
Beef Marketing Group (U.S)	N/A	N/A	- No Specific Protocols		IBP Price Premiums	-Ind. Or Group Carcass Data
Decatur Beef Alliance (U.S)	60(same sex)	- Sell Calves -Retain ownership	- No Specific Protocols -Scanning Tech.	-Electronic identification	$30-$50 per head	-Ind. Carcass Data
U.S. Premium Beef (U.S)	100	-Retain ownership -Lease shares	-No Specific Protocols -Qualified Custom Feedlots	-Electronic identification - Tags	$16-$46 per head	-Ind. Carcass Data - Dividends (% of profits) -↑in share value
Highland Premium Alberta Beef Alliance (Cdn)	35	SellCalves -Partner w/Feedlot -Retain ownership	-Feed Protocol -Health Protocol -Certification	- Tags	15% above live weight market price	-Ind. Carcass Data
Tee Creek Premium Meats (Cdn)	Not specified	-Retain ownership	-Feed Protocol -Health Protocol - Internal Cert. -Working w/CFIA to obtain cert.	- Tags - Individual monitoring	No Prem. currently paid	↑ in value of company
Ranchers Renaissance (U.S)	Classes: A- 150 B- 2,000	-Retain ownership	-Feed Protocol -Health Protocol -HACCP system -Internal Certification	-Electronic identification	$27-$52 per head	-Ind. Carcass Data

As shown in Table 6.2, cow-calf producer-driven alliances appear to be more formal and have often been structured as cooperatives where ownership is shared between the individuals involved in the program. An example of such a program is US Premium Beef. When feedlots or packers have developed alliances they are typically privately driven ventures that are more informal in their coordination of the supply chain. An example of a packer driven program is PM Beef Group and an example of a feedlot driven program is Decatur Beef Alliance. Other alliances have been initiated by external entities and have taken two different forms. Firstly, companies have emerged that facilitate coordination, as a service to different industry segments, without the company actually owning any facilities, livestock or end-products. GeneNet is an example of such a company that provides a service to producers, feedlots, and the packer with which it is aligned. Other external companies have emerged that also work to facilitate the coordination of different industry segments. These companies are different in that they purchase finished products and manage the marketing of these products to retailers and other end users. Examples of such companies include Laura's Lean Beef (LLB) and Nebraska Corn Fed Beef (NCFB).

The attributes being branded by the alliances are focused mainly on the production of high quality beef products that are tender, flavourful, and of a consistent quality. Laura's Lean Beef (LLB), Highland Premium Alberta Beef (HPAB), and Tee Creek Premium Meats (TCPM) produce natural beef products that are hormone and antibiotic free. The production of lean meat is also emphasized by LLB, while HPAB brands its product as being produced in Alberta. NCFB differentiates its product as being produced in Nebraska and corn-fed. Heartland Premium Beef (HPB) utilizes Holstein cattle derived from the calves from dairy farms and focuses strictly on this breed. Also unique is the Beef Marketing Group (BMG), which was developed by a group of feedlots in order to guarantee the processor, IBP, with a supply of product into a specific plant. While members of the group are focused on high quality production, the arrangement is not directly driven by the production of particular attributes. Instead, benefits are derived from guaranteeing the supply of a large volume of cattle to a nearby processor and therefore an assured market drives this alliance.

All of the individuals interviewed indicated that the involvement of a packer was critical to the success of their alliance. Accordingly, they were aligned or driven by a specific packer. In a few cases, alliances marketed beef through two or more different processors. An example is the Cow Camp Beef Alliance, which markets beef through National Beef and IBP. Alliances with retailers depend directly on their objectives and structure. Critical to alliances with a retailer is: who owns the brand name label(s) to which the alliance's beef production is dedicated?

Seven out of the thirteen programs presented in Table 6.2 were not linked to a particular branded beef program and, instead, direct their production into multiple commodity and brand programs that are owned by a processor. Processors typically market their brands through major retailers and distributors throughout North America. Four of the alliances own a brand name label and are aligned with specific retailers. Two programs focus on supplying products to specific retailer private labels. The ownership structure for a brand name label can affect the relationship between supply chain participants within an alliance and also how they are linked to end-users. This aspect of alliances will be discussed in more detail later in this chapter.

COORDINATION OF PRODUCTION

Pricing Method

In the production of high quality consistent products, many of the alliances actively seek to operate outside of the traditional commodity market that uses a live-weight pricing system based on average lot quality. Many individuals in both the cow-calf sector and the feedlot level appear frustrated that they are not rewarded for the production of high quality cattle. Consequently, they support the use of a grid-based pricing system. The majority of alliances used a grid-based pricing system, with the exception of two of the natural programs (Highland Premium Alberta Beef Alliance and Tee Creek Premium Meats) which are quite small in terms of the volumes produced.

The structure of the grid-based pricing systems varies, with some being more detailed than others in terms of the number and types of measurements used to determine overall carcass quality. Also, some grid-based pricing systems are exclusive and only available for cattle marketed through a specific alliance to a certain packer. Other grid-based pricing systems are developed by the processor and available to both individuals within an alliance and other alliances and individuals that are marketing cattle to that processor.

All of the individuals interviewed stated that their grid-based pricing systems changed on an ongoing basis, with adjustments being made to respond to consumer demands to encourage the production of particular types of animals. As more quality-based grids have emerged in the market, processors have had to remain competitive and increase the premiums paid to producers in order to procure adequate volumes of cattle with particular attributes. Processors have an incentive to ensure that their grid-based pricing systems are competitive, as individual suppliers have increasing opportunities to switch to other grid-based pricing programs. Those that do not remain competitive will not be able to procure adequate volumes of high quality cattle for their own branded programs and will incur increased search costs to procure these cattle through the cash market.

Program Requirements

A cow-calf operator or feedlot is typically required to have at least 40 head to enter into a program. This is because an individual's cattle must typically be segregated throughout production, or a portion of the production process. A certain number of head is therefore required in order to maintain an efficient lot size. New identification technologies have facilitated the tracking of cattle in mixed ownership lots, but have not yet been adopted on a widespread scale. When shipping cattle by truck, a load is approximately forty head. As a result, the requirement also ensures transportation costs are minimized and economies of scale are captured. Some of the alliances require larger volumes of cattle to ensure adequate volumes of production flow into their branded beef programs. Table 6.3 shows that US Premium Beef requires an annual minimum of 100 head of cattle and Ranchers Renaissance has a minimum requirement of 150 head.

The alliances varied significantly in terms of the production protocols they required participants to follow. From Table 6.3 the natural-based programs, such as Laura's Lean

Beef and Highland Premium Alberta Beef, all have specific feed and health protocols that producers and feedlots are required to follow. The quality-based programs vary in terms of the protocols that they have implemented. Alliances like Ranchers Renaissance require participants to follow quite detailed production and processing protocols that have been implemented to ensure consistent and high quality production. Other alliances, such as Decatur Beef Alliance, rely on the use of economic signals to direct production and have very few, if any, production requirements. Programs also had different requirements due to the attributes being produced and required cattle to be of a certain origin, of a certain breed, and other specifications. For example, Heartland Premium Beef Alliance marketed Holstein cattle and cattle marketed through Nebraska Corn Fed Beef must be fed within Nebraska.

Traceability and Certification Systems

The implementation of traceability and certification systems also varies among alliances. Electronic identification systems have been adopted by several of the alliances to facilitate the tracking of individual animals throughout production and processing. These systems are often tied directly to the provision of carcass quality data that can be applied to specific animals instead of on an overall lot basis. The natural programs examined did have third party certification by either the Canadian Food Inspection Agency or the US Department of Agriculture (USDA). While several of the quality-based programs have internal certification programs and require participants to sign affidavits, PM Beef is unique in that its system is USDA Process Verified, which is a third party certification system developed by the USDA to ensure compliance with specified production and processing protocols.

It is apparent that the mechanisms used to coordinate production and guarantee specific attributes can vary significantly, in terms of the pricing methods used, program requirements, and traceability systems implemented. This is partially a result of the attributes being provided by different alliances, but also a result of the level of consistency that programs are providing for particular attributes. An overview of the alliances examined shows that there is a significant variance in the structures used to produce consistently high quality, tender beef. Some programs are focused on achieving very high levels of consistency and have implemented more detailed pricing structures, program requirements, and traceability systems to achieve this. Others are focused on moving away from the inconsistencies that exist in the spot market and increasing quality, but are more relaxed in terms of their coordination and requirements and are more accepting of some variation between animals.

BENEFITS RECEIVED

Based on the interviews with individuals involved in alliances, the perceived benefits of improved coordination are numerous. Most significant is the improved flow of information along the supply chain. With increased coordination, more accurate information on consumers' demands is passed back from retailers and other end users to processors, feedlots, and cow-calf operators. Grid-based pricing systems convey more accurate economic signals regarding the quality of the product. Of particular importance is the ability of alliances to provide cow-calf operators access to demand information and grid-based pricing systems. The use of contracts and grid-based pricing systems to improve alignment between processors and feedlots has been quite common and facilitated the transfer of information to this sector, but flows of information further upstream in the supply chain have thus far been limited. Alliances provide cow-calf operators with access to grid-based pricing systems and information on the quality of their production, which was previously not available. Access to premiums provides cow-calf operators with increased incentives to improve their production and the information made available to them can assist in their production decisions.

Based on the interviews, alliances also provided substantial benefits for seedstock producers. Alliances often try and align with certain seedstock producers who produce animals that perform well in their program. This creates a dependable market for seedstock producers and is likely to result in increased demand for their seedstock if their progeny perform well and provides their customers (cow-calf operators) with increased returns. Seedstock producers have also purchased cattle back from their customers and marketed these cattle through an alliance. The purpose of buying cattle back from cow-calf producers is to obtain quality information on the progeny of their seedstock. This allows them to see what adjustments they should make to their breeding program and aids in selling seedstock, as they can outline to cow-calf operators what types of calves their seedstock will produce in terms of finished quality.

Processors benefit from having a more constant and stable flow of product that can be processed and marketed through their various commodity and branded beef programs. When they do not own the brand and either custom process cattle or have an alternative arrangement with an alliance, they still benefit from the constant flow through the plant. Alliances also facilitate the transfer of information to processors, retailers, and other end-users regarding the source and processes used in order to ensure the guarantees provided under a brand.

For retailers, the provision of a specific product through an alliance allows them to differentiate themselves from their competitors. Retailers that can provide their customers with differentiated high quality beef may be able to establish increased consumer loyalty to the store. Some retailers have limited the premium at which they sell their brand name product. An example is one of the retail brands Ranchers Renaissance produces for. In this case, the retailer has focused on using their brand name product to increase consumer loyalty. They have traded-off the lower returns they receive on their meat case for higher levels of consumer loyalty and an overall increase in grocery sales.

TRANSACTION CHARACTERISTICS

Specialized Investments

In Chapter 5, cow-calf operators indicated that the investments that they were required to make in order to participate in an alliance was the most important transaction characteristic affecting their willingness to participate in a particular alliance. Therefore, it is important to consider more closely the nature of specialized investments in the alliances examined in this chapter and how this potential barrier to participation is managed. From Table 6.3 it is apparent that the alliances examined varied widely in terms of what they required at the cow-calf level, with the most common requirement being that cattle follow a specific feed and health protocol.

Record and certification systems were also required by some alliances. Again, these varied with respect to the complexity of these systems and the amount of time or capital required by cow-calf operators. The more standardized and simplified the record keeping system is, the more willing cow-calf operators are to participate in an alliance given the reduced time required to manage records. One interviewee stated that the previously cumbersome record keeping process required by their system limited producer participation to some extent. As a result, the organization worked hard to create a standardized system that reduces the amount of time required to input information while improving the overall quality of the information that is obtained throughout the supply chain.

No significant farm improvement expenditures were required by any of the alliances interviewed. The most common element of farm improvement across the different alliances was the adoption of HACCP based programs that certify participating cow-calf operators, feedlots, and in some cases processors and retailers[1]. These types of programs appear to be best suited to ensuring standardization of production procedures, while requiring minimal investments by the majority of cow-calf operators. Other more detailed certification and audit programs were also apparent. For example, PM Beef has implemented a USDA process verified system that requires each individual animal to have a "passport", which includes detailed information on the animal and the production and processing procedures carried out. In addition, USDA audits the production and processing segments on an ongoing basis.

Overall, the investments in human and physical capital that cow-calf operators were required to make to participate in any of the alliances were quite small. Confirming the results of the conjoint analysis in Chapter 5, alliances have limited the amount of investment required in order to encourage participation. Recognizing that while individuals are willing to make small investments in either physical or human capital, large investments offset the benefits derived from participation and are likely to limit entry. Investments focused primarily on the implementation of feed and health protocols and record/certification systems, both of which had positive part-worth values in the conjoint analysis of cow-calf operators.

As cow-calf operators were required to make minimal investments in specialized assets in most of the alliances, the risk of opportunistic behaviour is expected to be low. This coincides with the observation that in most of the alliances coordination between cow-calf operators and the alliances was low. Cow-calf operators were willing to participate in the alliances without the use of contracts to ensure a buyer's commitment and to reduce their exposure to opportunistic behaviour.

The investments required by feedlots are in most cases similar to those required in the cow-calf sector. In some situations, the feedlots and processors initiating alliances incur costs associated with implementing computer vision scanning (CVS) technologies and tracking technologies. The investments associating with implementing these technologies can initially be quite high, but risk of opportunistic behaviour by other supply chain participants is expected to be low. CVS and electronic identification/ tracking technologies are highly transferable and can be easily adapted for different purposes. Although supporting database

---

[1] Hazard Analysis and Critical Control Point (HACCP) systems focus on identifying and preventing hazards within a production system. The objective of a HACCP-based system is to analyze a production system for potential

systems are often developed to specifically meet a particular program's needs, the risk of opportunistic behaviour is still expected to be low. Typically, information systems can be easily adjusted and, as a result, are transferable. Consequently, the transaction costs incurred to reduce the risk of opportunistic behaviour with investments in CVS, traceability systems, and information systems are expected to be low and will not affect the degree of coordination to any great extent.

Overall, the risk of opportunistic behaviour as a result of investment in specific assets is minimal and has not had a great impact on the degree of supply chain coordination. This may be, in part, due to the limited amount of investment alliances have required supply chain participants to make in order to encourage participation. It may also be due to the reciprocal nature of the relationship between buyers and sellers in the supply chain. Buyers need to be able to ensure adequate supplies of a differentiated product, which is not readily available in the spot market. If they act opportunistically sellers will not be willing to transact with buyers in subsequent years, thus increasing buyers costs associated with searching out and procuring new supplies. Similarly, if sellers act opportunistically, buyers will choose not to deal with them in the future and they will lose a market in which to sell their differentiated product. If both parties do not act opportunistically, an ongoing relationship can be established where market access is provided and a consistent flow of supply is realized.

Brand Ownership

The asset specific investment in a brand make the brand's ownership an important question in the examination of alliances in beef supply chains. It is expected that the degree of coordination between different supply chain segments is dependent on who owns a brand name label and how the product is supplied into a label. Developing and owning a brand name label results in both capital investments and transaction costs. Both physical and human capital investments are made in developing a brand and marketing it to consumers. If an alliance owns a brand they must pay listing fees to have their products stocked in retail stores. Listing fees can be quite expensive and may limit the feasibility of marketing a brand name product through a retailer. In order to avoid some of the high capital costs that are incurred with owning a brand name label, several of the alliances interviewed indicated that they chose instead to be the exclusive suppliers into retailer-owned branded beef programs. This reduces the amount of capital that is required, as the retailer incurs the costs of developing and marketing the brand.

For many alliances that are initiated by participants in the production sectors, avoiding brand ownership may be a more efficient alternative for three main reasons. Firstly, processors and retailers have more marketing expertise than those involved in cow-calf production and feedlots. Secondly, give the size of the majority of processors and retailers, they have greater access to large amounts of capital and can more easily absorb the capital costs involved with owning a brand name label. In the interview with PM Beef Group, another reason for retailer ownership of a brand was suggested – that consumers are already familiar with the retailer's reputation and brand name. Lower costs are incurred in educating

---

hazards and identify critical control points. Upon identification of critical control points, measures are established to reduce hazards. Ongoing monitoring and record keeping systems are then implemented.

consumers about the quality of the product, as a retailer already has an established reputation and has an incentive to maintain a positive self image, thus lowering information costs for consumers.

One of the biggest challenges identified by many of the alliances that either owned a brand name label or were the exclusive suppliers into a private label is maintaining a constant flow of product to meet year round demands. If adequate volumes are not maintained on a consistent basis, consumer loyalty is undermined and retailers and other end users are not willing to work with an alliance. At the same time, large volumes are often required in order to meet retailer and end user demands. It can become extremely costly to organize supply chain participants and to ensure adequate volumes of a differentiated product are available on an ongoing basis.

The costs of organizing the supply of a differentiated product through an alliance arise because additional product cannot be easily procured through the spot market. In a sense, a brand name is a specialized asset and the supply chain participant that owns a brand name label, or is the exclusive supplier to a brand name, faces the risk that both the suppliers and the buyers that they have aligned with will act opportunistically. This is because of the high sunk investments involved in developing and maintaining a brand name label. In the case of suppliers, cow-calf operators and feedlots could commit to providing a specific volume of product for the brand name program, but upon the sale they may demand a higher price for this product than was previously agreed. Due to downstream supply commitments and the inability to procure the differentiated product through the current spot market system, the program would be forced to pay a higher price and the overall profitability of the program would decrease.

In order to reduce the risk of opportunistic behaviour by suppliers, increased transaction costs will be incurred to determine the reputation of suppliers, and establish and enforce the commitments made by cow-calf operators and/or feedlots. Search costs may be incurred in order to procure adequate supplies for the program. The transaction costs associated with guaranteeing adequate supplies for a brand name program can be high, whether or not the label is owned internally or an alliance is the exclusive supplier to a brand name program. In order to minimize these costs, participants in a branded program may focus on several different measures to increase coordination and commitment.

Whether they owned a brand name label or were an exclusive supplier into a label, the majority of alliances required an increased level of commitment from participants when they were compared to alliances that were not linked directly to a specific brand name label. Commitment was ensured through the use of annual contracts and in some cases participants were required to commit capital to the program in the form of membership fees or the purchase of shares. The extent to which contracts and membership fees are used to ensure commitment varies between the alliances. Several used contracts that required cow-calf producers and feedlots to commit a certain volume of supply within a particular production period. These types of agreements reduce the overall information costs, but can increase ongoing negotiation and enforcement costs as individual contracts must be negotiated and enforcement costs may arise if supply commitments are breached. The ongoing negotiation costs may be minimal if contracts with cow-calf operators and feedlots are standardized and price is determined using a pre-specified grid-based pricing system.

The commitment of capital by alliance participants to reduce the risk of opportunistic behaviour also varied considerably. Some alliances required new members to pay entrance fees or to purchase shares that give them the right and obligation to deliver a certain number of animals each year. For example, as shown in Table 6.2, US Premium Beef requires participants to pay a membership fee, as well as purchase or lease shares. Similarly, Ranchers Renaissance requires a membership fee, with the fee tied to the number of cattle committed to the program. Further coordination and the commitment of capital to the program reduces the ongoing negotiation and enforcement costs incurred with the use of annual contracts, as the provision of capital by participants creates hostage assets. If participants do not fulfill their obligations to supply a particular volume of animals into the program, they can be removed and their shares or membership fees will not be reimbursed.

The creation of more formal alliances that require participants to purchase shares and/or pay membership fees appear to be used mainly in situations where the volume of supply being committed by individual participants is large and membership is closed. In these situations, no further supply can be procured and it is essential to ensure the supply commitments made by existing members are fulfilled. Both U.S. Premium Beef and Ranchers Renaissance require that participants invest in the cooperative in order to ensure their commitment of a certain number of animals into the program on an annual basis. Since these cooperatives are closed and no outside supplies of animals can be used, it is essential to ensure the commitment of members and eliminate any incentive for them to act opportunistically. The commitment of hostage assets achieves this purpose. The use of contracts is more successful when supply can be procured on an annual basis both from existing alliance members and new members. In these cases, a lower level of commitment is required from individual participants and supply can be procured from a greater number of sources.

It appears to make little difference, in terms of brand ownership, whether an informal structure that relies on contracts or a more formal structure using hostage assets is used to ensure commitment. At the same time, ensuring commitment of supply chain participants to maintain a constant flow of product is necessary. For the Nebraska Corn Fed Beef program, which owns its brand name label, supply commitment has been a very large issue. When cash prices outside the alliance rose substantially in the US due to the discovery of BSE in Canada in May 2003, much of the supply that had been committed to the program was withdrawn and sold in the cash market. The program had not required cow-calf operators or feedlots to sign contracts prior to this time. As a result, the program was unable to meet the supply commitments they had made with end users and consequently lost customers.

Nebraska Corn Fed Beef subsequently worked on implementing a contract system to ensure an adequate level of commitment by program participants. While NCFB requires the payment of annual fees to cover administration costs, it has not required participants to pay membership fees in order to ensure commitment. The choice to move to a structure that requires participant to invest capital is expected to be dependent on a combination of factors that are in addition to who owns a brand name label. These factors will be discussed later in this chapter and include issues surrounding information asymmetry and the number of buyers and sellers.

Alliances have used one additional measure to ensure commitment of supply into the program and minimize the associated transaction costs. A number of the alliances interviewed required that cow-calf operators retain ownership of their calves through to processing, or at least share ownership with feedlots. In a sense, cow-calf operators are providing the alliance with an increased capital commitment, as they incur the additional feeding costs at the feedlot level and also the opportunity costs of having their capital tied up for a longer period of time.

Retained ownership does not create a hostage asset, as finished cattle can still be sold into other markets. However, upon entry into an alliance that requires retained ownership, a cow-calf operator forgoes the opportunity to use their capital elsewhere. In order to recover their capital and make a return on it, they have an incentive to stay with the alliance, as opposed to exiting and having to incur search costs to locate another market for their cattle. Cow-calf operators are also accepting the risk that they may receive lower returns than if they sold their calves, which in itself signals a certain degree of commitment.

Retained ownership increases cow-calf operators' exposure to opportunistic behaviour. They have incurred a higher level of investment in producing a differentiated product and if they are unable to sell it through the previously agreed upon pricing method they could receive a discounted price in the spot market. However, the risk of buyers involved in a branded beef program acting opportunistically is unlikely as they need to ensure adequate supplies and sellers will choose not to deal with them if they have a reputation of acting opportunistically. As a result, the expected transaction costs arising because of opportunistic behaviour when ownership of cattle is retained by cow-calf operators are expected to be minimal and are unlikely to have an impact on the method of coordination chosen. The value associated with retained ownership, in terms of reduced transactions, will be discussed in greater detail later in this chapter.

Opportunistic behaviour by retailers and other end-users, when they are aligned with an alliance that owns their own brand or is the exclusive supplier into a private label, is also expected to be minimal. There is a risk that retailers and other end-users could refuse to take delivery of the pre-agreed volume of product and instead demand a lower price. However, it is unlikely that this will occur, as in order to satisfy their consumers they need a constant supply of the product that satisfies the guarantees they are providing to consumers and it is unlikely they would be able to easily obtain such product through the spot market system without incurring large information and search costs. Supporting the reciprocal nature of this relationship is the fact that in the alliances interviewed, minimal transaction costs are incurred to ensure end-user commitment, with most of the alliances relying on trust and verbal contracts.

Alignment With Packer-Owned Programs

In order to reduce the coordination and transaction costs associated with managing supply and ensuring an adequate flow of products on a consistent basis, some participants in the supply chain have taken an alternative approach. Cow-calf operators and feedlots have aligned themselves with specific packers, focusing on the production of high-quality tender beef that fits into multiple existing commodity and branded beef programs that are owned by the processor.

Typically under such an arrangement alliances are not required to ensure the supply of a particular volume of animals into the plant on an ongoing basis. Instead, the processor and alliance establish an approximate average annual volume that the alliance will market through the processor. Volume requirements are fairly flexible given that the percentage of product that the processor procures from the alliance may only be a small portion of its total processing needs. Many of these alliances indicated that the processor was willing to accept as much production as the alliance could produce. From Table 6.2, examples of alliances that are aligned with a specific processor and its beef programs include GeneNet, Decatur Beef Alliance, and the Beef Marketing Group.

Normally under such an arrangement, program requirements are minimal, thus asset specific investments are minimal. These alliances are more focused on using grid-based pricing systems to convey information back along the supply chain and to increase the value received when high quality cattle are produced. Based on carcass quality, and other requirements such as breed, cattle can be allocated into several different programs run by the processor. The benefit is that it may be possible to allocate animals that do not fit one program into an alternative branded program. Often alliances that are focused on marketing product through their own brand name or through an exclusive arrangement into a private label program face substantial discounts for cattle that do not meet the program requirements or when they have excess supply.

The transaction costs incurred when marketing to packer-owned beef programs are reduced. Lower information and negotiation costs are incurred by supply chain participants due to the lower level of asset specificity and reduced risk of opportunistic behaviour. As the processor benefits from the increased flow of high quality product into its plant, it has less incentive to act opportunistically towards sellers. The reciprocal nature of the relationship and mutual benefits received by both parties is important to the sustainability of this relationship.

There is also less concern over ensuring adequate volumes of supply on an ongoing basis, consequently negotiation costs incurred to ensure supply commitments are reduced. Typically, those alliances that direct production into multiple programs owned by a specific packer require little more than a verbal commitment or a feeding agreement when the cattle are put on feed. Program fees usually range between US$3.00 and US$7.00 per head. These fees are not typically used to ensure commitment; instead they cover the costs of tagging cattle and measuring quality. No long-term commitment is required by either party, and typically cattle can be entered into the program at anytime prior to the time that they are processed.

Price Uncertainty Associated With Quality Variability

Grid-based pricing systems are a more efficient method to transfer detailed information on consumer demands back within the beef industry when attributes such as tenderness are being produced. There is a reallocation of risk, as instead of the processor accepting the risk of quality variability, cow-calf operators and finishing feedlots are accepting the risk. Cow-calf operators and feedlots have the greatest impact on the quality of cattle being produced and the incentive to produce high quality products is greater when payment is based on carcass quality.

Price grids varied between the alliances analyzed. More detailed grids allowed information costs to be reduced. Cow-calf operators are provided with clear economic signals regarding the quality demanded by the target market. The incentive to improve production in order to access the premiums available is increased due to the grid's larger premiums and discounts. From Table 6.2, alliances with more detailed grids include GeneNet and PM Beef Group. When a more detailed grid is used, monitoring costs are lower than through a program that focuses on implementing more detailed production requirements and protocols. Monitoring costs do not have to be incurred to ensure compliance with program requirements, with the system focusing on the use of transparent economic signals to achieve the desired product quality.

While information costs associated with the transfer of information to upstream supply chain participants are reduced with grid-based pricing systems, it is important to note that cow-calf operators and feedlots incur information costs when they are initially planning to participate in this system. Costs are incurred in searching out information on grid-based pricing systems so that individuals can evaluate their expected performance on different pricing systems and to determine which alliance and grid-based pricing system best suits their production system. Most of the alliances examined used grid-based pricing systems, with the use of this type of pricing system increasing in the industry. Therefore, it is likely that the initial information costs incurred to reduce price uncertainty are low and are offset by the reduction in information costs that occurs when a grid-based pricing system is used.

Producer Acceptance Of Grid-Based Pricing Systems

On the whole, most of the individuals interviewed indicated that although the use of grid-based pricing systems is increasing, a portion of cow-calf producers are hesitant to price their cattle this way. This may in part be because, while cow-calf operators can search out information on price and reduce price uncertainty, it is difficult for them to completely eliminate uncertainty as to the price they will receive. Many cow-calf operators are risk averse individuals who prefer a live-weight pricing system where the price they receive is more predictable and they are not exposed to the risk that they will receive price discounts upon cattle being processed. The question arises as to how to encourage participation of cow-calf operators so that consumer demands can be met on a more consistent basis. The alliances examined focused on two methods to encourage participation.

Firstly, alliances have focused on helping individuals manage their exposure to risk. The base price that many alliances use, from which carcass quality premiums and discounts are added or subtracted, is established using an average weekly spot market price at the time of processing. Given the lag in time between when production decisions are made and returns are determined, it is difficult for producers to project what type of base price and net returns they can expect. For PM Beef, the base price is determined by the futures market price for the expected month of delivery. Producers have the option of locking in their price anytime up until cattle are processed. This provides them with a greater ability to determine and control their expected net return. Other alliances use similar techniques, assisting individuals in hedging their production on the futures market in order to lock in a base price or allowing producers to establish a forward contract with a specified base price.

Nebraska Corn Fed Beef continues to allow individuals to sell their cattle on a live weight basis, while providing them with quality information that outlines how their cattle would have performed on the grid-based pricing system. This has been very successful in encouraging participation and providing producers with an insight into how their cattle perform prior to taking on the risk of pricing cattle through a grid. Currently, over 75 percent of producers are pricing their cattle through the organization's quality grid, while the remainder either forward contract their cattle or sell them on a live weight basis.

In addition to assisting cow-calf operators in managing risk, alliances have focused on educating them about the other benefits of a grid-based pricing system. The majority of the alliances examined placed less emphasis on the ability of grids to provide premiums and more focus on the value of the information provided through grids. Prior to the creation of these pricing systems, access to information on the quality of production was limited. Those individuals that participate in alliances with grid-based pricing systems now have access to information on the quality of their production and, as a result, can make changes to improve quality and, hence, be more competitive.

One view was that, with the increasing use of grid-based pricing systems, a two-tiered market is slowly developing, with higher prices being received for cattle purchased on a grid-based pricing system. In the cash market buyers are taking on the risk that quality will be low and they are passing that risk onto feedlots and cow-calf operators through lower prices. Processors and other buyers are paying for the information on product quality made available through the grid, to which they do not have access when using live weight pricing mechanisms.

Given the potential emergence of a two-tiered market for cattle, the value of the information that can be obtained through a grid-based pricing system is expected to increase. In order to remain competitive and gain access to premium prices, individuals need information on the quality of their production and will place a greater value on this information if, in its absence, they are subject to large discounts in the spot market. In many of the alliances examined, individuals whose cattle did not perform well left after the first year and used the information obtained on the quality of their production to make the changes to their production processes. They then returned to the alliance a few years later in order to gain access to premiums through the grid. Educating participants on the changing industry structure and the value of quality information assists in encouraging participation. Joining an alliance aids in ensuring long-term competitiveness by increasing cow-calf operator's and feedlot's access to information and their ability to access markets with higher prices.

Grid-Based Pricing And Alliances

The question arises as to why alliances are necessary if a grid-based system can be used between processors and production sectors to improve information flow and increase the quality of cattle. From the interviews, three main reasons became apparent. Firstly, alliances work to coordinate the cow-calf sector with the rest of the industry. Alliances align cow-calf operators with feedlots and processors through standardized methods. Instead of negotiating multiple separate transactions with individuals, an alliance aligns cow-calf producers with specific feedlots and from there coordinates transactions with a processor. Negotiations between the different supply chain participants are limited and the associated costs are reduced, with the alliance negotiating on behalf of multiple individuals for a large volume of cattle. Upon processing, the alliance administers the transfer of information back along the supply chain. Without the standardized coordination of transactions along the supply chain, it is costly to link the large number of cow-calf operators, with small numbers of cattle, to the rest of the supply chain and improve coordination.

Monitoring costs are also reduced under an alliance structure. Grid-based pricing systems may result in monitoring costs for producers in ensuring that processors do not falsify carcass grades to pay lower prices. Under an alliance, these monitoring costs are reduced because a processor has an incentive to maintain a positive relationship with the alliance given the benefits it receives from having a more consistent flow of high quality product into its processing plants. Also, the alliance transacts with a processor on a more frequent basis than would individuals. Consequently, there is a greater reliance on trust to ensure proper carcass grading, and monitoring costs are minimal.

Information Asymmetry

The alliances examined branded experience, credence, and search attributes. Program requirements and certification methods have been implemented to ensure that the production of different credence attributes can be guaranteed to downstream customers. Three of the alliances focused on the production of natural beef with no hormones or antibiotics. In addition to providing natural beef, Highland Premium Beef Alliance also brands a portion of their product with the guarantee that the beef was raised in Alberta. Nebraska Corn Fed Beef guarantees that product is corn fed and raised in Nebraska. PM Beef provides consumers with a guarantee that the source and process for all of its beef can be verified. With the exception of Nebraska Corn Fed Beef, all of the alliances guaranteeing credence attributes rely on affidavits and third-party certification to ensure compliance and reduce the problems associated with information asymmetry. Typically, the third party certification systems require alliances to submit regular records. Random audits are performed throughout the supply chain on an ongoing basis.

Nebraska Corn Fed Beef verifies the production of its credence attributes through an internal certification and audit process. Participants in the alliance are required to following the Beef Quality Assurance program, which works to reduce quality and consistency problems through the implementation of specific feed, health, and management protocols. Participants are also required to keep detailed and accurate production records and are subject to random internal audits on an ongoing basis.

The systems used to guarantee the production of experience and search attributes, namely tenderness and leanness, vary significantly. Some alliances have implemented detailed production and management protocols to reduce overall variability and increase the production of tenderness and/or leanness attributes. The more detailed protocols become, the more costly it is for individuals to comply with them. As a result, the incentives to cheat increases because attributes are not easily detected prior to consumption and information asymmetries exist. In order to reduce information asymmetries and ensure compliance, alliances with detailed program requirements have often implemented internal certification and audit systems.

In some cases, the move from a more informal alliance to a formal new generation cooperative structure has also facilitated compliance with more detailed program requirements. For example, Ranchers Renaissance and other new generation cooperatives increase the incentive to comply with program requirements, as participants have committed capital to the cooperative that is non-refundable. Consequently, the monitoring costs incurred to ensure compliance with more detailed program requirements are lower when a more formal alliance structure is chosen. New generation cooperatives provide for greater control and the closer alignment of incentives.

Number of Buyers and Sellers

Tighter program specifications reduce the number of buyers and sellers due to the transaction specific quality of the product and, as a result, closer coordination is necessary to ensure adequate supplies. For example, Laura's Lean Beef requires that cattle are of an exotic breed and have been raised with no hormones or antibiotics. Requiring cattle to be both of an exotic breed and natural places significant limits on the number of cattle that are eligible to be marketed through the program and it is very difficult to procure adequate volumes through the regular market system.

From the buyer's perspective, significant search costs are incurred to procure adequate volumes of lean and natural cattle. To ensure adequate volumes of these cattle, negotiation costs are also incurred, with contracts being used to ensure the commitment of sellers. Sellers are also concerned with ensuring market access due to the specialized nature of the product they are selling and the limited number of buyers that are willing to pay a premium for that product. Consequently, they will incur search and information costs in order to find buyers and determine their reputations. The increased transaction costs are expected to result in closer vertical coordination.

If both the numbers of buyers and sellers for a specialized product are small, a mutually beneficial relationship exists and the risk of opportunistic behaviour by either party is low. For example, Highland Premium Alberta Beef has limited access to alternative suppliers that can fulfill their needs, and sellers also have limited access to alternate markets to sell their natural cattle. This creates a mutually dependent relationship and a low risk that either party will break commitments. A similar situation exists for other alliances that operate in niche markets with a small number of buyers and sellers. In these situations, it appears that transaction costs are minimized and, while increased coordination may be required to ensure the production of particular attributes, a small number of buyers and sellers does not necessitate increased coordination.

The situation changes as an increasing number of sellers are available when a differentiated product is being produced. With many of the programs that are producing tenderness, such as GeneNet and PM Beef Group, there are a larger number of cow-calf operators and feedlots available. At the same time there are few buyers in the market due to industry concentration in the processing and retailer sectors. Alliances such as PM Beef Group, which are focused on providing a high level of consistency and, as a result, have detailed program requirements that increase their costs, will be subject to a greater risk of opportunistic behaviour by buyers. Based on the alliance structures present in the industry, it appears that although there is an increased risk of opportunistic behaviour in this situation it does not affect the type of alliance structure chosen. This may be because a program's guarantees are often dependent on the more detailed production specifications. For example, PM Beef Group guarantees its beef is produced under its Ranch to Retail verified production system. As a result, there is no incentive for them to act opportunistically given that it would be difficult for them to procure high-quality, tender process verified cattle from alternative sources, and thus a mutually dependent relationship exists.

Transaction Frequency

Discussion in the previous chapters indicated that a significant challenge in coordinating the beef industry was the differences in the frequency of transactions between supply chain participants. While transactions between other sectors of the beef industry occur on a more frequent basis, cow-calf operators typically market cattle in one or two transactions per year. The focus of most of the alliances is to improve coordination between cow-calf operators and the rest of the supply chain by acting as a facilitator. As alliances transact with all segments in the supply chain on a more frequent basis it aids in creating trust-based relationships and improving the flow of information to cow-calf operators. Using alliances to overcome the challenges associated with less frequent transactions reduces transaction costs resulting from asset specificity and transaction uncertainty and, as a result, increases the incentives of cow-calf operators to participate in alliances and produce differentiated beef products. Whether or not an informal or formal alliance is chosen to overcome the challenges associated with less frequent transactions does not seem to matter. The choice between alliance structures appears to be more dependent on the premium structure, degree of asset specificity, brand ownership structure, and amount of transaction uncertainty associated with producing different beef products.

CRITICAL SUCCESS FACTORS AND CHALLENGES FOR ALLIANCES

The previous section provided insights from the alliances examined on the importance of the different transaction characteristics outlined in the predictive model developed in Chapter 4. The following section examines additional factors that have an impact on improved supply chain coordination.

Creating Value Along the Supply Chain

One of the most significant challenges that many of the individuals interviewed identified was creating value along the entire supply chain. In order to encourage participation in the alliance, the benefits of participation have to be greater than the associated costs. The production of differentiated attributes can increase transaction costs and production costs. Changes to existing production and processing practices may also create inefficiencies that do not exist in the commodity oriented system. These inefficiencies are often associated with the restricted use of different technologies, such as hormones and antibiotics, and lower volumes that flow through the supply chain when differentiated products are produced.

With many niche market products that have high production and processing costs, the price charged to consumers is significantly higher than the price of commodity oriented beef products. Only a small segment of consumers are willing to accept the large price differential. Consequently, the market size for many products is limited and the potential to create value and ensure that increased transaction and operation costs are covered within each segment of the supply chain is limited.

In a sense, the market is in disequilibrium. Some alliances that are currently operating are unable to ensure that the benefits received by all supply chain segments are greater than the costs incurred by these segments. In the long run, it is likely that these alliances will move in one of three directions. Firstly, they may choose to restructure to ensure value is distributed along the supply chain based on the increased costs incurred by each sector. Secondly, when overall costs are greater than benefits, alliances may restructure their existing focus and program requirements to better meet consumer demands. Finally, if they are unable to restructure it is likely these alliances will disband in the long run, with participants exiting the alliance.

One alliance had examined branding beef based on an enhanced food safety program implemented throughout the production process. However, while there is a demand for enhanced food safety, consumers' willingness to pay a premium appeared to be limited. As a result, it is unlikely that the alliance would be able to recoup the increased production and transaction costs. Similarly, the emergence of process and source verification systems is likely to increase in the future in order to guarantee other attributes. However, it is unclear whether these attributes alone would command a price premium. This may be because consumers are coming to expect verification of all beef products consumed, as part of ensuring both the quality guarantees provided and food safety.

While the market may be in disequilibrium, short-term market fluctuations may arise where costs for some participants may exceed the increase in value received through an alliance. Getting participants to accept that in the short term there may be periods where the price received through the alliance is lower than in the cash market has been a priority for many of the alliances. Over the long run, it is important that the benefits exceed the costs. It is necessary that participants in an alliance understand whether the market is in short run disequilibrium or a structural failure exists and the alliance is not viable in the long run. Newer alliances faced greater uncertainty regarding how to manage market fluctuations and in understanding whether costs exceeded benefits over the short and long run. It appears that those alliances where the costs exceed the benefits in the long run will exit from the industry, while those that face short-term fluctuations will be able to overcome the situation and operate in the long run.

If in the short run disequilibrium exists, it is necessary that participants in an alliance understand and have a long-term focus and commitment to the program. As exit in the short term is not beneficial to participants, it will result in the failure of the alliance. At the same time, the alliance must be flexible and facilitate communication to ensure that all participants are represented and to adapt the alliance if a long-run structural problem becomes apparent.

Marketing The Entire Carcass

Alliances also face a challenge in selling the whole carcass at a premium in order to offset the increased costs associated with producing differentiated beef products. In general, only a portion of the carcass can be sold at a premium. Some cuts are not as popular with customers and, as a result, their willingness to pay a premium for these cuts is lower. Therefore, in order to recoup increased costs, larger premiums must be charged on a small portion of the carcass, while lower or no premiums are available for the rest of the carcass.

Being able to market an adequate portion of the carcass at a premium to offset increased costs has been identified by many alliances as a challenge. It is especially important for those alliances that market product into their own brand name label or an exclusive private label. Typically, they have higher average costs than alliances that market products into multiple processor-owned brand programs. It is expected that their transaction costs will also be higher given the greater need to ensure commitment of supply chain participants in order to guarantee a consistent flow of product. Alliances that market product into multiple processor-owned brand programs typically incur a lower level of transaction costs associated with ensuring participants' commitment, as it is not as necessary to maintain a consistent and constant supply of product. Alliances that market product into multiple brand programs also have an advantage because they are typically able to market product into multiple brands and sell a larger portion of the carcass at a premium.

In order to offset the costs, several alternative approaches have been used to improve the marketability of the carcass. Firstly, alliances such as GeneNet, Cow Camp Beef Alliance and the Beef Marketing Group have chosen to market product into multiple brand name labels rather than developing their own brand or an exclusive supply relationship with a private label. This lowers their average production and transaction costs. It also increases the available markets in which to sell different portions of the carcass at a premium and reduces the discounts that are often incurred by programs that have access to few alternative markets.

Alternatively, NCFB has chosen to establish their own brand name label, but purchases back from the processor only those cuts of meat that can be sold at a premium. The processor sells the cuts back to the alliance with a processing margin added back into the price. The remainder of the carcasses or portions of the carcass are sold through the processor's branded and commodity based programs using a grid pricing system. While this method does not aid in increasing the portion of the carcass that can be sold at a premium through the brand name label, it does enable the alliance to have access to an alternative market to sell other product. This may reduce the discounts these types of alliances typically face in selling the remainder of the carcass and assists in increasing value along the supply chain.

Other programs have worked to increase the percentage of the carcass that is sold at a premium through the brand name label. Research and development has been undertaken to produce alternative value-added products from those cuts of meat that are otherwise difficult to sell at a premium. For example, Laura's Lean Beef has expanded into the production of pre-cooked products, frozen patties, and other convenience oriented products. Ranchers Renaissance has taken a different approach and brands the whole beef case in the retail stores to which it sells. They are able to obtain a large premium for their tender-verified products, while also obtaining a smaller premium for those products that are not tender-verified but guaranteed to be consistent and process verified.

Many alliances have focused on selling to multiple end-users to increase the percentage of the carcass sold at a premium. The demand for specific beef cuts for many end-users in the service sector is limited to only the most popular cuts. Therefore, focusing solely on this market reduces the percentage of the carcass that can be sold at a premium. Consequently, alliances have focused on selling into multiple retail and end-user markets and increasing the percentage of the carcass that can be sold at a premium.

Objectives Of Cow-Calf Operators

In Chapter 5 the effect of different transaction characteristics on the willingness of cow-calf operators to participate in alliances and produce differentiated cattle were investigated. The chapter did not assess the effect of the characteristics of a producer's operation on their decision to participate in an alliance. Cow-calf producer's operations are often diversified, with beef production being only a portion of their total farm enterprise. In many situations they are involved in beef production as a method to utilize existing grass and forage resources that are unsuited to crop production, with beef production not being the primary source of income for the overall farm operation.

It is expected that producers are rational profit maximizers, who seek to maximize the net returns from their farm enterprise. As a result, it would appear that even when beef production is not their primary source of income they would want to increase quality and participate in an alliance in order to gain access to differentiated markets that have higher returns. At the same time, because producers are often managing multiple operations, and have limited access to both human and capital resources, the additional gain from participating in an alliance needs to outweigh the costs, including the opportunity costs of diverting human and capital resources from other farm enterprises. The reallocation of human and capital resources into beef production may actually result in a decrease in net returns and, as a result, less focus may be placed on improving quality and making the changes required to produce differentiated beef products through an alliance. It is expected that as the portion of the operation that is allocated to beef production decreases it is less likely that human and capital resources will be reallocated to improve quality and differentiate the beef cattle produced. Whereas, those operations that are more specialized in beef production will have a greater incentive to allocate the increased human and capital resources that are often required when participating in an alliance.

If many cow-calf operators are involved in beef production as a method to utilize existing forage resources, average herd size is expected to remain small due to the limited additional resources that can be reallocated from other aspects of their farm operation into beef production. Alliances have struggled to encourage participation by these types of producers, who are not as focused on improving quality and becoming more competitive in the beef industry. The question arises as to how to encourage participation in alliances when cow-calf operators' objectives do not always match those held by the rest of the industry. Educating individuals about the benefits that can be derived from participation in an alliance, aside from the premiums received, is one approach to encouraging greater participation in alliances.

For many ranchers, their expertise does not lie in the marketing of beef cattle. Alliances can reduce an individual's marketing costs, as the alliance does the marketing. This allows cow-calf operators to concentrate on the production of beef cattle and their other farm operations, while maximizing the returns they receive. They spend less time and incur lower costs in searching out markets and negotiating transactions, with the alliance performing and specializing in these functions. If a two-tiered market emerges and price differenced become more defined, the value of the benefits received is expected to increase, which may encourage further participation from mixed farm operations producing beef cattle.

Managing Product Flow

The management of product flow throughout the supply chain has been identified as a significant challenge for several reasons. Firstly, in order to ensure supply on an ongoing basis, many alliances that own their own brand name label or have an exclusive relationship with a retailer-owned label, have tried to encourage producers to adjust their calving periods. For example, NCFB and several other alliances encourage fall calving rather than the more common practice of calving cows in the spring. This provides a more consistent flow of finished cattle on a year round basis, but its acceptance at the cow-calf operator level has been limited due to increased costs in terms of the human and capital resources required. On mixed farm operations, producers may prefer to complete calving prior to seeding and/or harvesting crops. Additional labor would be needed if calving occurred at the same time as either seeding or harvesting and result in increased costs to the producer. Calving later in the year also requires the maintenance of calves into the winter, which can result in higher costs and lost revenues due to lower rates of gain in areas where winters are harsh.

Encouraging producers to adopt alternative calving patterns requires offsetting the increased costs incurred. Nebraska Corn Fed Beef pays premiums for cattle that will be finished in periods of the year where product supplies are typically lower. Producers entering into the program are required to commit cattle at specific time periods, with higher premiums for those periods where supply is low. Although this has encouraged some cow-calf operators to alter their calving period, success with mixed farm operations is lower. In situations where acceptance has been low, programs have chosen alternate measures to manage supply.

Some programs, such as Ranchers Renaissance and U.S. Premium Beef, have worked to pull supplies from different regions, where due to climatic differences average calving and finishing times vary and result in a more consistent flow of supply through the alliance. Supply flow is also managed through grazing programs and other feeding regimes that adjust the finishing times of cattle to better suit demand. Alliances that supply into multiple packer-owned programs, and do not own their own label or exclusively supply into a retailer-owned label, are not required to maintain as consistent a flow of animals into the processor and thus are less focused on encouraging producers to make changes to their existing production schedule. Examples of such programs include Cow Camp Beef Alliance, GeneNet, and Decatur Beef Alliance. Producers are more likely to participate in these types of alliances if they operate mixed farms and do not wish to change their production schedule.

The second challenge related to managing product flow is with respect to the relationship between processors and alliances. Processors have looked to alliances as a method of securing adequate flows of both specialized inputs and commodity inputs. Alliances lower the information and search costs associated with procuring cattle and ensuring adequate supplies are available to fulfill the requirements of different branded programs. In turn, processors are able to make supply commitments to downstream end users when adequate supplies of inputs are available. In some circumstances, alliances have been used as a method to ensure a more consistent and adequate flow of cattle into the plant without a direct focus on increasing supplies into their branded programs. Given the increasing size of processing plants and substantial decrease in profitability that occurs if they do not operate at capacity, ensuring a portion of cattle supplies through the use of alliances is beneficial.

The Beef Marketing Group (BMG) is an example of an alliance that was formed specifically to provide an IBP plant in eastern Kansas with an ongoing base supply of cattle, with the plant having previously struggled to obtain the volumes it required on a consistent basis. In exchange for the supply of cattle, IBP has developed a preferential pricing agreement with the alliance. A legal challenge to this relationship from feed yards and the US government in the late 1990s alleged that the Beef Marketing Group received unfair preferential treatment. The lawsuit was not successful, but the opposition of some beef industry participants to such an arrangement is important, as such actions could impact the formation of alliances and future degree of supply chain coordination in the beef industry.

Whether an alliance is ensuring supplies or working to coordinate the production of a differentiated beef product, opposition to such arrangements has surfaced. This opposition arises mainly because of concerns that alliances result in reduced competition and a movement away from the spot market. Essentially, there is opposition to the emergence of a two-tiered market where cattle that are sold in the spot market may be discounted. This opposition has resulted in a push for regulatory intervention and lawsuits against organizations involved in closer vertical alliances, with arrangements including exclusive pricing agreements, supply contracts or custom feeding of cattle by a processor.

At the Alberta Cattle Feeders Association's 2004 annual meeting a motion was passed that would limit the number of cattle that packers could own to 10% of their monthly kills. This came just after a US case involving Tyson Foods in which a jury recommended US$1.28 billion be awarded to cattle producers to compensate for Tyson Foods allegedly manipulating cattle prices by controlling approximately 1/3 of the cattle that they processed. The decision against Tyson Foods was subsequently overturned, but it is important to understand as both situations focus on limiting processor control. The importance of the issue is that while packers may not always directly own cattle, many of the arrangements used to improve coordination and produce differentiated products to meet consumer demands may be limited in the future due to regulatory intervention. For example, Decatur Beef Alliance struggled to establish an exclusive pricing agreement with Excel. This arrangement could increase the value received by alliance participants and overall alliance participation, but Excel appeared at the time hesitant to enter into an arrangement as a result of the increased opposition and the associated lawsuits.

Whether improved coordination occurs to increase the production of differentiated beef products and/or maintain an adequate flow of product throughout the supply chain it appears that the industry is moving in this direction. With the emergence of a two-tiered market system, where cattle are sold either through the spot market or by methods of closer coordination, it is expected that individuals in the spot market will receive lower returns. At the same time, regulatory intervention to prevent such a situation will disrupt the market and may limit the ability of industry participants to improve coordination and respond to consumer demands. The opposition to increased coordination also brings into question how new generation cooperatives will be managed. US Premium Beef is a producer-owned cooperative that is the majority owner of the fourth largest processor National Beef. While opposition to such cooperatives has not currently occurred to any great extent, they are in a sense a vertically integrated company that limits market access and results in preferential treatment. If regulatory intervention limits packer-ownership and control of supplies, presumably these operations will also be affected.

Concentration In The Processing And Retailer Sectors

The processing and retailing sectors in Canada are even more concentrated than those in the US and the degree of concentration is expected to increase in the future. This may affect the development of alliances in two ways. First, it has been found in the US that after a processor or retailer has aligned itself with a few programs, they typically do not want to align with themselves with any additional alliances. This reluctance results from increased management costs, including the opportunity cost of human and capital resources required to organize additional programs, administer several different grid-based pricing systems, and segregating processing runs. In addition, retailers are reluctant to run more than one or two branded programs in their stores. Retailers are more likely to develop a single brand name label and have a limited number of supply chain relationships to procure product for that label.

The high degree of concentration in the processing and retailing sector, combined with their limited willingness to adopt multiple branded programs, will affect how alliances develop in the future. Alliances will likely be required to supply substantial volumes of cattle in order to fulfill the requirements of branded programs. This was not a problem for many of the existing alliances examined, as when they were initiated very few similar programs were in existence and processors and/or retailers were willing to work with them even if they initially only marketed small volumes of cattle. These alliances were able to grow slowly to their current size. However, as more alliances have emerged, and concentration in the processing and retailing sectors continues to increase, it is less likely that they will be willing to work with alliances that supply small volumes of cattle at the outset. At the same time, supplying large volumes of cattle is less feasible for new alliances. The inability of new alliances to start small and expand slowly may be a limiting factor in the number of new alliances that emerge within the industry, and the Canadian industry in particular, in the future.

Within the U.S. industry, participants have also had the alternative opportunity of creating alliances with mid-size processors and retailers. Mid-size processors and retailers benefit, as they are able to create a differentiated value-added market where they do not have to compete with their larger competitors based on price. Alliances benefit, as typically they do not have to supply the substantial volumes of cattle that are required by larger processors and retailers. This allows them to grow and develop more slowly. PM Beef Group and NCFB are two alliances in the US that have created relationships with mid-size processors and/or retailers. They have been very successful, as they have been able to establish themselves on a smaller scale and ensure an adequate supply flow prior to increasing the volumes they supply into processor-owned or private label programs. In addition, those alliances with their own brand name are typically smaller. Large processors are not willing to work with them due to the decrease in their operational efficiency associated with segregating small volumes of production. Similarly, large retailers are less willing to market small volumes of product.

In Canada, very few mid-size processors or retailers exist. The industry is oligopolistic, with a few large firms dominating both sectors. This could limit the types of alliances that emerge. New alliances may choose not to have their own brand name given the substantial costs associated with developing and marketing a label. In addition, maintaining the substantial volume of cattle that would be required under such a structure results in high transaction costs. In order to minimize marketing and transaction costs, alliances in the Canadian beef industry are more likely to focus on marketing into existing processor-owned or private label branded programs. Less exclusive relationships where multiple alliances supply into packer-owned programs or private label retailer programs, using the same grid-based pricing arrangement and more general program requirements, may also occur. This would reduce overall complexity and, as a result, possibly increase the acceptance of additional alliances that supply lower volumes of cattle.

ADDITIONAL OPPORTUNITIES TO IMPROVE COORDINATION

Aside from increased supply chain coordination through the use of contracts and alliances, additional opportunities exist to improve coordination and reduce the transaction costs incurred by supply chain participants when producing differentiated beef products.

Retained Ownership Of Cattle By Cow-Calf Operators

Most of the alliances interviewed either required or strongly encouraged cow-calf operators to retain ownership of cattle throughout production until they were processed. Retained ownership can affect the degree of coordination required when providing differentiated beef products. When producers retain ownership of cattle, transactions at the cow-calf operator/feedlot interface change and the feedlot becomes a "hotel" where cattle are fed on a custom basis. Cow-calf operators transact directly with a processor. While an alliance typically facilitates the interaction between cow-calf operators and the processor, the direct interaction between these two parties may increase the incentive for cow-calf operators to produce high-quality cattle with specific attributes. The returns to cow-calf operators become directly dependent on the finished quality of cattle.

The better alignment of incentives should result in lower transaction costs associated with determining the reputation of sellers and monitoring production in order to ensure compliance with program requirements. At the same, transaction costs are also reduced as information, in the form of data and economic price signals, is transferred directly from the processor to the cow-calf operator. This creates a more transparent flow of information to guide cow-calf operator's production decisions. It is unclear whether negotiation costs are reduced. While pricing arrangements are only negotiated between producers and processors when ownership is retained, a flat rate custom feeding fee must be negotiated between cow-calf operators and feedlots. It is expected that the negotiation costs associated with a custom feeding fee are minimal, as a result of it being standardized.

Retained ownership may also increase the value received by cow-calf operators. Instead of receiving premiums by selling their calves through an alliance to a feedlot, they are able to capture all of the premiums that are paid upon cattle being processed. Whether or not the increase in premiums received will offset the opportunity costs associated with retaining ownership will vary depending on each cow-calf operator's situation. It is likely that producers who operate mixed farms will be less willing to retain ownership, as they would have to use capital resources allocated for other farm enterprises to pay feeding charges. They may also depend on the revenue derived from the sale of their calves to finance other enterprises and they would not have access to these funds until the sale of the finished cattle.

In order to encourage smaller cow-calf operators to retain ownership, other alternatives have been provided, such as feedlots partnering and sharing ownership of an operator's cattle through to processing. GeneNet, PM Beef Group, Cow Camp Beef Alliance, and several other alliances allow cow-calf operators to partner with feedlots and share ownership. This reduces the capital that producers are required to commit, while still maintaining the more direct link between a producer's returns and the finished quality. For example, NCFB, Laura's Lean Beef, and Highland Premium Alberta Beef allow calves to be purchased by feedlots. Alliances that allowed cow-calf operators to partner with feedlots or sell their calves to feedlots, said that initially providing cow-calf operators with these options often encourages them to retain ownership over the long run. When cow-calf operators receive information on the quality of cattle produced and the premiums paid at the feedlot level they are often encouraged to increase their involvement in order to capture the potential premiums available from retained ownership.

Certification Institutions

For many of the credence attributes being produced, a third party that verifies production and processing methods and provides certification is often necessary. Highland Premium Alberta Beef and Tee Creek Beef are both Canadian-based alliances that produce natural beef. When interviewed, both of these alliances indicated that obtaining third-party certification for their product has been a significant challenge, as currently there is no standardized institution to provide such certification in Canada. Both of the alliances approached the Canadian Food Inspection Agency and have developed a system, but this took a substantial amount of time and effort. As the Canadian beef industry continues to develop and produce increased numbers of differentiated products, it needs to recognize the importance and facilitate the provision of third party certification institutions. These institutions reduce the monitoring costs that would otherwise be incurred through internal auditing. Third party certification institutions are expected to provide a more standardized and simplified certification process that reduces the amount of effort and coordination required to monitor supply chain participants.

Electronic Identification And Computer Vision Scanning Systems

Electronic identification has the potential to improve traceability and verify the source of individual animals in the beef industry. The computer vision scanning systems (CVS) and data management systems used with electronic identification also potentially facilitate the transfer of substantial amounts of information regarding the quality of individual animals. Information can be gathered on the production and processing methods used, live animal quality, and carcass quality. In addition, electronic identification enables cattle to be mixed with other cattle in feedlots and at processing plants, as electronic identification tags can link an individual animal with a specific owner. This may enable cow-calf operators with a small number of cattle to retain ownership. Previously, as cattle had to be maintained in separate lots through the feeding process it was more difficult for small cow-calf operators to retain ownership because many feedlots preferred larger lots of animals for operational efficiency.

The Decatur Beef Alliance uses electronic identification to sort and co-mingle cattle at the feedlot level. The alliance uses the Micro Beef Technology ACCU-TRAC™ Electronic Cattle Management System, which measures and manages individual animals using CVS, in order to optimize finishing quality. Every animal in the alliance is measured with the ultrasound technology, which evaluates carcass quality characteristics of the live animal. Key to the success of the system is the use of electronic identification that can link a specific animal back to its owner. When the cattle are sorted based on carcass quality characteristics they are commingled into mixed ownership lots. Cattle can then be sold when they reach the point at which they will maximize returns. Previously, cattle from each owner had to remain in separate lots as it was too difficult to manage the record keeping associated with mixed ownership lots. Cattle were managed based on the average finishing time of cattle within the lot rather than on an individual animal basis. In the Decatur Beef Alliance, a producer's cattle can be sold over several different periods, while the associated record management costs are reduced through the use of electronic identification tags.

Electronic identification tags can also be used in conjunction with other systems that produce credence attributes where it is necessary to implement a traceability system to ensure compliance with program requirements. Information on individual animals and the production and management processes that have been used is entered into a database, with information being tied to an animal's electronic identification tag. The multiple uses of electronic identification tags can potentially be beneficial in improving coordination and transferring information throughout the supply chain. The adoption of this technology is currently limited. This may be because cow-calf operators must incur the costs of purchasing the tags and, unless they retain ownership of calves, they do not necessarily receive any benefits or information due to the low level of coordination that currently exists between cow-calf operators and the rest of the supply chain. Consequently, the adoption of electronic identification tags by cow-calf operators has been minimal. The use of electronic identification technology has also been limited because very few feedlots and processors have implemented the scanning technologies and associated databases, which are required in order to read and use electronic identification tags. This equipment can be costly and, as a result, industry segments have been slow to implement it.

Information Management Systems

Information management systems that are used in conjunction with individual animal identification have the potential to improve the transfer of information on quality and on the production of other attributes along the supply chain. As a result, some industry players are increasingly focused on developing more efficient and comprehensive systems to gather and interpret information, and increase the availability of this information throughout the supply chain.

Within Canada's beef industry, the creation of new information management systems has occurred. Examples include those produced by ComputerAid Professional Services and Viewtrak Technologies. Both of these companies work with supply chain participants and alliances to develop customized information management platforms to gather and analyze both production and financial data. The establishment of these types of information management systems has utilized developments in technology that have allowed for long term retention of information in extensive databases. Being able to retain large volumes of data is of a significant value and facilitates more informed management decisions related to production and processing methods. Supply chain participants can use this data to create an increased understanding as to the changes that have occurred, with it enabling management decisions to be made based on more comprehensive data analysis.

The mandatory CCIA tagging program in Canada could potentially facilitate the transfer of information along the supply chain and reduce the transaction costs associated with transferring information. The transfer of information between the cow-calf sector and the rest of the supply chain is especially poor. This is because information management systems are very costly and most cow-calf operators cannot justify such an investment given the size of their operation and the value they would obtain from incurring such an investment. In order to increase coordination and improve the flow of information between cow-calf operators and other supply chain participants, the CCIA could be used as a conduit to facilitate information transfer. Instead of having multiple private corporations developing separate data management systems it may be more efficient to develop a national system from which data could be drawn from by different supply chain participants. A single system may reduce the overlapping development costs that would be incurred by private corporations that are working to achieve similar objectives.

In addition, when multiple information collection systems exist, supply chain participants incur transfer costs if they choose to move from one system to another. Consequently there are barriers to entry and exit. If cow-calf operators or other supply participants are required to enter into one system and pay to input information into that system, they are limited to transacting with those buyers within that particular supply chain. As a result, there is an increased risk of opportunistic behaviour and transaction costs will be increased in order to mitigate this risk. Whereas with a single system, participants have access to a large number of buyers, with no transfer costs being incurred to access these buyers. In this type of system, the risk of opportunistic behaviour and associated transaction costs may be reduced.

Understanding the benefits and costs associated with developing private data systems or a nationally-based data system is an area that could be further researched in order to determine the benefits and costs involved under either scenario. It is especially important to note while significant benefits appear to exist under the creation of a single system, significant challenges are also involved as a result of confidentiality and data ownership issues. Research in this area would facilitate a greater understanding of the options the industry has in increasing information flow along the supply chain to improve coordination.

CONCLUSIONS

Alliances appear to be a central component of revitalizing the North American beef industry's competitiveness. There are, however, operation characteristics that are unique to the beef industry that have a significant impact on the development of beef supply chain coordination programs. The industry has been innovative in its approaches to dealing with the special needs of beef industry participants. The integration of many cow-calf operations into quality improving branding programs and other quality enhancement programs remains a challenge. As a result, the fully transition from beef being marketed as a commodity to beef being differentiated on quality will be inhibited. Further supply chain innovations will likely be required to complete the transition.

Chapter 7

INSIGHTS FOR THE AGRI-FOOD SECTOR

KEEPING UP WITH CONSUMERS

In recent years, the beef industry has been forced to examine improving coordination along the supply chain in response to declining consumer demand for beef. Consumers are demanding more convenient, consistent, high quality, differentiated products – products the beef industry's competitors have been adept at providing. In order to regain their competitiveness, participants in the beef industry have begun to seriously examine the production of differentiated and branded beef products. This transformation has been slow to occur due, in part, to the substantial reorganization of the beef supply chain that is required to transform existing commodity production systems into more coordinated, vertically aligned supply chains.

There has been limited research on supply chain coordination within the beef industry and on how the relationship between different supply chain participants evolves with differentiated beef products. This research is critical for identifying what makes a successful supply chain alliance and understanding both the opportunities and constraints to improving coordination along the beef supply chain. An understanding of how different product attributes affect transaction costs and result in the formation of particular supply chain structures is a first step towards determining what makes a successful supply chain alliance.

In order to increase the production of differentiated beef products, improved coordination will be needed. At the same time, improving coordination will only be successful if the value received by the industry more than offsets the increase in production and transaction costs. These costs are dependent on both the types of attributes being produced and the level of consistency that is guaranteed. The optimal supply chain structure that minimizes transaction costs is influenced by the transaction characteristics that emerge when producing a specific beef product and the associated transaction costs. Additional opportunities and constraints to improving coordination in the beef industry have been identified in this book.

COW-CALF OPERATIONS AND SUPPLY CHAIN COORDINATION

If one compares the beef supply chain with the modern supply chains of its major competitors, pork and chicken, one difference stands out. The beef supply chain is still very much anchored in the land. Cow-calf operations are located so as to utilize forage resources. Forage does not come in packages that can be bundled into convenient packages that match the economies of scale that define modern meat supply chains. Due to the geographic dispersion of grazing and forage resources, many cow-calf operations will remain small and widely spread. While this dispersion was once the case in the poultry and hog industries, it is no longer the case – they were not "tied to the land" in the way cow-calf operations are. Hog and chicken production has proved much more amenable to economies of scale and the types of coordination that allow the development of differentiated and branded products. If the beef industry is to improve its competitiveness relative to pork and chicken, it will have to find inventive ways to coordinate a supply chain that incorporates cow-calf operations. Effective research is integral to the design and successful development of branded beef programs and improved supply chain coordination. The conjoint experiment and additional survey questions presented in Chapter 5 provides insights into why the participation of cow-calf operators in value chain alliances has been minimal. Closer vertical coordination, through the use of value chain alliances, can result in substantial benefits, but there are also costs involved with the production of differentiated beef products. The results in Chapter 5 indicate that transaction characteristics and the associated transaction costs limit the willingness of cow-calf operators to participate in branded beef programs.

The creation of successful programs is therefore dependent on a program's characteristics being such that the benefits to cow-calf operators are greater than the increase in transaction costs. The emphasis on premiums in the conjoint analysis and the questions regarding program fees show that, while cow-calf operators are willing to make trade-offs and accept increased costs, they are only willing to do this when benefits are greater than costs. This is readily apparent because respondents indicated a willingness to make the required investments and increase their exposure to opportunistic behaviour. Beyond a certain point, however, when large expenditures or one-time fees are required, the information and negotiation costs incurred to reduce the risk of opportunistic behaviour may well exceed the benefits received and limit participation.

It appears that cow-calf operators are most concerned with the balance between premiums received and the costs associated with the investments required to produce different beef attributes. Lower importance is placed on the number of buyers and the pricing method used. This implies that price uncertainty is less of a concern and, as a result, lower transaction costs are incurred to ensure the reputations of buyers, searching out information on grid-based systems, and negotiating agreements to secure price and market access.

Aside from premiums, other benefits were not included in the conjoint reported in Chapter 5. This was necessary to keep the conjoint experiment tractable for participants. Additional benefits that often arise as a result of increased coordination are the assurance of access into a premium market and the ability to receive information on the quality of cattle after they have been processed. Cow-calf operators were asked to explicitly rate the importance of these benefits and they were rated as high. However, this does not tell us how cow-calf operators make trade-offs between these benefits and other characteristics (i.e. expected premiums, investments, pricing method, and number of buyers). Further research examining the trade-offs made between these benefits and other program characteristics would be beneficial. It is expected that cow-calf operators would be willing to accept certain transaction characteristics with low or negative part-worth values in exchange for quality information and market access.

The relationship between pricing method and the receipt of quality information is worth emphasizing. Cow-calf operators indicated a preference for a combination live weight and carcass quality pricing system, where a base price is determined and premiums and discounts are then applied based on carcass quality. Even though using this method means that some of the risk associated with variability in cattle quality is transferred to them, it may be that they are willing to accept the increased risk of price discounts – as in exchange they typically receive quality information. If this is the case, it is an indication that cow-calf operators place a high value on the receipt of quality information and are willing to make trade-offs to receive it. At the same time the lower relative preference for a pricing system based solely on carcass quality, as opposed to a live weight pricing system, demonstrates that cow-calf operators are limited in their willingness to make trade-offs. Namely, the value of carcass quality information is offset by the greater transfer of risk that occurs under a pricing system that is based solely on carcass quality. Cow-calf operators, on average, do not appear to be willing to make this trade-off and would prefer a live weight system where no carcass quality information is received.

The research reported in Chapter 5 also identified differences in the relative importance of transaction characteristics based on specific socio-economic factors including herd size, participation in an alliance, sources of farm income, and age. Differences between operations and production characteristics were shown to influence the relative importance of the transaction characteristics. Understanding the differences between cow-calf operations needs to be considered when branded beef and value chain alliance programs are developed. The pork and poultry industries have to a considerable degree been able to apply a "one size fits all" model when developing their modern supply chains – they either selected or fostered only those operations that fit their requirements. "One size fits all" will not work in the beef industry.

INSIGHTS FROM EXISTING SUPPLY CHAIN ALLIANCES

To evaluate the importance of different transaction characteristics from the perspective of alliances, interviews were conducted with key managers and directors of different alliances throughout North America. Several insights emerge. First, asset specific investments have typically been limited to compliance with specific feed and health protocols and the implementation of record/certification systems. As a result, the risk of opportunistic behaviour appears to be minimal and the transaction costs to reduce opportunistic behaviour associated with asset specificity are small. Consequently, the degree of coordination is not affected to, any great degree, by the level of investments required.

Instead, the degree of coordination appears to be a result of how an alliance is aligned with a particular brand name label. Those alliances that own a brand name label or have an exclusive relationship with a retailer-owned brand name label face an increased risk that sellers will act opportunistically given the fixed nature of their supply and the ongoing need to fulfill downstream obligations. In order to minimize the transaction costs incurred to reduce the risk of opportunistic behaviour, alliances often chose a formal structure, which uses contracts and/or membership fees, to ensure a greater level of commitment from participants and to reduce their incentive to act opportunistically. Whereas, when an alliance is aligned with a specific processor and sells into multiple programs owned by a processor, there is greater flexibility in terms of the quantity of cattle that alliances are required to provide on an ongoing basis. Since processors are able to procure supply through other marketing arrangements, the volumes provided by an alliance can vary and, as a result, there is a lower risk of opportunistic behaviour by suppliers. Consequently, transaction costs will be lower and the degree of coordination necessary to minimize costs is also lower, with more informal alliance structures emerging.

Alliances have readily adopted the use of grid-based pricing systems in order to reduce the degree to which incomplete information is available on quality and to realign incentives. Participants receive more transparent signals regarding the quality of products. These systems reduce information costs from searching out quality information and, as a result, reduce the degree of coordination required. It is also feasible for grid-based pricing systems to reduce monitoring costs. Alliances have implemented grid-based pricing systems with more detailed specifications that result in higher premiums and discounts being paid based on carcass quality. When detailed program requirements are implemented in an alliance to ensure a more consistent level of quality, participants must be monitored in order to ensure that they comply as there is an incentive to cheat. Less monitoring is required when price is directly tied to the quality of production through a more detailed grid. Participants have a clear incentive to ensure a more consistent level of quality, to avoid being discounted under a more accurate grid.

The numbers of buyers and sellers did not seem to have a substantial impact on the degree of coordination chosen by alliances. This mirrors the results from the cow-calf operator survey, where the relative importance of the number of buyers was low compared to other transaction characteristics. In large part, this appears to be a result of the reciprocal nature of the relationship between buyers and sellers along the supply chain. Sellers with specialized products need to be guaranteed access into the markets that sell these products. Buyers also need a constant supply of specialized products, which cannot be easily procured through the spot market, in order fulfill their downstream obligations. Consequently, the risk of opportunistic behaviour by either buyers or sellers is expected to be minimal and does not have a large impact on the degree of coordination.

The relatively low concern over the number of buyers, even when the number of buyers is limited, is apparent in that most of the alliances did not have formal contracts or arrangements to secure the commitment of buyers. Alliances rely on the fact that buyers receive benefits from obtaining an ongoing and consistent supply of product and have an incentive to maintain positive relationships with their suppliers.

FUTURE DEVELOPMENTS IN NORTH AMERICAN BEEF SUPPLY CHAINS

Improved coordination between supply chain participants facilitates the development of differentiated products that are more consistent and of a higher quality. Several critical success factors and challenges to the successful development of branded beef alliances are apparent.

Critical Success Factors

The production of specific beef attributes can result in an increase in both production costs and transaction costs throughout the supply chain. While consumers are often willing to pay premiums for differentiated branded beef products, there is a limit to the level of premiums they are willing to accept. As a result, the premiums available throughout the supply chain do not always offset the increase in production and transaction costs. This problem may be a result of short term market fluctuations. In this situation, the long term commitment of supply chain participants is necessary in order to ensure the ongoing success of an alliance. It is also important to note that aside from weighing costs against the premiums received, the value of other benefits needs to be considered. Access to markets and the ability to obtain increased information are significant benefits of alliances and need to be considered when determining the net gain received from participating in a program.

In certain situations, it may be difficult to overcome periods where production and transaction costs exceed the benefits received by different supply chain participants. The results from the cow-calf operator survey reported in Chapter 5 clearly show that when programs are developed to improve coordination and to produce different beef attributes, the importance of different transaction characteristics needs to be kept in mind. While cow-calf operators can have a significant impact on the production of different attributes, coordination between this sector and the rest of the supply chain has been limited. To improve coordination between cow-calf operators and other supply chain participants, programs need to work with all supply chain participants and consider the trade-offs they make between different transaction characteristics and the benefits received.

Improved information flows are also important to the success of coordination initiatives and the production of differentiated branded beef products. Cooperation and flexibility within a program is necessary to facilitate the transfer of information both upstream and downstream along the supply chain. The industry needs to continue to work on transferring information along the entire supply chain, especially to feedlots and cow-calf operators. Up to this point, the transfer of quality information and accurate price signals to cow-calf operators has been limited. Key to the increased transfer of such information is the development of different methods that enhance the flow of information, while minimizing the associated transaction costs. These methods include the continued advancement of grid-based pricing systems to provide more transparent price signals to cow-calf operators and feedlots. Further, integrated information management systems are important. This technology has the potential to reduce information costs while substantially improving the flow of detailed information throughout the supply chain.

Critical to improving the flow of information, while minimizing the association transaction costs, is how alliances are linked to processors and retailers. All of the alliances examined were linked to specific processors and in some cases they were linked directly to the retail sector. While the success of alliances did not seem dependent on direct alignment with the retail sector, alignment with a processor, or processors, was considered to be essential to the success of an alliance. Processors appear to be the main interface between end-users and the production sectors and key to the transfer of information between end-users and the rest of the supply chain. They facilitate the production of their own branded and commodity beef products and also custom process for brand name labels owned by retailers.

With some products the cooperation of processors is crucial to ensure the traceability of animals and products is maintained and that other guarantees provided under a brand name are fulfilled. Alignment with a specific processor that is willing to fulfill traceability requirements and any other program requirements is usually necessary. Otherwise, the monitoring costs that would have to be incurred by other supply chain participants to ensure traceability and/or other program requirements would likely be prohibitive.

Critical Challenges

Although alignment with a processor is usually necessary to the success of an alliance, the high concentration of the processing and retailer sectors limits the number of alliances that can be expected to develop and be sustainable. This is partly a result of the large volumes of cattle required to fulfill the requirements of processor or retailer-owned brand name labels. Coordination to ensure adequate supplies becomes quite costly, with high negotiation and search costs being incurred. This is because the low concentration in the cow-calf sector requires transactions with a large number of cow-calf operators to ensure sufficient volumes of cattle to fulfill program requirements.

Coordination with processor and retailer-owned brand name labels is also expected to be limited in the future. Once processors and retailers have developed a few brand name labels and aligned themselves with a couple of alliances they may not need to form additional alliances or develop additional brand name products. This reduces the transaction costs associated with organizing multiple production runs when production has to be segregated, multiple grid-based pricing systems have to be managed, and multiple sets of negotiations must occur.

The structure of alliances will be further impacted by how they are aligned with a brand name label. When an alliance owns a brand name label or is the exclusive supplier into a retailer-owned brand name label, marketing and transaction costs are expected to be higher throughout the supply chain. This is a result of the increased costs incurred to ensure adequate supplies and the commitment of alliance participants. Due to the higher costs incurred when an alliance owns a brand name label or is the exclusive supplier into a retailer-owned label, it appears that some alliances have opted to operate under a different structure.

In particular, there has been an increased emergence of more informal alliances that align themselves with a specific processor and market product through multiple processor-owned branded and commodity beef programs. This type of relationship also overcomes the limited willingness of processors to work with several different alliance-based programs. When alliances are aligned with a specific processor, multiple alliances can be established that supply product into processor-owned programs using similar agreements, pricing arrangements, and program requirements. This limits the number of brand name labels and the production and transaction costs involved with having many different exclusive arrangements. At the same time, it allows for a greater number of alliances to be aligned with a processor. This may enable alliances to supply smaller volumes, reducing the transaction costs associated with ensuring adequate supplies.

The structure of cow-calf operations also presents a challenge to the development of alliances and improved coordination within the industry. Cow-calf operators often run mixed farming operations and, as a result, the opportunity costs of reallocating human and capital resources from other enterprises into cow-calf production may be high. This may limit the willingness of cow-calf operators to participate in alliances. The participation of cow-calf operators is necessary in the production of many different attributes and, as a result, the opportunity costs incurred by cow-calf operators could be an important limitation to program development.

Opportunities

Even though challenges exist to improving coordination in the beef industry, several opportunities exist to lower transaction costs and facilitate improved coordination. For example, cow-calf producers have been encouraged to retain ownership of their calves throughout production. This may allow increased transparency and reduces information and negotiation costs. Alliances have provided financing incentives for retained ownership and often facilitate feedlots sharing ownership of calves to reduce the effects on the timing of cash flow.

Industry infrastructure also aids in lowering transaction costs. Certification institutions implement standardized procedures in order to reduce the monitoring costs of producing credence attributes. Quality assurance programs are similar in that they implement standardized procedures to increase the quality and consistency of products, with the key attribute being tenderness. The creation of certification institutions for credence attributes and quality assurance programs facilitates coordination, while minimizing the associated transaction costs.

The mandatory individual animal identification program in Canada is another institution that was implemented to trace cattle, but is being looked at carefully as a method to tie individual animal identification with information systems that could transfer detailed production and quality information throughout the supply chain. The further development and use of other technologies, such as comprehensive information management systems, electronic identification, and computer vision scanning (CVS), could also facilitate the reduction of information and monitoring costs while improving coordination within the beef industry.

The beef industry plays a significant role in North American agriculture. However, increasing value in the industry is partially dependent on the production of differentiated beef products that better respond to consumer demands and increases the value received by industry participants. The industry must improve coordination to increase the transfer of information regarding consumers' demands and product quality along the supply chain. In improving coordination, the importance of different transaction characteristics to supply chain participants is critical. It is also important to understand the trade-offs supply chain participants are willing to make between the benefits received from improved coordination and transaction costs arising when producing different beef attributes. The trade-offs will have a substantial impact on the optimal method of coordination for branded beef products. This book has taken a first step towards understanding the importance of different transaction characteristics and how they impact supply chain coordination in the beef industry.

THE NORTH AMERICAN BEEF INDUSTRY AND THE AGRI-FOOD SECTOR

The North American beef industry is on the move. After decades of focusing on improving the competitiveness of their commodity but losing market share to more consumer-savvy competitors, differentiated and branded beef products have become the focus of the industry. New supply chain arrangements are emerging that can facilitate the transition of the beef industry from a commodity business into one that is responsive to the multi-faceted desires of consumers that expect products that cater to their specific tastes. While devising supply chain arrangements that can encompass the diversity of cow-calf operations remains a major challenge, the combination of innovative coordination mechanisms and new technologies is showing considerable promise.

Differentiated and branded beef products will provide fierce competition for beef's competition. There is little doubt that beef is still the preferred meat of North American consumers. They have more often chosen poultry or pork in recent years because beef did not have some of the attributes they wanted, particularly convenience and consistency. As the beef industry is able to provide a range of new attributes through the re-orientation of its supply chains, consumers can be expected to return to beef. They will pay a premium for beef with the new attributes. The agri-food sector needs to anticipate this change and think about providing complementary products that will augment the consumers' re-discovery of beef.

The North American beef industry also needs to work as a continental unit. Borders should no longer matter. The North American market is integrated. The border closures associated with the discovery of BSE showed just how disruptive borders can be. Broken supply chains impose costs on all members of the beef industry. While effective disease management is a priority, protectionism should have no place in decisions. The focus of North American beef producers should be on making their supply chains models of efficiency and responsiveness. That is the key to competitiveness in the meat industry and prosperity in the beef industry across North America.

REFERENCES

Agri-Food Trade Service Fact Sheets. (2003) *Trade Statistics*. Agriculture and Agri-Food Canada, www.ats-sea.agr.ca.

Alberta Agriculture, Food and Rural Development. (2001) *A Review of the Competitive Position of Alberta's Primary Beef Production Sector*. Edmonton: Government of Alberta.

Allan, J. (2002). Retail's View. *Beef*, February 15, http://www.beef-mag.com.

Anderson, J.L., and Bettencourt, S.U. (1993). A Conjoint Approach to Model Product Preferences: The New England Market for Fresh and Frozen Salmon. *Marine Resource Economics*, 8, pp. 31-49.

Anton, T.E. (2002). *Not All Beef Marketing Are the Same: A Review of Alliance Types*. FE-362 Cooperative Extension Service. Institute of Food and Agricultural Sciences, Gainesville: University of Florida.

Atkins, F.J., Kerr, W.A., and McGivern, D.B. (1989). A Note on Structural Change in Canadian Beef Demand, *Canadian Journal of Agricultural Economics*, 37 (3), pp. 513-524.

Barichello, R. (2007). Administrative Procedures, the Distribution of Costs and Benefits, and Incentives in Anti-dumping Cases. In W.A. Kerr and J.D. Gaisford, *Handbook on International Trade Policy*. (pp. 360-367). Cheltenham: Edward Elgar.

Barkema, A.D. (1994). The Changing Structure of the U.S. Food System. *Canadian Journal of Agricultural Economics*, 42, pp. 541-547.

Barkema, A.D. and Drabenstott, M. (1990) A Crossroads for the Cattle Industry. *Economic Review - Federal Reserve Bank of Kansas City*, 75 (6), pp. 47-66.

Barkema, A.D., Drabenstott, M., and Novack, N. (2001). The New U.S. Meat Industry. *Economic Review - Federal Reserve Bank of Kansas City*, Second Quarter 2001., pp. 33-56

Bastian, C. (2001). *The New Beef Industry: What Will it Mean to Feeder Cattle Producers?* Laramie, University of Wyoming.

Beef Trade Website. (2003). *Beef Grades*. Calgary: Beef Information Centre, www.beefinfo.org

Beshear, M., and Lamb, R. (1998). From the Plains to the Plate: Can the Beef Industry Regain Market Share? *Economic Review. Federal Reserve Bank of Kansas City*, 83 (4), pp. 49-66.

Bliss, T.J., and Ward, C.E. (1992). *Assessing Group Marketing Alternatives for Livestock*. F-525, OSU Extension Facts, Oklahoma Cooperative Extension Service, Stillwater:Oklahoma State University.

Boehlje, M.D., Hofing, S.L., and Schroeder, T.C. (1999). *Value Chains in Agricultural Industries.* Staff Paper 99-10, Department of Agricultural Economics, West Lafayette, Purdue University.

Boland, M., and Katz, J.P. (2000). A New Value-Added Strategy for the US Beef Industry: the Case of US Premium Beef Ltd. *Supply Chain Management,* 5 (2), pp. 99-109.

Brester, G. W. (2002). Meeting Consumer Demands with Genetics and Market Coordination: The Case of the Leachman Cattle Company. *Review of Agricultural Economics,* 24 (1), pp. 251-265.

Brester, G.W., Mintert, J., and Schroeder, T.C. (1995). *Positioning the Beef Industry for the Future.* MF – 2123, Department of Agricultural Economics, Manhattan: Kansas State University.

Brewin, D., and Ulrich, A. (1999). *Consistency and Quality: Some Lessons from Saskatchewan's Beef Supply Chain.* Saskatchewan Agriculture Development Fund, Saskatoon: University of Saskatchewan.

Bruce, C.J., and Kerr, W.A. (1986). A Proposed Arbitration Mechanism to Ensure Free Trade in Livestock Products. *Canadian Journal of Agricultural Economics,* 34 (3), 347-360.

Butler, J. (2003). President and CEO of Ranchers Renaissance, personal communication, March 17.

Canfax Research Services. (2003). *Alberta Packing Plant Procurement Summary.* Canadian Cattlemen's Association, Calgary, www.cattle.ca/canfax/

Canfax Research Services. (2002). *Canfax Annual Report.* Canadian Cattlemen's Association, Calgary, www.cattle.ca/canfax/

Canfax Research Services. (2001). *Canfax Statistical Briefer.* Canadian Cattlemen's Association. Calgary, www.cattle.ca/canfax/

Caswell, J.H., and Mojduszka, E.M. (1996) Using Informational Labeling to Influence the Market for Quality in Food Products. *American Journal of Agricultural Economics,* 78, pp. 1248-1253.

Certified Angus Beef Website, www.certifiedangusbeef.com

Coase, R.H. (1937). The Nature of the Firm. *Economica,* n.s. 4 (16), pp. 386-405.

Considine, J.I., Kerr, W.A., Smith, G.R., and Ulmer, S.M. (1986). The Impact of a New Grading System on the Beef Cattle Industry: The Case of Canada. *Western Journal of Agricultural Economics,* 11 (2), 184-194.

Decatur Beef Alliance Fact Sheet (2003). Decatur County Feed Yard, Oberlin, Kansas, USA.

Den Ouden, M., Dijkhuizen, A.A., Huirne, R.B.M., and Zuurbier, P.J.P. (1996). Vertical Cooperation in Agricultural Production-Marketing Chains, with Special Reference to Product Differentiation in Pork. *Agribusiness,* 12 (3), pp. 277-290.

Frank, D., and Henderson, D.R. (1992). Transaction Costs as Determinants of Vertical Coordination in the U.S. Food Industries. *American Journal of Agricultural Economics,* 74 (4), pp. 941-950.

Fuez, D.M., and Umberger, W.J. (2001). *Consumers Willingness to Pay for Flavour in Beef Steaks: An Experimental Economics Approach.* Cornhusker Economics, Institute of Agriculture and Natural Resources, Department of Agricultural Economics, Lincoln: University of Nebraska.

Gillis, K.G., White, C.D., Ulmer, S.M., Kerr, W.A., and Kwaczek, A.S. (1985). The Prospects for Export of Primal Beef Cuts to California. *Canadian Journal of Agricultural Economics,* 33 (2), 171-194.

Green, P.E., and Rao, V.R. (1971). Conjoint Measurement for Quantifying Judgmental Data. *Journal of Marketing Research*, 8, pp. 355-363.

Green, P.E., and Srinivasan, V. (1978). Conjoint Analysis in Consumer Research: Issues and Outlook. *The Journal of Consumer Research: An Interdisciplinary Quarterly*, 5 (2), pp. 103-123.

Green, P.E., and Wind, Y. (1973). *Multiattribute Decisions in Marketing: A Measurement Approach*. Hinsdale: The Dryden Press.

Hair, J.E., Anderson, R.E., Tatham, R.L., and Black, W.C. (1992). *Multivariate Data Analysis with Readings*, 3rd Edition. New York, USA : Macmillan Publishing Company.

Halbrendt, C.J., Bacon, R., and Pesek, J. (1992). Weighted Least Squares Analysis for Conjoint Studies: The Case of Hybrid Striped Bass. *Agribusiness*, 8 (2), pp. 187-198.

Hammack, S.P. (1998) *Cattle Types and Breeds Characteristics and Uses*. L-5206, Texas Adapted Genetic Strategies, Texas Agricultural Extension Service.

Hayenga, M., Hayes, D., Lawrence, J., Purcell, W., Schroeder, T., Vukina, T., and Ward, C. (2000). *Meat Packer Vertical Integration and Contract Linkages in the Beef and Pork Industries: An Economic Perspective*. Washington, USA : American Meat Institute.

Hayenga, M., Schroeder, T., and Lawrence, J. (2002). Churning Out the Links: Vertical Integration in the Beef and Pork Industries. *Choices: The Magazine of Food, Farm and Resource Issues*, Winter, pp. 19-23.

Hayes, D., and Kerr, W.A. (1997). Progress Toward a Single Market: The New Institutional Economics of the NAFTA Livestock Sectors. In R.M.A. Loynes, R.D. Knutson, K. Meilke, and D. Sumner (Eds.), *Harmonization/Convergence/Compatibility in Agriculture and Agrifood Policy: Canada, United States and Mexico*. (pp. 1-21). Winnipeg: University of Manitoba, Texas A and M University, University of Guelph, University of California, Davis.

Hayes, D.J., Lence, S.H., and Stoppa, A. (2003). *Farmer-Owned Brands?* Center for Agricultural and Rural Development, Ames: Iowa State University.

Hill, R.C., Griffiths, W.E., and Judge, G.G. (2001). *Undergraduate Econometrics*. Second Edition. New York, USA: John Wiley and Sons, Inc.

Hobbs, J.E. (1996a). A Transaction Cost Approach to Supply Chain Management. *Supply Chain Management*, 1 (2), 15-27.

Hobbs, J.E. (1996b). A Transaction Cost Analysis of Quality Traceability and Animal Welfare Issues in UK Beef Retailing. *British Food Journal*, 98 (6), pp. 16-26.

Hobbs, J.E. (1996c). Transaction Costs and Slaughter Cattle Procurement: Processors' Selection of Supply Channels. *Agribusiness*, 12 (6), pp. 509-523.

Hobbs, J.E. (1998). Innovation and Future Direction of Supply Chain Management in the Canadian Agri-Food Industry. *Canadian Journal of Agricultural Economics*, 46, pp. 525-537.

Hobbs, J.E., and Kerr, W.A. (1999). Transaction Costs. In S. Bhagwan Dahiya (ed.), *The Current State of Economic Science*. Vol. 4, (pp. 2111-2133) Rohtak: Spellbound Publications PVT Ltd.

Hobbs, J.E., and Kerr, W.A. (1998). Structural Developments in the Canadian Livestock Subsector: Strategic Positioning within the Continental Market. In R.M.A. Loynes, R.D. Knutson and K. Meilke (Eds.), *Economic Harmonization in the Canadian/US/Mexican Grain-Livestock Subsector*. (pp. 125-143). Guelph: University of Guelph.

Hobbs, J.E., and Kerr, W.A. (1994). Responding to Japan's Deregulation of Beef Imports: A Multifaceted Challenge for Canadian Export Managers. *Asia Pacific Journal of Management*, 11 (1), 47-65.

Hobbs, J.E., Kerr, W.A., and Klein, K.K. (1996). Coordination and Competitiveness of Supply Chains: Implications for the Western Canadian Livestock Industries. *Canadian Journal of Agricultural Economics*, 44, pp. 403-408.

Hobbs, J.E, Kerr, W.A., and Klein, K.K. (1998). Creating International Competitiveness Through Supply Chain Management: Danish Pork, *Supply Chain Management*, 3 (2), pp. 68-78.

Hudson, W.T., and Purcell, W.D. (2003). Risk Sharing and Compensation Guides for Managers and Members of Vertical Beef Alliances. *Review of Agricultural* Economics, 25 (1), pp. 44-65.

International Beef Industry Congress. (2003). *International Beef Industry Congress Proceedings*. Calgary, July.

International Livestock Congress. (2002). 2002 Beef Section: Surviving and Thriving in the Next Decade. *2002 International Livestock Congress Proceedings*. Houston, February.

International Livestock Congress. (2000). 2000 Beef Section: Global Beef Best Demand Initiatives. *2002 International Livestock Congress Proceedings*. Houston, February.

Isaac, G.E., Perdikis, N., and Kerr, W.A. (2004). Cracking Export Markets with Genetically Modified Crops – What is the Entry Mode Strategy? *International Marketing Review*, 21 (4/5), 536-548.

Ishmeal, W. (2002). Why Future Beef Went Under. *Beef*, November 1, http://www.beef-mag.com.

Kerr, W.A. (1982). The Supply of New Germ Plasm to the Canadian Beef Cattle Industry. *Technological Forecasting and Social Change*, 21, 103-132.

Kerr, W.A. (1984). Selective Breeding, Heritable Characteristics and Genetic-Based Technological Change in the Canadian Beef Cattle Industry. *Western Journal of Agricultural Economics*, 9 (1), 14-28.

Kerr, W.A. (1985). The Changing Economics of the Western Livestock Industry. *Canadian Public Policy*, 11, 294-300.

Kerr, W.A. (1988). The Canada-United States Free Trade Agreement and the Livestock Sector: The Second Stage Negotiations. *Canadian Journal of Agricultural Economics*, 36 (4), 895-903.

Kerr, W.A. (1991). Technological Transfer Through Pure-Bred Herds in British Columbia. *Agricultural History*, 65 (1), 72-100.

Kerr, W.A. (2006a). Dumping: Trade Policy in Need of a Theoretical Make Over, *Canadian Journal of Agricultural Economics*, 54 (1), 11-31.

Kerr, W.A. (2006b). NAFTA's Underdeveloped Institutions: Did They Contribute to the BSE Crisis? In K.M. Huff, K.D. Meilke, R.D. Knutson, R.F. Ochoa and J. Rude (Eds.), *Agrifood Regulatory and Policy Integration Under Stress*, (pp. 213-226). Guelph: Texas A and M University/University of Guelph/Intituto Interamericano de Cooperacion para la Agricultural-Mexico.

Kerr, W.A., and Correll, R.J. (1993). *The International Competitiveness of the Prairie Livestock and Red Meat Sector*. Winnipeg: Manitoba Red Meat Forum.

Kerr, W.A., and Cullen, S.E. (1985). Canada-U.S. Free Trade - Implications for the Western Canadian Livestock Industry. *Western Economic Review*, 4 (3), 24-36.

Kerr, W.A., Cullen, S.E., and Sommerville, M.S. (1986). *Trade Barriers and the Western Canadian Livestock Industry*. Working Paper 11/86, Marketing and Economics Branch, Ottawa: Agriculture Canada.

Kerr, W.A., and Hall, S.L. (2003). Mandatory Country-of-Origin Labeling (MCOOL), Its Economic and Trade Policy Implications, Proceedings of a conference entitled WTO: Competing Policy Issues and Agendas for Agricultural Trade sponsored by the Farm Foundation and USDA Economic Research Service, Washington, D.C., Sept. 17, www.farmfoundation.org/projects/documents/KerrPaper.pdf.

Kerr, W.A., and Hobbs, J.E. (1992). U.S. Beef Exports to Western Canada: Exploiting Opportunities for Intra-Industry Trade. *Journal of Agribusiness*, 10 (1), 29-40.

Kerr, W.A., Klein, K.K., Hobbs, J.E., and Kagatsume, M. (1994). *Marketing Beef in Japan*. New York: Haworth Press.

Kerr, W.A., Loppacher, L.J., and Hobbs, J.E. (2007). International Standards for Regulating Trade When BSE is Present: Why are They Being Ignored? *Current Agriculture, Food and Resource Issues*, 8, 1-15.

Kerr, W.A., and Ulmer, S.M. (1984). *The Importance of the Livestock and Meat Processing Industries to Western Growth*. Discussion Paper No. 255, Ottawa: Economic Council of Canada.

Kinsey, J., and Senauer, B. (1996). Consumer Trends and Changing Food Retailing Formats. *American Journal of Agricultural Economics*, 78 (5), pp. 1187-1192.

Kovanda, J. and Schroeder, T.C. (2003) Beef Alliances: Motivations, Extent, and Future Prospects. in S. Koontz (ed.) *Economics of Red Meat and Dairy Industries*. TheVeterinary Clinics of North America, (pp. 397-417) Philadelphia: W B Saunders Co.

Kroes, E.P. and Sheldon, R.J. (1988) Stated Preference Methods. *Journal of Transport Economics and Policy*, 22 (1), pp. 11-25.

Kubas, L., and Simmons, A. (2000). Looking Ahead. *Canadian Retailer*. November/December, http://www.retailcouncil.org/media/cdnretailer/

Lamp, G. (1998). 50% Branded by 2005. *Beef*, May 1, http://www.beef-mag.com

Lancaster, K. (1971). Consumer Demand A New Approach. New York: Columbia University Press.

Lawrence, J.D., Schroeder, T.C., and Hayenga, M.L. (2001). Evolving Producer-Packer-Customer Linkages in the Beef and Pork Industries. *Review of Agricultural Economics*, 23 (2) pp. 370-385.

Loppacher, L.J., and Kerr, W.A. (2005). The Efficacy of World Trade Organization Rules on Sanitary Barriers: Bovine Spongiform Encephalopathy in North America, *Journal of World Trade*, 39 (3), 427-443.

Louviere, J.J. (1988). Conjoint Analysis Modelling of Stated Preferences. *Journal of Transport Economics and Policy*. 22 (1), pp. 93-119.

Lusk, J. (2001). Branded Beef Is It "What's for Dinner?" *Choices: The Magazine of Food, Farm and Resource Issues*, 16 (2), p. 27

Lusk, J., Fox, J., Schroeder, T., Mintert, J., and Koohmaraie, M. (1999). *Will Consumers Pay for Guaranteed Tender Steak?* Research Bulletin. Research Institute on Livestock Pricing. Agricultural and Applied Economics, Blacksburg: Virginia Technical University.

Marsh, T.L., Mintert, J., and Schroeder, T.C. (2000). Beef Demand Determinants: A Research Summary. *Beef Marketing*. MF-2457, Department of Agricultural Economics, Manhattan: Kansas State University.

Martinez, S.W., Smith, K.E., and Zering, K.D. (1998). Analysis of Changing Methods of Vertical Coordination in the Pork Industry. *Journal of Agricultural and Applied Economics*, 30 (2), pp. 301-311.

McCullough, J., and Best, R. (1979). Conjoint Measurement: Temporal Stability and Structural Reliability. *Journal of Marketing Research*, 16, pp. 26-31.

Meeting the Market: Growth through Strategic Alliances. (2002). *Agriculture and Food Council Conference Proceedings*. Red Deer, November.

Moodley, R.D., Kerr, W.A., and Gordon, D.V. (2000). Has the Canada-US Trade Agreement Fostered Price Integration? *Weltwirtschaftliches Archiv*, 136 (2), 334-354.

Ness, M.R., and Gerhardy, H. (1994). Consumer Preferences for Quality and Freshness Attributes of Eggs. *British Food Journal*, 96(3), pp. 26-36.

Oxley, J.E. (1997). Appropriability Hazards and Governance in Strategic Alliances: A Transaction Cost Approach. *Journal of Law, Economics, and Organization*, 13 (2), pp. 387-409.

Patterson, P.M., Burkink, T.J., Lipsey, R.S., Lipsey, J., Roth, R.W., and Martin, M.K. (2003). Targeting Tourists with State Branding Programs. *Agribusiness*, 19 (4), pp. 525-538.

Pearcy, B. (2000). *Rancher's Renaissance*. Report 9-900-008, Boston: Harvard Business School Publishing.

Peterson, H.C., and Phillips, J.C. (2001). *Segmentation and Differentiation of Agri-Food Niche Markets: Examples from the Literature*. Staff Paper 2001-05, Department of Agricultural Economics, East Lansing: Michigan State University.

Peterson, H.C., and Wysocki, A. (1998). *Strategic Choice Along The Vertical Coordination Continuum*. Staff Paper 98-16, Department of Agricultural Economics, East Lancing, Michigan State University.

Prentice, B.E., and Benel, D. (1992). Determinants of Empty Returns by U.S. Refrigerated Trucks: Conjoint Analysis Approach. *Canadian Journal of Agricultural Economics*, 40 (1), pp. 109-127.

Purcell, W.D. (1993). *Consumers' Buying Behavior for Beef: Implications of Price and Product* Attributes. Research Bulletin, Research Institute on Livestock Pricing, Agricultural and Applied Economics, Blacksburg: Virginia Technical University.

Purcell, W.D. (2000). *Measures of Changes in Demand for Beef, Pork, and Chicken, 1975-2000*. Research Institute on Livestock Pricing, Department of Agricultural and Applied Economics, Blacksburg: Virginia Technical University.

Purcell, W.D. (2002). *Demand for Meats: Past, Present, and a Look Ahead*. Research Institute on Livestock Pricing, Department of Agricultural and Applied Economics, Blacksburg: Virginia Technical University.

Ranchers Renaissance Website, www.ranchersrenaissance.com.

Roybal, J. (2001). The Dawn of Future Beef. *Beef*, August, p. 16.

Sanderson, P.K. (2001). *Consumer Preferences: The Bison Meat Industry*. Unpublished MSc. Thesis, Department of Agricultural Economics, Saskatoon: University of Saskatchewan.

Schroeder, T., Lawrence, J., Ward, C.E., and Fuez, D.M. (2002). *Fed Cattle Marketing Trends and Concerns: Cattle Feeder Survey Results*. MF-2561 Agricultural Experiment Station and Cooperative Extension Service, Manhattan: Kansas State University.

Shelanski, H.A., and Klein, P.G. (1995). Empirical Research in Transaction Cost Economics: A Review and Assessment. *The Journal of Law, Economics, and Organization*, 11 (2), pp. 335-361.

Sporleder, T.L. (1994). Assessing Vertical Strategic Alliances by Agribusiness. *Canadian Journal of Agricultural Economics*, 42, pp. 533-540.

SPSS Inc. (1997). *SPSS Conjoint 8.0.*, Chicago: SPSS Inc.

Smith, R. (2000). Beef Cattle Producers Urged to Align to Deliver Guarantees Consumers Want. *Feedstuffs*, 72 (52), p. 8.

Statistics Canada Website. www.statcan.ca

Steenkamp, J.-B.E.M. (1987). Conjoint Measurement in Ham Quality Evaluation. *Journal of Agricultural Economics*, 38, pp. 473-480

Stevens, T.H., White, S., Kittredge, D.B., and Dennis, D. (2002). Factors Affecting NIPF Landowner Participation in Management Programs: A Massachusetts Case Study. *Journal of Forest Economics*, 8 (3), pp.169-184.

Sy, H.A., Faminow, M.D., Johnson, G.V., and Crow, G. (1997). Estimating the Values of Cattle Characteristics Using an Ordered Probit Model. *American Journal of Agricultural Economics*, 97(2), pp. 463-476.

Unterschultz, J. (2000). *New Instruments for Coordination and Risk Sharing Within the Canadian Beef Industry*. Project Report 00-04, Department of Rural Economy, Edmonton: University of Alberta, Edmonton, Canada.

Ward, C.E. (2001a). *Beef Industry Alliances and Vertical Arrangements*. WF-563, OSU Extension Facts, Oklahoma Cooperative Extension Service, Stillwater: Oklahoma State University.

Ward, C.E. (2001b). *Vertical Integration Comparison: Beef, Pork, and Poultry*. WF-552, OSU Extension Facts, Oklahoma Cooperative Extension Service, Stillwater: Oklahoma State University.

Weibert, W. (2004). Decatur Beef Alliance, personal interview, February 10.

Williamson, O.E. (1971). The Vertical Integration of Production: Market Failure Considerations. *American Economic Review*, 61 (2), pp. 112-123.

Williamson, O.E. (1986a). Chapter Seven. Transaction Cost Economics: The Governance of Contractual Relations. *Economic Organization: Firms, Markets, and Policy Control*. pp. 101-130, Brighton, USA: Wheatsheaf Books.

Williamson, O.E. (1986b). Chapter Nine – What is Transaction Cost Economics? *Economic Organization: Firms, Markets, and Policy Control*. pp. 174-191, Brighton, USA: Wheatsheaf Books.

APPENDIX A
COW-CALF OPERATOR SURVEY

The following questions are about branded beef programs. You do not need to have participated in a program to complete the survey. We are interested in your opinions about different types of programs. You will not be identified in the survey.

Section A

Please circle an answer for each of the following questions, from 1-5, where #1 is not important and #5 is very important to you as a producer. (Circle the number)

1. How important is it to you to secure a buyer for your calves a considerable time before you plan to sell them?

    Not important ....Very important
        1   2   3   4   5

2. How important is it to you that you receive a premium price for your calves?

    Not important ....Very important
        1   2   3   4   5

3. How important is it to you that you are able to lock in a price for your calves early on?

    Not important ....Very important
        1   2   3   4   5

4. How important is it to you that you are able to obtain detailed data about the carcass quality of the calves that you produce?

    Not important ....Very important
        1   2   3   4   5

Please circle an answer for each of the following questions, from 1-5, where #1 is not very good and #5 is very good. (Circle the number)

5. How good do you think a branded beef alliance would be in improving market access and securing a buyer for your calves?

   Not very good ....Very good
       1   2   3   4   5

6. How good do you think a branded beef alliance would be in securing you a premium price for your calves?

   Not very good ....Very good
       1   2   3   4   5

7. Do you think branded beef alliances would be a good method for you to obtain information regarding the carcass quality of your calves?

   Not very good ....Very good
       1   2   3   4   5

8. Do you think branded beef alliances are a good method for you to lock in certain price for your calves?

   Not very good ....Very good
       1   2   3   4   5

Section B

We are now going to show you some descriptions, or "profiles of different branded beef programs. Each description combines different features of a branded program. Remember that it is not necessary for you to have been involved in a program to answer these questions.

Please Continue to the Next Page

PROGRAM FEATURES

The following exercise will describe 4 features of branded beef programs. Please read through them carefully. If you have any questions, just ask. Once you have read through these features you can proceed to the exercise on the next page.

1. **Investment:** An Investment that you would need to make in order to join a branded beef program.
   a. No additional investments are required
   b. Adoption of a specific Feed and Health Protocol
      (Requires that you purchase specific inputs and invest time in the maintenance of records in order to prove compliance with a program's standards)
   c. Capital Expenditures for Farm Improvement:
      (Requires that you invest capital into your current operation, for example, in order to improve the corral system currently used, pen size, the water drainage system, or other capital improvements)
   d. Record/Certification System
      (Requires that you invest time and increase your knowledge/management skills in order to implement a new record keeping system that allows for third party verification and the certification of your production)

2. **Pricing Method:** How price will be determined when your calves are sold to backgrounding/finishing feedlots.
   a. Carcass Quality
      (Price for calves is determined based on the quality of the carcass upon processing)
   b. Live Weight
      (Price for your calves is determined at the time you sell them based on their live weight)
   c. Live Weight & Carcass Quality
      (An initial payment for your calves is determined at the time you sell them, with a final payment being made after processing when the quality of the carcass can be determined)

3. **Number of Buyers:** The number of buyers that you will have access to when selling your calves.
   a. Single Buyer
      (Only one buyer is available for you to sell your calves to)
   b. Small Number of Buyers
      (A limited number of buyers are available for you to sell your calves to)
   c. Large Number of Buyers
      (A large number of buyers are available for you to sell your calves to)

4. **Expected Premium:** The premium that you expect to receive (above current market price) for producing calves with specific attributes.
    a. No Premium
    b. 0-5%
    c. 5-10%
    d. 10-15%

We will now show you descriptions of branded beef programs that combine different aspects of these features. Below is an example. As is shown in the example, we will be asking you to score each profile on a scale of 1-12 representing how likely you would be to produce calves for a branded program with these features.

Example:

The left hand side lists features of the branded program and the right hand side describes these features.

Investment	Farm Improvement Expenditures
Pricing Method	Live Weight & Carcass Quality
Number of Buyers	Large Number of Buyers
Expected Premium	0-5%

Please rate the scenario based on how willing you would be to produce calves for a program with these features.

Unlikely to produce... Likely to produce

1   2   3   4   5   6   7   8   9   10   11   12

Please score each of the following profiles based on your willingness to produce calves in branded beef programs with these features, where 1 = highly unlikely to produce for this type of program and 12 = highly likely to produce. You can refer back to page 3 for details of each feature.

Appendix A

Please try to use the full range of the scale when scoring these profiles

Profile 1 **Investment**: Record/Certification System **Pricing Method**: Live Quality **Number of Buyers**: Large Number of Buyers **Expected Premium**: 5-10% Unlikely to produce Likely to produce 1 2 3 4 5 6 7 8 9 10 11 12	**Profile 2** **Investment**: Feed & Health Protocol **Pricing Method**: Carcass Quality **Number of Buyers**: Small Number of Buyers **Expected Premium**: 5-10% Unlikely to produce Likely to produce 1 2 3 4 5 6 7 8 9 10 11 12
Profile 3 **Investment**: Record/Certification System **Pricing Method**: Carcass Quality **Number of Buyers**: Single Buyer **Expected Premium**: 0-5% Unlikely to produce Likely to produce 1 2 3 4 5 6 7 8 9 10 11 12	**Profile 4** **Investment**: Record Certification System **Pricing Method**: Carcass Quality **Number of Buyers**: Single Buyer **Expected Premium**: 10-15% Unlikely to produce Likely to produce 1 2 3 4 5 6 7 8 9 10 11 12
Profile 5 **Investment**: No Additional Investment **Pricing Method**: Live Weight **Number of Buyers**: Small Number of Buyers **Expected Premium**: 10-15% Unlikely to produce Likely to produce 1 2 3 4 5 6 7 8 9 10 11 12	**Profile 6** **Investment**: Farm Improvement Expenditures **Pricing Method**: Live Weight **Number of Buyers**: Single Buyer **Expected Premium**: No Premium Unlikely to produce Likely to produce 1 2 3 4 5 6 7 8 9 10 11 12
Profile 7 **Investment**: Farm Improvement Expenditures **Pricing Method**: Carcass Quality **Number of Buyers**: Large Number of Buyers **Expected Premium**: 10-15% Unlikely to produce Likely to produce 1 2 3 4 5 6 7 8 9 10 11 12	**Profile 8** **Investment**: Record/Certification System **Pricing Method**: Live Weight & Carcass Quality **Number of Buyers**: Small Number of Buyers **Expected Premium**: No Premium Unlikely to produce Likely to produce 1 2 3 4 5 6 7 8 9 10 11 12
Profile 9 **Investment**: Farm Improvement Expenditures **Pricing Method**: Live Weight & Carcass Quality **Number of Buyers**: Single Buyer **Expected Premium**: 5-10% Unlikely to produce Likely to produce 1 2 3 4 5 6 7 8 9 10 11 12	**Profile 10** **Investment**: No Additional Investment **Pricing Method**: Carcass Quality **Number of Buyers**: Single Buyer **Expected Premium**: 5-10% Unlikely to produce Likely to produce 1 2 3 4 5 6 7 8 9 10 11 12

Profile 11	Profile 12
Investment: Feed & Health Protocol **Pricing Method:** Carcass Quality **Number of Buyers:** Large Number of Buyers **Expected Premium:** No Premium Unlikely to produce Likely to produce 1 2 3 4 5 6 7 8 9 10 11 12	**Investment:** Farm Improvement Expenditures **Pricing Method:** Carcass Quality **Number of Buyers:** Small Number of Buyers **Expected Premium:** 0-5% Unlikely to produce Likely to produce 1 2 3 4 5 6 7 8 9 10 11 12
Profile 13	Profile 14
Investment: No Additional Investment **Pricing Method:** Live Weight & Carcass Quality **Number of Buyers:** Large Number of Buyers **Expected Premium:** 0-5% Unlikely to produce Likely to produce 1 2 3 4 5 6 7 8 9 10 11 12	**Investment:** No Additional Investment **Pricing Method:** Carcass Quality **Number of Buyers:** Single Buyer **Expected Premium:** No Premium Unlikely to produce Likely to produce 1 2 3 4 5 6 7 8 9 10 11 12
Profile 15	Profile 16
Investment: Feed & Health Protocol **Pricing Method:** Live Weight & Carcass Quality **Number of Buyers:** Single Buyer **Expected Premium:** 10-15% Unlikely to produce Likely to produce 1 2 3 4 5 6 7 8 9 10 11 12	**Investment:** Feed & Health Protocol **Pricing Method:** Live Weight **Number of Buyers:** Single Buyer **Expected Premium:** 0-5% Unlikely to produce Likely to produce 1 2 3 4 5 6 7 8 9 10 11 12
Profile 17	Profile 18
Investment: Feed & Health Protocol **Pricing Method:** Carcass Quality **Number of Buyers:** Single Buyer **Expected Premium:** No Premium Unlikely to produce Likely to produce 1 2 3 4 5 6 7 8 9 10 11 12	**Investment:** Record/Certification System **Pricing Method:** Carcass Quality **Number of Buyers:** Large Number of Buyers **Expected Premium:** 10-15% Unlikely to produce Likely to produce 1 2 3 4 5 6 7 8 9 10 11 12

Section C

The following section of the survey will ask you some questions regarding your individual operation. Please circle the appropriate answer for each question.

Appendix A

9. What percentage of your farm income is derived from cow-calf production?
    a. None
    b. 0-25%
    c. 25-50%
    d. 50-75%
    e. 100%

10. Please circle any other sources of income that are applicable to your operation.
    a. Background Cattle Feeding
    b. Finishing Feedlot
    c. Grain Farming
    d. Other Livestock
    e. Other (Please Specify) _____

11. Are you or have you ever been involved in any sort of branded beef program or alliance with other producers or beef industry segments (i.e. feedlots, packers, and/or retailers)?
    a. Yes
    b. No

If you answered yes to question #11 please proceed to questions #12 - #14. If you answered no to question #11 please skip to question #15.

12. What type of an alliance are you or were you involved in? (You can choose more than one)
    a. Marketing Contract (where price, date, and delivery location are specified)
    b. Production Contract (where inputs/production processes, price, and buyer rights to inspect are specified)
    c. Brand Licensing Program (e.g. Certified Angus Beef)
    d. Marketing Alliance (e.g. Laura's Lean Beef)
    e. Producer Cooperative (e.g. Ranchers Renaissance)
    f. Other (Please Specify) _____

13. What proportion of your production (beef) is marketed through the alliance?
    a. 0-25%
    b. 26-50%
    c. 51-75%
    d. 76-99%
    e. 100%

14. What is the name of the alliance you are involved in? (Optional)
    _____

All respondents: please continue and answer all of the questions below.

15. What was your gross farm/corporate revenue last year?
    a. Under $10,000
    b. $10,000 to $24,999
    c. $25,000 to $49,999
    d. $50,000 to $99,999
    e. $100,000 to $249,999
    f. $250,000 to $499,999
    g. $500,000 +

16. How large is your cow-calf operation? (# of cows)
    a. 0-50 head
    b. 50-100 head
    c. 100-150 head
    d. 150-200 head
    e. 200-300 head
    f. 300+

17. How do you typically sell your calves?
    a. Cash Market (i.e. local auction market)
    b. Order Buyer
    c. Forward Contract
    d. Other (Please Specify) _____

18. Please indicate your age.
    a. 18 – 25
    b. 25 – 35
    c. 35 – 45
    d. 45 – 60
    e. 60 +

19. Please indicate the highest level of education obtained (Circle one):
    a. Less than grade 9
    b. Grade 9 to 12
    c. High school graduate
    d. Technical School
    e. College Diploma
    f. Bachelor's Degree
    g. Master's Degree
    h. Doctorate Degree

20. Please rate each of the following different branded beef products based on whether you think consumer demand for each product is High, Medium, or Low. Circle the appropriate answer (High, Medium, or Low)

Animal Welfare Friendly	High	Medium	Low
Tender	High	Medium	Low
Organic & GM Free	High	Medium	Low
Natural (no hormones or antibiotics)	High	Medium	Low
Environmentally Friendly	High	Medium	Low
Lean	High	Medium	Low
Breed (i.e. Angus, Hereford, etc.)	High	Medium	Low
Product Origin (i.e. Alberta Beef)	High	Medium	Low
Grass Fed	High	Medium	Low
Convenience	High	Medium	Low

21. Many branded beef programs require that producers and other participants pay membership fees. These fees are often used to ensure that participants are committed to the program and to cover ongoing administration costs. Typically these fees come in two different forms.
    1. Lump-sum payments that must be paid to become a member of the program.
    AND/OR
    2. A Yearly fee per head of cattle marketed through the program

a. Suppose you joined a branded beef program that required you to pay a one-time lump sum payment of $15,000 to enter the program and then a $5 yearly fee per head for each of the calves that you market through the program. What would be the minimum premium (above current market price) that you would be willing to accept and still enter the branded beef program:
   a. 0-5%
   b. 5-10%
   c. 10-15%
   d. 15-20%

b. Suppose you joined a branded beef program that required you to pay a one-time lump sum payment of $2,500 to enter the program and then a $5 yearly fee per head for each of the calves that you market through the program. What would be the minimum premium (above current market price) that you would be willing to accept and still enter the branded beef program:
   a. 0-5%
   b. 5-10%
   c. 10-15%
   d. 15-20%

c. Suppose you joined a branded beef program that required you to pay a $5 yearly fee per head for each of the calves that you market through the program. What would be the minimum premium (above current market price) that you would be willing to accept and still enter the branded beef program:
   a.   0-5%
   b.   5-10%
   c.   10-15%
   d.   15-20%

22. What are the key factors that have limited your involvement in value chain alliances and branded beef programs?

_____

_____

_____

_____

_____

23. Do you have any further comments about branded beef programs that you would like to share with us?

_____

_____

_____

_____

_____

Thank You For Your Participation!

APPENDIX B
BEEF ALLIANCE SURVEY

The following interview questions are about marketing alliances and branded beef programs. They focus on the ownership structure of different marketing alliances, organizational characteristics, program requirements, program pricing methods, and market access issues.

1. Organizational Characteristics

a. What is the name of the branded beef program(s)/marketing alliance(s) your company is currently involved in? What products are currently being produced?

_____

_____

_____

_____

b. What is the focus of the program? What are the attributes being provided (branded) under the program? (E.g. organic, breed, etc.)

_____

_____

_____

_____

c. How long has the program been in existence? How long has your company been involved in the program?

d. Who initially established the program? Were there any significant challenges to be overcome? How were they overcome?

e. What is the size of the existing program in terms of the number of cattle processed through the program each year? In terms of sales?

f. How important is the branded beef program to your company? (In terms of % of company sales or some other measure) Is all the beef from the animals that qualify for the program marketed through the program, or do some cuts still get marketed through traditional (non-branded) channels? Has the sale of lower quality cattle/cuts been an issue? How has this been handled?

g. What type of growth do you project over the next several years for your program? Do you foresee any significant changes in the focus of the program?

2. Structure/Ownership of the company/program

a. How is the program structured? For example is it run through a cooperative, a marketing alliance, contracts, or some other method?

b. What supply chain members are involved in the program and how are they linked together (e.g. cow-calf producers, feedlots, packers, distributors, retailers)? Which are the links that are crucial to providing the branded attributes you are marketing?

c. In aligning with other members of the supply chain what is your major priority? (E.g. to ensure ongoing supplies, access to specific qualities of animals, easier monitoring of quality....etc?)

d. Who are your major customers (supermarkets, restaurants, specialty stores)? How were these connections developed? Have there been any challenges in dealing with certain types of end-users as opposed to other types of end-users?

e. What are some of the main issues that have to be dealt with in developing downstream markets for branded beef programs? How have the requirements of your downstream customers affected how you interact with upstream suppliers, e.g. in terms of sharing risks, program requirements, etc.?

3. What is required of producers in order to participate in your program?

    a. In terms of investments, changes in practices, by producers
- i. Feed/Health Protocol
- ii. Record/Certification System
- iii. Capital Expenditures
- iv. Other program specific investments

b. In terms of commitment
   i. What level of commitment do you require from producers/feedlots that participate in your program? (Length of time, Number of cattle)
   ii. How do you ensure a certain level of commitment?
      1. Equity Investment
      2. Contractual Obligations

c. Have you been involved in any previous programs that failed to get enough participation by producers or other supply chain members? What were the main reasons this occurred?

d. In the current program, have any of the existing or previous program requirements limited producer participation? If so what has been done to overcome these limitations?

4. Payment/Reward System

a. How are producers and feedlots paid through the program?
   i. Grid Pricing System
   ii. Live Weight Pricing
   iii. Other

b. What are the key components of the pricing system if a grid pricing system is used? (Check current use of institutions both for grading and for other attributes)

c. Previous analysis of branded beef programs has indicated that producers were not as willing to participate in programs that used carcass quality grid-based pricing systems? (Transfer of risk) Have you found this to be a problem under your program? How has your grid been designed to ensure that there is still incentive for producers to enter into the program?

d. Based on previous years, what kind of premium can producers expect when participating in your program?

e. Are there other program incentives that seem to encourage producer participation in the program – market access, quality information, etc?

5. Market Access

a. As program requirements become increasingly detailed and specific in nature the market available for producers to sell their product (at a premium) tends to decrease and they are increasingly dependent on only a few buyers or a single buyer. This sometimes discourages producers from participating in a program. What have you done to assure producers that they will have ongoing market access under the program and encourage their commitment to the program?

6. Future Directions

a. Are there any current limitations/barriers that the program is facing, which have limited its growth? What has been done to overcome these limitations?

b. In addition to premium prices are there other less obvious benefits that can be obtained from increased coordination and involvement in a branded beef program? For whom?

7. Industry concerns

a. With the occurrence of BSE what changes do expect with respect to marketing alliances both in general and more specifically the program you are involved in?

b. What would be the value of a standardized tagging/tracking system such as the CCIA to your program and alliances in general?

INDEX

A

access, 4, 9, 15, 22, 47, 56, 67, 95, 96, 97, 99, 101, 117, 119, 123, 125, 127, 130, 131, 136, 138, 142, 144, 159, 169
accounting, 13
accuracy, 75, 89
acquisitions, 4
adaptability, 2
administration, 24, 121, 165
age, 13, 86, 99, 102, 103, 143, 164
agent, 31
aging, 12
agricultural market, 7
agriculture, 27, 147
agri-food, vii, viii, 2, 3
alternative(s), 14, 15, 26, 28, 35, 36, 37, 38, 39, 40, 72, 75, 77, 80, 83, 117, 119, 122, 123, 127, 128, 130, 132, 134, 136
American culture, viii
amortization, 41
Angus, 2, 16, 18, 19, 20, 21, 23, 68, 150, 163, 165
animal health, 6, 23
animal welfare, viii, 2, 12, 13, 47, 50, 51, 52, 64
animals, 3, 4, 5, 8, 9, 14, 16, 19, 22, 24, 28, 32, 33, 38, 39, 51, 54, 103, 109, 110, 115, 116, 117, 121, 122, 123, 132, 137, 146, 168, 169
antibiotic(s), 12, 15, 47, 48, 50, 52, 62, 114, 126, 127, 128, 165
arbitrage, 4
arbitration, 60
artificial insemination, 5
Asia, 4, 152
assets, 30, 37, 38, 39, 40, 41, 49, 50, 51, 64, 90, 91, 99, 101, 102, 106, 118, 119, 121
assumptions, 35, 36
asymmetric information, 36

asymmetry, 37, 39, 43, 64, 66, 67, 77
attention, viii, 12, 45
attitudes, 74, 107
auditing, 136
Australia, 7
automobiles, 2
availability, 138
average costs, 130

B

bacteria, 15
baked fresh, 1
bakeries, 2
bankruptcy, 25, 110
bargaining, 37, 38, 57
barriers, 4, 5, 42, 109, 138, 173
barriers to entry, 138
beef sector, vii, 28
behavior, 52
benefits, 4, 6, 21, 22, 30, 32, 42, 71, 77, 79, 96, 97, 100, 104, 106, 107, 109, 110, 114, 116, 117, 118, 123, 125, 126, 128, 129, 131, 132, 137, 138, 142, 144, 145, 148, 173
benign, 4
biological processes, 33
birth, 8
blocks, 1
bovine, 4
bovine spongiform encephalopathy (BSE), 4, 5, 7, 121, 148, 152, 153, 174
brand loyalty, 18
breakfast, 1
breeding, 8, 16, 109, 117
British Columbia, 152
bundling, 45
butchers, 2, 62

buyer, 29, 38, 47, 59, 60, 77, 78, 92, 95, 98, 103, 104, 118, 127, 157, 158, 159, 163, 173

C

California, 3, 4, 150, 151
Canada, vii, viii, 3, 4, 5, 7, 8, 9, 10, 11, 12, 13, 15, 20, 34, 54, 61, 73, 84, 85, 109, 110, 121, 134, 135, 136, 138, 147, 149, 150, 151, 152, 153, 154, 155
Canada-US Trade Agreement (CUSTA), 3, 4, 5
canned, 1
capital cost, 67, 119
capital expenditure, 77, 90, 97
cash flow, 147
category a, 47
cattle, viii, 3, 4, 5, 7, 8, 9, 16, 17, 19, 20, 21, 22, 24, 25, 26, 27, 29, 31, 32, 33, 34, 39, 41, 42, 47, 50, 52, 55, 56, 61, 68, 69, 73, 78, 79, 98, 99, 102, 103, 110, 114, 115, 116, 117, 118, 121, 122, 123, 124, 125, 127, 128, 131, 132, 133, 134, 135, 136, 137, 142, 143, 144, 146, 147, 150, 165, 168, 171
census, 84, 85
certificate, 86
certification, 18, 47, 50, 54, 66, 69, 70, 77, 79, 90, 96, 97, 116, 118, 126, 136, 143, 147, 159
channels, 73, 168
Chicago, 155
chicken(s), 2, 5, 7, 10, 11, 142
cholesterol, 1, 12, 16
classes, 24
classification, 34, 47
closure, 4
Colorado, 3, 8, 23
Columbia University, 153
commercial, viii, 8, 9, 55, 62
commodity(ies), vii, 3, 26, 27, 38, 114, 115, 117, 122, 128, 129, 130, 132, 139, 141, 146, 148
communication, 18, 28, 31, 46, 129
competition, 1, 133, 148
competitiveness, 2, 125, 139, 141, 142, 148
complementary products, 148
complexity, 39, 41, 49, 66, 69, 74, 79, 82, 103, 107, 118, 135
compliance, 24, 49, 50, 55, 60, 66, 69, 116, 124, 126, 135, 137, 143, 159
components, 172
composition, 80, 81
computation, 82
concentration, 8, 9, 10, 33, 61, 107, 127, 134, 146
confidence, 14
confidentiality, 139
conflict, 40

conflict resolution, 40
conformity, 24
Congress, 7, 9, 10, 12, 13, 14, 23, 152
consolidation, 9, 10, 34
constraints, 6, 9, 107, 141
construction, 26
consumer loyalty, 117, 120
consumer markets, 4
consumer satisfaction, 55
consumer taste, vii
consumers, vii, viii, 1, 2, 5, 6, 10, 11, 12, 13, 14, 15, 16, 18, 19, 23, 26, 27, 30, 31, 33, 34, 38, 46, 47, 48, 49, 50, 51, 55, 57, 58, 63, 66, 69, 104, 107, 116, 119, 122, 126, 129, 145, 148
consumption, vii, 8, 10, 11, 13, 126
consumption patterns, 10, 11
control, 9, 10, 18, 28, 29, 30, 31, 33, 37, 39, 102, 119, 124, 127, 133, 134
convex, 81
corn, 1, 114, 126
corporations, 138
correlations, 89
cost saving, 5, 10, 29, 32, 71
Costco, 1, 2
costs, 2, 5, 8, 9, 10, 11, 14, 15, 18, 20, 21, 22, 23, 24, 26, 28, 29, 32, 33, 35, 36, 37, 38, 39, 40, 41, 42, 43, 45, 49, 51, 52, 53, 54, 55, 56, 57, 59, 60, 61, 62, 63, 64, 66, 67, 68, 69, 70, 71, 73, 77, 78, 79, 91, 97, 100, 101, 105, 106, 107, 115, 118, 119, 120, 121, 122, 123, 124, 125, 126, 127, 128, 129, 130, 131, 132, 134, 135, 136, 137, 138, 141, 142, 144, 145, 146, 147, 148, 165
country of origin, 5
credibility, 73
crop production, 131
crops, 132
Crow Rate, 3
cues, 47
cultural heritage, viii
current limit, 33, 109, 173
customers, 1, 21, 25, 27, 63, 117, 121, 126, 130, 170

D

dairies, 2
dairy, 5, 114
data analysis, 138
database, 56, 118, 137
decisions, 72, 73, 74, 97, 117, 124, 135, 138, 148
definition, 57, 77
delivery, 17, 41, 69, 122, 124, 163

demand, 6, 10, 11, 12, 13, 14, 15, 19, 26, 27, 38, 40, 46, 48, 55, 58, 62, 63, 104, 105, 107, 117, 120, 122, 129, 131, 132, 141, 165
demographic factors, 12
Department of Agriculture, 19, 46, 116
dependent variable, 38, 45, 72, 80
desire(s), 6, 27, 51, 148
diet(s), viii, 8, 13
differentiated products, vii, 12, 14, 40, 71, 128, 133, 136, 141, 145
differentiation, 12, 13, 14, 27
disclosure, 47
disequilibrium, 34, 129
dispersion, 8, 33, 43, 142
disposable income, 12
distortions, 3, 4
distribution, 2, 27, 35, 36, 84, 85
diversification, 4
diversity, 2, 6, 12, 148
dividends, 17
division, 19
drainage, 159
dumping, 4, 149

E

earnings, 12
eating, 2, 14, 48
economic incentives, 6
economic indicator, 21
economic losses, 26
Economic Research Service, 153
economic theory, 37
economics, 3, 35, 36, 37
economies of scale, 2, 5, 6, 9, 27, 62, 115, 142
education, 84, 85, 86, 88, 99, 103, 164
elasticity, 97
elasticity of supply, 97
email, 109
employees, 36, 40
end-users, 18, 34, 60, 111, 114, 117, 122, 131, 146, 170
energy, 8
entrepreneurs, 2
environment, 23, 35, 107
environmental awareness, 47
environmental sustainability, viii, 13, 49
equilibrium, 34, 35
equipment, 137
equity, 17, 25, 26, 30, 42
estimating, 73, 75
ethnic diversity, 12
evidence, 4, 5

excess supply, 123
exchange relationship, 30
exclusion, 16, 75
execution, 75
exercise, 29, 159
expenditures, 6, 92, 95, 96, 98, 118, 142
experimental design, 82
expertise, 119, 131
exports, 7
exposure, 118, 122, 124, 142

F

failure, 5, 13, 26, 27, 28, 104, 129
family, 12, 72
farm(s), 1, 2, 7, 8, 9, 19, 47, 77, 84, 85, 90, 92, 95, 96, 97, 98, 99, 101, 103, 114, 118, 131, 132, 136, 143, 163, 164
farmers, 2, 31
fast food, 1
fat, vii, 1, 12, 16, 46
Federal Reserve Bank, 149
females, 12
fertilizers, 48
finance, 136
financing, 147
firms, vii, 1, 3, 6, 9, 10, 14, 30, 35, 36, 37, 39, 41, 47, 52, 66, 135
fishmongers, 2
fixed costs, 61
flexibility, 23, 57, 70, 144, 145
flour mills, 2
fluctuations, 31, 129, 145
focusing, 26, 48, 61, 75, 122, 124, 131, 148
food, vii, viii, 1, 2, 3, 5, 6, 7, 8, 10, 12, 13, 14, 46, 47, 48, 50, 52, 129, 141, 148
food industry, vii, 1, 2, 3
food products, 1, 2, 5, 12
food safety, vii, 12, 13, 14, 47, 48, 50, 52, 129
foreign firms, 5
foreign investment, 4
freeze dried, 1
freezing, 2
fresh, 1, 46
frozen, 1, 130
fruit packers, 2
fuel, 12
funds, 24, 136
futures, 124

G

general stores, 2
generation, 5, 16, 17, 23, 25, 31, 68, 100, 126, 134
genetic traits, 33
genetically modified organisms, 48
genetics, vii, 5, 23, 25, 33, 38, 46, 50, 62, 107
geography, 5
globalization, 2
goals, 28, 35
goods and services, 73
governance, 38
government, 2, 15, 23, 46, 84, 133
grades, 2, 13, 14, 15, 19, 42, 46, 91, 126
grading, 4, 13, 15, 19, 20, 23, 27, 40, 46, 50, 56, 68, 126, 172
grass, 16, 47, 48, 66, 105, 131
grazing, vii, 5, 6, 8, 132, 142
grazing resources, 5
green grocers, 2
greenfield, 4
grids, 31, 115, 123, 125
gross domestic product, 7
groups, 14, 21, 73, 99, 100
growth, 12, 20, 21, 25, 50, 52, 109, 169, 173
growth hormone, 50
guidance, 19
guidelines, 21, 50, 54, 55

H

hands, 1
harassment, 5
harmonization, 4
harvesting, 132
hazards, 40, 118
head, 1, 8, 9, 20, 21, 22, 24, 25, 29, 85, 86, 99, 106, 110, 111, 112, 113, 115, 123, 164, 165, 166
health, 9, 12, 13, 46, 48, 50, 77, 90, 97, 116, 118, 126, 143
heart, 1
hedging, 124
high school, 86
higher education, 84
higher quality, 29, 37, 46, 54, 145
hiring, 52
hog, 5, 142
hormone(s), 12, 15, 47, 48, 52, 62, 114, 126, 127, 128, 165
host, vii, viii, 2
households, 12
housing, 5

human capital, 14, 38, 50, 64, 68, 69, 118, 119
human resources, 51
hypothesis, 74

I

identification, 9, 19, 22, 39, 47, 48, 58, 76, 112, 113, 115, 116, 118, 119, 137, 138, 147
identity, 14, 19, 23, 31, 38, 53, 55, 64
implementation, 40, 41, 50, 54, 55, 61, 63, 69, 77, 79, 97, 116, 118, 126, 143
in situ, 36, 37, 39, 41, 46, 60, 121
incentives, 2, 3, 16, 17, 19, 20, 24, 25, 29, 31, 40, 41, 43, 55, 62, 107, 117, 126, 127, 128, 135, 144, 147, 172
income, 2, 12, 22, 85, 99, 101, 103, 131, 143, 163
increased access, 98
independence, 23, 30
independent variable, 38, 45, 80
indication, 143
indicators, 21, 48, 54, 90
industry, vii, viii, 1, 2, 3, 4, 5, 6, 7, 8, 9, 10, 11, 12, 13, 14, 15, 17, 18, 19, 22, 23, 25, 26, 27, 28, 30, 31, 32, 33, 34, 35, 37, 40, 43, 52, 54, 57, 58, 60, 61, 66, 67, 69, 70, 71, 72, 74, 78, 79, 84, 101, 102, 107, 109, 110, 114, 123, 124, 125, 127, 128, 129, 131, 133, 134, 135, 136, 137, 138, 139, 141, 142, 143, 145, 147, 148, 163
inflation, 11
information asymmetry, 37, 38, 39, 42, 52, 55, 66, 67, 79, 121, 126
information systems, 119, 147
information technology, 109
infrastructure, 147
injury, iv
innovation, 6, 10, 11, 151
insight, 18, 58, 98, 105, 124
inspection(s), 24, 46, 116, 136
institutions, 54, 55, 56, 64, 70, 136, 147, 172
integration, vii, 3, 4, 5, 28, 31, 32, 33, 43, 67, 139
integrity, 19
intensity, 28
interaction(s), vii, 67, 135
interdependence, 4
interface, 33, 55, 58, 61, 71, 135, 146
internalizing, 43
internet, 85, 112
interval, 5
intervention, 133
interview, 109, 119, 155, 167
investment, 4, 10, 18, 23, 25, 26, 30, 31, 37, 38, 39, 49, 50, 51, 64, 66, 68, 69, 77, 89, 95, 97, 101, 118, 119, 122, 138

investors, 25, 64
irritants, 4

J

Japan, 4, 7, 152, 153
judgment, 75, 83

K

Korea, 4

L

labor, 8, 10, 12, 46, 132
labor force, 12, 46
lamb, 3, 7
land, 8, 32, 33, 43, 142
large scale, 2, 5
lawsuits, 133
lawyers, 52
lead, 5, 26, 77, 79
legislation, 5
licenses, 19, 20
lifestyle(s), vii, 8, 12, 48
likelihood, 15, 38
limitation, 43, 75, 147
linear model, 81
links, 45, 61, 62, 70, 169
literature, 14, 72, 80
livestock, 3, 9, 12, 13, 14, 27, 28, 47, 48, 54, 114, 149, 150, 151, 152, 153, 154, 163
location, 22, 84, 109, 163
logistics, vii
longevity, 17, 39, 42
low cholesterol, 1
low fat, 1
low risk, 127
lower prices, 35, 125, 126
loyalty, 117

M

mad cow disease, 4
management, 6, 8, 9, 15, 17, 18, 20, 21, 22, 26, 30, 33, 40, 50, 51, 63, 68, 69, 74, 105, 107, 126, 132, 134, 137, 138, 145, 147, 148, 159
management practices, 20, 33
market access, 22, 31, 79, 100, 109, 119, 127, 134, 142, 143, 158, 167, 172, 173
market prices, 30, 57

market segment, 34
market share, 3, 5, 9, 10, 11, 13, 15, 57, 58, 148
market structure, 8, 28
marketability, 130
marketing, 13, 15, 16, 17, 18, 19, 20, 21, 22, 23, 25, 27, 28, 29, 30, 31, 32, 34, 41, 61, 66, 72, 83, 100, 103, 104, 114, 115, 119, 123, 131, 135, 144, 146, 167, 169, 174
Massachusetts, 155
meals, 12, 13, 46
measurement, 13, 16, 23, 29, 56, 72, 73, 75, 105
measures, 25, 54, 89, 90, 91, 119, 120, 132, 137
meat, 2, 7, 8, 10, 12, 13, 14, 15, 17, 20, 24, 27, 28, 50, 71, 114, 117, 130, 142, 148
media, 153
membership, 17, 18, 24, 31, 68, 105, 107, 120, 121, 144, 165
merchandise, 19
Mexico, 3, 7, 151, 152
microwave, 1
Missouri, 109
models, 33, 148
money, 26
monopoly, 58
monopsony, 58
Montana, 22
moral hazard, 37
motion, 133
motivation, 29
movement, 26, 27, 28, 32, 133
multivariate, 73

N

Nabisco, 1
Nebraska, 8, 22, 34, 49, 109, 110, 111, 113, 114, 116, 121, 124, 126, 132, 150
needles, vii
negotiating, 35, 36, 41, 42, 59, 125, 132, 142
negotiation, 29, 36, 40, 41, 42, 52, 55, 56, 57, 59, 61, 67, 68, 77, 78, 91, 120, 121, 123, 127, 135, 142, 146, 147
New England, 149
New York, 151, 153
niche market, 4, 14, 18, 48, 58, 127, 129
non-tariff barriers, 4, 5
North America, vii, viii, 1, 3, 4, 5, 7, 8, 9, 10, 12, 25, 26, 57, 58, 78, 109, 114, 139, 143, 145, 147, 148, 153
North American Free Trade Agreement (NAFTA), 3, 4, 5, 151, 152
nutrition, vii, 12, 13

O

obligation, 30, 121
observations, 89
Oklahoma, 149, 155
operator(s), 21, 22, 53, 55, 58, 62, 65, 70, 71, 72, 73, 75, 77, 78, 79, 84, 85, 93, 97, 98, 99, 100, 101, 106, 107, 115, 122, 125, 131, 132, 135, 136, 144, 145
opportunism, 36, 37, 40, 77
opportunity costs, 121, 131, 136, 147
organic, 1, 12, 15, 39, 47, 48, 54, 105, 167
organization(s), vii, 3, 16, 21, 24, 25, 31, 35, 42, 58, 66, 68, 84, 109, 118, 125, 133
orientation, 3, 4, 148
Ottawa, 153
ownership, 21, 22, 24, 25, 28, 56, 110, 112, 113, 114, 115, 119, 121, 122, 128, 134, 135, 136, 137, 139, 147, 167
ownership structure, 110, 114, 128, 167

P

Pacific, 152
packaging, 2, 6
partnership(s), 21, 22, 23
penalties, 18
penalty, 40
perception, 73
perceptions, 73, 74, 84, 98, 104
performance, 3, 21, 22, 24, 30, 51, 84, 104, 124
personal, 109, 150, 155
personal communication, 150
pesticides, 48
planning, 124
plants, 2, 9, 10, 24, 29, 61, 62, 69, 126, 133, 137
pleasure, 12
poor, 28, 42, 54, 55, 138
population, 12, 84
population growth, 12
pork, 3, 5, 6, 7, 10, 32, 33, 34, 142, 143, 148
positive relationship, 126, 144
poultry, 3, 5, 6, 11, 12, 32, 33, 142, 143, 148
power, 4, 57
preference, 5, 14, 72, 73, 75, 80, 81, 82, 83, 89, 93, 95, 143
preferential treatment, 133, 134
premium meats (PM), 110, 111, 114, 116, 118, 119, 123, 124, 126, 127, 134, 136
premiums, 17, 18, 19, 20, 22, 24, 27, 29, 41, 52, 62, 81, 90, 91, 93, 95, 96, 97, 98, 99, 100, 101, 106, 107, 109, 115, 117, 123, 124, 125, 130, 131, 132, 136, 142, 143, 144, 145
price index, 11
price mechanism, 35
price signals, 16, 40, 63, 135, 145
prices, 2, 3, 4, 11, 16, 29, 31, 35, 36, 38, 39, 40, 41, 65, 121, 125, 133, 173
probability, 38
process control, 24
processing stages, 15, 54, 63
producers, viii, 4, 5, 8, 16, 17, 19, 23, 38, 39, 40, 41, 42, 45, 50, 52, 62, 104, 107, 114, 115, 116, 117, 120, 124, 125, 126, 131, 132, 133, 135, 136, 147, 148, 163, 165, 169, 170, 171, 172, 173
product attributes, vii, 2, 39, 41, 141
production costs, 8, 9, 11, 17, 37, 38, 39, 128, 145
productivity, 5
profit, 10, 19, 23, 24, 25, 111, 131
profit margin, 10
profitability, 13, 14, 17, 33, 120, 133
profits, 10, 23, 27, 32, 42, 113
program administration, 105
promote, 5, 15
property rights, 18
prosperity, 6, 148
protectionism, 148
proteins, 13
protocol(s), vii, 9, 15, 21, 41, 46, 50, 51, 66, 68, 77, 90, 97, 107, 115, 116, 118, 124, 126, 143

Q

quality assurance, 23, 147
quality control, 23, 28
quality production, 114, 116
quasi-rent, 37, 38, 41, 59

R

range, viii, 1, 2, 4, 8, 12, 20, 58, 71, 72, 90, 95, 97, 102, 106, 123, 148, 161
rating scale, 73
ratings, 73, 89, 90, 103
rationality, 36, 39, 41, 49
ready to eat, vii
realism, 82
reduction, 42, 56, 57, 90, 91, 96, 98, 124, 147
regional, 3, 8, 50
regression, 80, 88
regulations, 24
relationship(s), vii, 2, 6, 20, 24, 26, 29, 30, 38, 40, 49, 50, 52, 53, 56, 59, 61, 64, 66, 70, 71, 78, 79,

80, 81, 88, 90, 91, 106, 114, 119, 122, 123, 127, 128, 130, 132, 133, 134, 135, 141, 143, 144, 146
relative prices, 11
reliability, 75
Renaissance, 17, 18, 23, 24, 25, 26, 31, 68, 110, 112, 113, 115, 116, 117, 121, 126, 130, 132, 150, 154, 163
rent, 23, 37
reputation, 39, 42, 46, 53, 55, 59, 60, 61, 77, 78, 119, 120, 122, 135
research design, 76
residues, vii
resolution, 30
resources, vii, 5, 6, 8, 23, 32, 33, 35, 37, 50, 98, 99, 131, 132, 134, 136, 142, 147
responsiveness, 97, 148
restaurant chains, 2
restaurants, 19, 170
retail, 2, 8, 10, 11, 13, 14, 19, 23, 25, 62, 117, 119, 130, 131, 146
retention, 138
retirement, 102
returns, 21, 32, 39, 41, 42, 56, 99, 101, 117, 122, 124, 131, 132, 133, 135, 136, 137
revenue, 30, 136, 164
rewards, 19, 27
rice, 124
risk, 4, 15, 25, 32, 40, 42, 52, 53, 56, 57, 59, 60, 64, 73, 77, 78, 79, 82, 89, 90, 98, 106, 118, 119, 120, 122, 123, 124, 125, 127, 138, 142, 143, 144, 172
rolling, 24

S

safety, vii, 28, 47, 48, 129
sales, 7, 10, 12, 13, 24, 34, 117, 168
sample, 81, 84, 89, 104
sanitary and phytosanitary standards, 5
savings, 14, 29, 32
scaling, 2
scatter, 11
scatter plot, 11
school, 86, 164
scores, 73, 80, 82, 89, 90, 99, 100, 101
search, 36, 38, 41, 46, 47, 48, 50, 53, 56, 57, 62, 64, 69, 78, 91, 115, 122, 124, 126, 127, 132, 146
searching, 14, 21, 42, 56, 59, 60, 78, 119, 124, 132, 142, 144
security, 4
seeding, 132
segmentation, 30
segregation, 14, 30, 73
selecting, 41

self-interest, 37
sex, 21, 113
shareholders, 112
shares, 17, 111, 113, 120, 121
sharing, 26, 30, 136, 147, 170
short run, 129
shy, 26
sign, 21, 116, 121
signals, 13, 15, 27, 28, 30, 31, 55, 62, 116, 122, 123, 144, 145
sites, vii, 49
skills, 50, 159
smoked, 1
software, 89, 90
sorting, 21, 42
South Korea, 7
specific knowledge, 50
specificity, 36, 37, 38, 39, 40, 41, 43, 49, 50, 51, 52, 60, 64, 66, 67, 69, 77, 97, 123, 128, 143
speed, 5, 32
spot market, 28, 29, 32, 38, 39, 40, 41, 52, 53, 55, 64, 66, 67, 116, 119, 120, 122, 124, 125, 133, 144
SPSS, 72, 73, 82, 83, 89, 90, 155
stability, 17, 24, 26, 30, 31, 75
stages, 18, 20, 28, 30, 31, 32, 33, 35, 36, 43, 47, 52, 54, 62, 79
standardization, 2, 5, 6, 118
standards, 4, 13, 18, 23, 24, 27, 41, 52, 53, 54, 55, 64, 68, 69, 70, 159
statistics, 34, 89
strategies, vii
strength, 73, 83
stress, 4
subsidy, 3
substitution, 11
sugar, 1
summaries, 30
supermarket chains, 2, 10, 12
suppliers, vii, 6, 9, 21, 22, 24, 27, 29, 37, 41, 42, 60, 62, 67, 115, 119, 120, 127, 144, 170
sustainability, 123
systems, 9, 13, 15, 16, 17, 27, 30, 40, 41, 45, 50, 54, 56, 57, 61, 63, 66, 68, 69, 78, 98, 107, 109, 115, 116, 118, 119, 123, 124, 125, 126, 129, 134, 137, 138, 141, 142, 143, 144, 145, 146, 147, 172

T

tariffs, 4
technological developments, 10
technology, 10, 20, 21, 137, 138, 145
temporal, 75
Texas, 8, 23, 34, 151, 152

theory, 28, 35, 36
threat, 10
time periods, 132
timing, 25, 147
total product, 7, 60
total utility, 72, 80, 89, 90, 92, 96, 97
tracking, 9, 19, 22, 56, 63, 70, 115, 116, 118, 174
trade, 1, 4, 5, 38, 73, 79, 82, 83, 92, 95, 96, 97, 98, 107, 142, 143, 145, 148
trade-off, 73, 82, 83, 92, 95, 96, 97, 98, 107, 142, 143, 145, 148
trading, 3, 38, 41, 79, 110
trading partners, 38, 41
training, 3, 50
traits, 16, 31, 33
transaction costs, 14, 35, 36, 37, 39, 40, 43, 49, 51, 53, 55, 56, 57, 59, 60, 61, 63, 64, 66, 68, 70, 71, 72, 73, 75, 78, 79, 90, 91, 97, 100, 106, 107, 119, 120, 121, 122, 123, 127, 128, 129, 130, 135, 138, 141, 142, 143, 144, 145, 146, 147, 148
transactions, vii, 4, 6, 29, 30, 31, 33, 34, 35, 36, 37, 38, 39, 40, 42, 52, 54, 55, 60, 61, 62, 63, 64, 66, 68, 78, 122, 125, 128, 132, 135, 146
transformation, 26, 34, 141
transition, vii, 139, 148
transparency, 23, 25, 147
transport, 3, 6
transportation, 2, 4, 5, 49, 115
trend, 9, 11, 12, 34, 102
trust, 6, 23, 30, 31, 61, 122, 126, 128
turnover, 10

U

UK, 151
ultrasound, 21, 137
uncertainty, 14, 35, 36, 38, 39, 49, 52, 54, 57, 58, 59, 60, 61, 64, 65, 67, 77, 78, 79, 91, 98, 124, 128, 129, 142
undergraduate, 86
uniform, 17, 29, 54
unit cost, 10
United States, vii, 7, 10, 19, 20, 22, 46, 73, 110, 151, 152

urban centres, 3
USDA, 13, 16, 20, 46, 112, 113, 116, 118, 153
users, 23, 29, 31, 62, 63, 114, 116, 120, 121, 122, 131, 133, 146, 170

V

vacuum, 2
validity, 82, 89
values, 58, 72, 75, 80, 81, 82, 88, 89, 90, 92, 95, 96, 97, 102, 105, 106, 107, 118, 143
variability, 24, 52, 54, 55, 57, 65, 67, 77, 78, 79, 123, 126, 143
variable costs, 9, 40
variable(s), 9, 13, 40, 41, 45, 46, 49, 54, 55, 58, 74, 77, 79, 88, 89, 105, 107
variance, 64, 80, 100, 116
variation, 5, 17, 33, 35, 61, 100, 116
vector, 81
vertical integration, 6, 28, 32, 33, 37, 43, 66, 67
Virginia, 153, 154
vision, 118, 137, 147
vulnerability, 26

W

wages, 40
Walmart, 1, 2
Washington, 151, 153
welfare, 16, 23, 28, 47, 48, 50, 52
wheat, 1
Whole Foods, 1
winter, 132
women, 12, 46
World Trade Organization (WHO), 153
worry, 75
writing, vii, 36

Y

yield, 13, 16, 17, 22, 25